You & Your Puppy

You & Your Puppy

Training and Health Care for Puppy's First Year

James DeBitetto, D.V.M., and Sarah Hodgson

HOWELL
BOOK
HOUSE

All photos except where credited are by Sarah Hodgson and James DeBitetto, DVM.
Medical illustrations are by James DeBitetto, DVM.

Howell Book House
MACMILLAN
A Simon & Schuster Macmillan Company
1633 Broadway
New York, NY 10019–6785

Library of Congress Cataloging-in-Publication Data

DeBitetto, James.
    You and your puppy : training and health care for puppy's first
year / James DeBitetto, DVM, and Sarah Hodgson.
        p. cm.

ISBN 0-87605-784-9

1. Puppies. 2. Puppies—Training. 3. Puppies—Health.
I. Hodgson, Sarah. II. Title.
SF427.D 38 1995
636.7'07—dc20   95–12044

Manufactured in the United States of America
10   9   8   7   6

Our Reward

Treat me with respect, teach me your rules and train me
with patience.
Let me know what pleases you, for if
you don't, my unbridled enthusiasm may place
unnecessary and stressful demands on you.
There is not an animal on the planet that could
offer you the same unconditional devotion that
I can, if you show me the
path to your heart.
Through my puppyhood I may test you, but only because
I am a puppy.
Persist, for I will remember your structure
as I grow into doghood.
Do not take advantage of me.
Though I have many needs, I cannot speak.
Be my leader, my keeper, my friend and my voice.
Your efforts will be our reward.

Sarah Hodgson

Contents

PART 1: Put Yourself in My Paws!

PART 2: Training: First Day Through First Year

PART 3:   Mister or Miss Manners

PART 4:   Your Puppy's Health

About the Authors

James DeBitetto, D.V.M, is the owner and director of the Country Home Veterinary Clinic in Bedford Hills, New York. He is a 1985 graduate of the New York State College of Veterinary Medicine, Cornell University, and a member of the American Veterinary Medical Association, American Animal Hospital Association, and the New York State Veterinary Medical Society. Dr. DeBitetto is also a concert violinist. He and his wife, Donna, share their lives with Myles, a Labrador Retriever.

Sarah Hodgson is owner of The Cooperative Canine, a private dog-training business in Goldens Bridge, New York. She received her B.A. in biology with an emphasis on animal behavior from the State University of New York at Purchase. Ms. Hodgson is a member of the Dog Writer's Association of America, the Society of North American Dog Trainers, and the Association of Pet Dog Trainers. She is also a registered Therapy Dogs International evaluator.

Acknowledgments for Sarah Hodgson

So many people to thank. Wow! Where to start? Three men. Three women.

First the women. Moira Hoff. Mo. You added dimples to every page of this book. It would not be the same without your input. Tina Balch—a great artist with the tolerance of a saint. Dominique Davis—my editor. Thank you all.

Now the men. Sean Frawley. Seymour Weiss. Jim DeBitetto. You all believed in me. This vision could not have become a reality without you. Super guys.

I have a place in my heart and in my head for all the trainers who started before me, watched me grow, and influenced my work with theirs. Job Michael Evans, Mordecai Siegel, Carol Benjamin, Robin Kovary, Larry Berg, Micky Niego, Arthur Haggerty, Barbra Giella, Debbie Feliziani, Sidney Mihls, Jack Shultz, and Liz Teal. I hope I didn't forget anybody. You've all been great!

A wave, a hello, and a thank you to all the veterinarians, pet supply stores, groomers, and breeders who send me warm-hearted people seeking help in their relationship with their dogs. I'm glad I can help.

Thanks to all my clients who from the start of my practice cheered me on. It's nice to have so much support. Thank you for that and for following through with my suggestions. I'm sorry I can't list all of you.

A special thanks to everyone who helped and endured my photo shoots. I wish I could list all of you too, but my space is limited.

Finally, to the one person who lifted me up when I was just a chick, Job Michael Evans, your belief in me and your guidance were like a nest in this wild and windy world. I'm not sure I was ready to fly. Though I miss you still, your song is forever impressioned in my heart.

Acknowledgments for James DeBitetto, D.V.M.

A book of this magnitude requires the help of many people. First, I'd like to thank my coauthor, Sarah Hodgson, for her unyielding energy and breadth of knowledge of the dog world. I would like to thank my editor, Dominique Davis, for her skillful editing and for all the energy that she put in to making this book so valuable for puppy owners. I'd like to thank my publisher, Sean Frawley, and all the wonderful people at Howell Book House. Next, I'd like to thank my staff at Country Home Veterinary Clinic: Katie, Penny, and Jacqueline, for their patience and for putting up with me for the two years this book was in production. A special thanks to my groomer, Pam Koerner, for her help in the grooming section and for the use of her beautiful puppies in a few of the photo shoots. A sincere thanks to Arlene Oraby, a dear friend, for teaching me the written word and for her enormous help with editing the manuscript. Her endearing and generous devotion to the Great Pyrenees is appreciated by many.

I'd like to thank a longtime friend, Joanne DeLuca-Isola, for her expert advice on graphic arts and for the immeasurable support she always gives. Also, thanks to all my clients who let me photograph their puppies and whose good questions prompted us to write this book. A dear thanks to the late Job M. Evans who was such a positive influence in the dog world and who gave us invaluable guidance at the very beginning of this project.

Perhaps most of all I'd like to thank my parents and family for their support through the years, with a special thanks to my wife, Donna, because without her, none of the last 10 years would have been possible. She has helped me in every aspect of my life, including this book; I love her so. Finally, thanks to my 10-year-old Labrador, Myles, my best friend, to whom my part of the book is dedicated.

Introduction

If you're searching for the one book that will walk you through the first year of your puppy's life, look no further. This book has it all. In it you'll learn about puppy personalities. Training. Health care. It's fun, informative, and easy to understand. Read on—you and your puppy will be glad you did!

The authors, one a veterinarian and the other a dog trainer and behavior specialist, believe that the best dog-owner relationship begins with the well-thought-out selection of a suitable breed. The right puppy in the right home, given the best care and training will grow up to be a responsive, polite and happy four-footed family member.

The training section, Parts 1–3, takes you on an entertaining journey through your puppy's life. You'll learn training techniques to cope with the stages of infants, adolescents, puberty, and teens. All the typical problems of puppy raising are addressed in simple, easy-to-follow steps. And lots of games make learning fun for all family members—two or four-legged!

The section on health care, Part 4, provides a wealth of important information. Read about common diseases and ailments and find out about the role your veterinarian plays in your puppy's health program. You'll also find comprehensive information about first aid and holistic alternatives.

This book focuses on caring for and training your puppy during the first year, but it can serve as a reference guide for years to come.

Raising a puppy is a wonderful experience. You'll laugh, you'll wonder, you'll fight to hold on to your patience. Now that you've brought a puppy into your life, make it a decision you'll never regret!

Part 1

Put Yourself in My Paws!

1

A Puppy's Eye View

Imagine yourself in a puppy's paws. Suddenly you're taken from a warm and familiar setting and brought to an unfamiliar place. You don't speak or understand the language or customs. Everyone is giving directions, and when you can't possibly understand them, they start yelling. Ahhh! And as if that wasn't enough, they lock you in a room and disappear for a few hours. It's a pretty scary scenario. . . . What would you do? Cry? Run? Pee on the floor? All of the above? Probably. I know I would. Then imagine that you find someone to translate and explain everything to you in a calm and friendly way. Suddenly, this new place seems less daunting. Things would definitely be looking up.

Puppies are like this; maybe they can't articulate or speculate on their new situation, but they do sense a change from life with their littermates. They experience fear and panic or happiness and excitement just as surely as we do. The problem we must contend with is that puppies can't reason, and they don't understand English. They don't understand complex sentences or yelling and hitting, either. These tactics only frighten them. These adorable little foreigners need someone to speak to them in their own language and to understand how it feels to be in their paws. A little doggy empathy, please!

Arlene Oraby

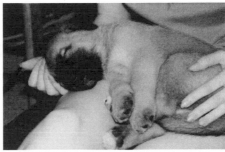

Your puppy's native language is "Doglish." In the next chapter I'll give you a crash course, and you'll be an expert in no time. With patience and understanding, you'll be able to explain your expectations fluently. In turn, your puppy will feel more secure. Everybody wins!

Get ready, destiny is calling you. It's time to act like a dog.

Dogs need lots of attention; certain breeds more than others. Unlike guinea pigs or gerbils, dogs don't accept social isolation very well. You can't expect them to enjoy sitting in a room all day with newspapers and a bowl of water. But busy people need dog love, too! If you're an always-on-the-go type, choose an independent breed with a medium-to-low energy level, *and make time in that schedule for your pup!*

If your schedule is unpredictable from week to week, you'll need to plan ahead for your new pup. New puppies need regular feedings and lots of outings when learning about housebreaking. Older puppies can adapt to a more flexible schedule as long as you don't forget a feeding.

If you're a home-all-day type, you (and your future puppy) are in luck. Although your schedule can be complicated and hectic, you probably have the flexibility to pay lots of attention to the new arrival.

2

Doglish

Congratulations! You are the proud parent of a playful, precious puppy. She's so cute and lively, you may be tempted to place all training efforts on hold and just cuddle and spoil her while she's so young and helpless. There's only one problem with that approach: It won't work. Nothing in life is that easy. If you are reading this with an older puppy, you may know the consequences firsthand of this idealized approach. The sooner you start to teach your puppy, the easier it is.

Your first job is to set up a leadership hierarchy. Because your puppy thinks of you (and everyone else in your family) as another dog, she will identify with you as either a leader or a follower—someone to pay attention to or someone to direct. Since being puppy trained is not a good thing, it's important to communicate leadership to your puppy as soon as possible. If you don't, you'll notice she'll start training you, and as anyone caught in that predicament can tell you, it's a disaster! A puppy who thinks she's number one is hyperactive, destructive and sometimes aggressive. Being in charge is a high-pressure job, and it's just too much for a pup. It's up to you to do it! Once you're in charge your pup will feel much safer.

So how do you set up a hierarchy? And what about a multi-person household? Remember this rule: If you walk on two legs, you're in control. If there are four humans in the household, your puppy must learn to take direction from everyone. In the hierarchy she'd be number five. The first step in learning to influence your puppy's behavior is to master good dog communication skills. Dogs naturally accept humans as other dogs and will learn better if you talk to them in their language. Of course, you must learn it to use it, so let's begin.

1 2 3 4 5

In a four-person household, the dog is at the bottom of the hierarchy. (Tina Engle-Balch)

DOGLISH

Doglish is a dog's version of our English. It has three components.

Eye Contact

Whenever you communicate approval or disapproval, look your puppy square in the eye. If you're pleased, smile so wide that your eyes squint. If you're upset, frown deeply and look very disappointed. This is your chance to be very theatrical! It will encourage her to watch you for direction.

Body Language

To direct your puppy's behavior, stand in front of her and stand tall. If you stand behind her, you'll look wimpy. If you bend over, you're doing what's known as the play bow. It's a play posture, and you simply won't be taken seriously. Straighten that back and look important!

Tonality

How you use your voice when communicating with your puppy is crucial because a dog understands how you sound, not what you say. Test this out—tell your puppy she's very bad in a happy tone. She'll probably wag her tail.

Your puppy understands four tones:

- *Directional Tone:* This is your Serious Voice. When you give a command like Sit or Come avoid sounding sweet. Otherwise, your puppy will take advantage. Speak clearly and sound like you mean it. Follow all commands with praise.
- *Praise Tone:* This is your Happy Voice. It should be warm and comforting, not strident or shrill.
- *Discipline Tone:* This is your Shame Voice. Act disappointed when your puppy acts naughty. *Do not yell.* Yelling may startle her, but it doesn't communicate anything.

- *The High-Pitched Squeal*: This is the only tone that works against you! Children and others with high voices may get a bit high-pitched when playing with or praising a puppy. Please try to avoid this. Because your puppy will be reminded of her littermates when she hears this tone, she may shift into rough play and mouthing behavior.

 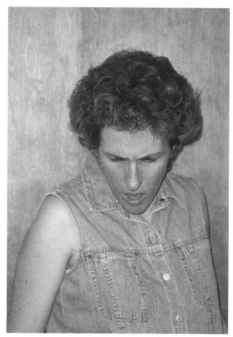

When praising, smile so wide your eyes squint.

When disciplining, speak in a shameful tone—don't yell.

As you can see, Doglish is quite different from English. Many people assume their puppy understands English, and she's no less than a fuzzy little human. In reality, puppies can't reason or comprehend anger. Every human reaction gets translated into Doglish. For example, if you correct your puppy for chewing on the couch with a stern "No" and a push, but ignore her when she's sitting in the corner with her own chew bone, what do you think she'll do the next time she wants attention? Your English says, "Don't chew on the couch," but your Doglish says, "I'll pay attention to you for chewing the couch, but not for chewing your bone." We'll discuss chewing in Chapter 13, but bear in mind, your puppy is watching you from a canine's eye, so you better start acting like one!

Let me give you a few more hints that will help you better understand your puppy:

- Your puppy loves attention! She doesn't care if it's negative or positive. Frantically chasing a sock stealer around the house may not seem like fun for you, but it's heaven to a pup. Sure, there may have been some stern words, but it's a surefire attention getter.
- Your puppy is habitual. She not only loves attention but is addicted to it. Once she finds a behavior that gets your attention, she'll repeat it over and over until it becomes a habit. Jumping is a great example of a negative habit. The most common corrections are physical: the shove, the knee in the chest, a little vocal disapproval, and some threatening eye contact. Now who can tell me what all these reactions have in common? They give attention to the puppy. Negative, perhaps, but most puppies will interpret these corrections as playful. You're talking human, she's thinking fun. She jumps up. You push her off. She jumps, you push. She stops temporarily but can't wait for the next person to walk through the door. Low and behold, a habit is forming. (We'll discuss how to rehabilitate the "joyful jumpers" in Chapter 13).
- Your puppy loves to learn. Her mind is like a sponge. Like kids, she'll do anything to make you proud. Your pup would much rather please you than anger you, but you must show her how.

Yes, there is more to that fuzzball than blinking eyes and puppy breath. In the following chapters you will be led stage by stage through training techniques and appropriate corrective measures. Puppies have different learning capabilities at different ages of development.

If you're starting this book with an adolescent puppy or older dog, reading each chapter will give you valuable insights that can be applied regardless of age.

Before we begin the training chapters, however, we still need to explore your puppy's individual personality and how it applies to your training techniques. Then we'll look at some humane and innovative training equipment to make life more enjoyable for both of you.

3

Understanding Your Puppy's Personality

Like children and snowflakes, each puppy is unique. Whether you've lived with your puppy for a couple of weeks or a few months, you'll notice he has his own special personality. This chapter outlines five basic personality types. Understanding and appreciating your puppy's special personality will give you an edge when formal training begins—you'll know what's going on behind those innocent eyes.

The Boss

This puppy has a strong sense of self. Bold and curious, he never misses a chance to investigate a new situation. He plays rough and often mouths excessively. Tug-of-war is big on his fun list, and if he can't provoke you with a toy, he'll use his leash or your clothing. He may be particularly rough with children, interpreting any corrections as an invitation to play harder. There are two subtypes to this personality:

The Bully

This boss takes himself too seriously. A dog of this nature can be extremely difficult to train. He is excessively physical and often mounts people. If his owners are too permissive, this dog may develop aggressive tendencies. Training must be very consistent and firm. If this is your pup, lay down the law *now*. Professional training may be needed.

Bold and curious, this puppy never misses a chance to investigate. (Pamela Levine)

Comic Relief

This boss doesn't want to lose any friends. He believes everything he does is very funny, and he must be firmly persuaded to cooperate. This guy *wants* to behave, he just finds it hard because there are so many fun things to do! Rarely will this personality develop aggression, although it's not unheard of. Given clear and consistent instruction, he takes to training well. His puppyhood will test your patience, but he'll be a wonderful dog if trained. This is my dog Calvin's basic personality type—Mr. Comedian.

Eager Beavers

If you like to train dogs, you'll love this personality. He's so eager to learn, he seems to read your mind. A genius! Left untrained, however, he may be a problem because he'll do anything for attention of any kind. If jumping gets a response, then jumping is good! If sitting on command gets a response, then sitting is good! Train this dog properly, and you'll have a Wonder Dog on your hands.

Joe Cool

He walks into your house and fits right in. Laid back and relaxed, he's not much interested in training. He likes to nap during formal lessons. Though this dog may sound dreamy, he has his drawbacks. Because of his laissez-faire attitude toward structure, training may fall by the wayside. Without it, he will not behave off leash. Joe Cool may be unmanageable in social situations too. So if you have a J.C. under your roof, don't neglect his training!

Joe Cool is laid back and relaxed.
(Arlene Oraby)

Sweet Pea

Docile and mild, this dog prefers to observe rather than to influence his world. He adores his people and trains best under a soft hand. There's little to say against this dear dog. Like the Joe Cools, it's easy to skip over training, but he needs it for the

Docile and mild, this dog prefers to observe rather than to influence his world.

same reasons. Firm corrections frighten him, but he'll learn quickly with loving praise.

Somewhat Shy

This dog likes to view the world from behind his owner's legs. Easily startled by strange situations and loud noises, he even becomes frightened when his owners fight. While it's very tempting to coddle this fellow when he's scared, comforting reassurances make the situation worse because he's getting praise for being wary. If you've got a shy guy on your hands, act confidently in new situations. Step away if he ducks behind you, and only pet him when he's in control. Training is essential for this pup because it will make him more confident. He'll respond best to a gentle hand.

A Puppy Personality Test

Here are six exercises that you'll use to access each puppy's personality. Rate each puppy according to the following scale: *A*—Active (top dog); *N*—Neutral (middle-man type); and *P*—Passive (a shy guy).
Test each puppy while it's awake and active.

Gentle Caress

1. *Gentle Caress:* Sit next to the puppy and gently stroke him at least 15 times. Does he immediately jump to-ward your face or scamper away toward a more stimulating distraction? Score *A*. Does he relax and sit quietly or climb in your lap? Score *N*. Does he cower, tuck his tail, pin his ears, or pull his mouth back in tension? Score *P*.

2. *Wacky Walk:* Stand up, shake your legs, clap your hands, and encourage the pup to follow you. Bend down like a monkey if you must, just

do what it takes to get his attention. Does he attack your legs or get distracted by a more interesting stimulation? Score *A*. Does he follow enthusiastically, looking up to your face for reinforcement? Score *N*. Does he sit and watch you quietly or withdraw in fear? Score *P*.

Flip-Flop

3. *Flip-Flop*: Next, lift the puppy and cradle him upside down like a baby. Does he squirm and try to grab at you with his mouth? Score *A*. If he wiggles a bit then settles happily, he gets an *N* score. If he whimpers or pulls his mouth back in tension (a submissive grin), he gets a *P*.

Uplift

4. *Uplift:* Cradle your puppy mid-body and suspend him four inches off the ground. If he squirms wildly and reaches out to mouth you, score *A*. If he squirms a bit but then relaxes, give him an *N*. If he shudders in fear or pins his ears back and tucks his tail, give him a *P*.

5. *What's That?* You'll need two spoons for this exercise. When the puppy is distracted, tap the spoons together above his head. If he jumps up and tries to wrestle the spoons, score *A*. If he ignores the sound or sniffs the spoons calmly, score *N*. If he cowers in fear or runs away, score *P*.

Crash Test

6. *Crash Test:* Walk at least six paces away from the puppy. Drop to the floor suddenly as if you've fallen and hurt your knee. Don't get carried away, but make it look realistic. Does the puppy take this as an invitation to play? Score *A*. Walk over and act curious? Give him an *N*. Does he run away or cower? Score *P*.

Just a Note

It's very rare that I come across a psychotic puppy, but they do exist, and I would be irresponsible if I didn't address this issue. Some puppies have been bred very poorly and suffer brain damage as a result. These puppies will develop into very vicious dogs and are a danger even as very young puppies. This problem is identified by erratic or fearful aggression responses in very atypical situations. There are two categories.

Erratic Viciousness

At unpredictable intervals, this puppy will growl fiercely from his belly. It may happen when his owner passes his food bowl, approaches when he's chewing a toy or even walks by him. At other times, the dog is perfectly sweet—a Jekyll-and-Hyde personality.

Fear-Biters

These puppies show dramatic fear or startled bite responses to nonthreatening situations like turning a page of the newspaper or moving your arm. They can act extremely confused or threatened when strangers approach. (*Please note:* Many well-educated dog people use this term incorrectly. There is a big difference in a dog/puppy that bites out of fear and a fear-biter. Don't automatically assume the worst if someone labels your dog with this term.)

Please don't panic if your dog occasionally growls at you or barks at the mailman. A lot of puppies growl when protecting a food dish or toy, and the guarding instinct is strong in many breeds. These are behavioral problems that can be cured or controlled with proper training. Even many biters can be rehabilitated. The situations I'm speaking of involve *severe* aggression—bared teeth, hard eyes, a growl that begins in the belly, and a bite response you'd expect from a trained police dog. These personality disturbances are seen very early, usually by four months of age.

It's both frightening and tragic because nothing can be done to alter these puppies' development. Their fate has been sealed by irresponsible, greedy people. If you suspect that your puppy might have either of these abnormalities, speak to your breeder and veterinarian immediately, and call a specialist to analyze the situation. These puppies must be euthanized. In my career, I've seen only four cases, and all were bought from unknown or suspect breeders.

Part 2

Training: First Day through First Year

4

Equipment Essentials

First things first! You need to set yourself up with the proper equipment. In this chapter I discuss the use of gates; a crate; indoor pens; the Teaching Lead, Flexi-Leash, and short lead; training collars; and chew toys.

Your puppy's age will determine how you use this chapter. Please read through it entirely before you begin, and make a note of any age-specific instructions. Don't put undue pressure on a very young pup!

GATES

Gates are essential to enclose a play area. This area must be kept clear of loose household objects that might be tempting to chew or could be harmful if swallowed. Ideally, this area should have linoleum or tiled floors in case of accidents. Kitchens are often ideal areas because they don't isolate your puppy from you.

Gates can also be used to discourage puppies from entering off-limits rooms, and they are necessary to block off dangerous stairways, ledges, or porches.

THE CRATE

Crates must be used properly. If you plan to be gone more than six hours, your puppy is better off enclosed in a kitchen or bathroom. Indoor pens are also available at your local pet store. If you're home, crate your pup only when necessary. Crates are a valuable training aid. In certain situations, they are extremely useful:

Advantages

- when your puppy must be left unattended for less than six hours;
- during sleeping hours with a young, unhousebroken puppy;
- as a feeding station for distractible pups (*see* Chapter 10).

The crate encourages good sleeping habits and discourages elimination. Convenient and effective, crates are widely recommended. But they're not perfect.

Confining your puppy in a crate works as a preventative measure. Your puppy can't get into much trouble in there, but isolation provides little actual *training*, and it has other drawbacks:

Disadvantages

- It doesn't communicate leadership.
- It separates you from your puppy when you're at home.
- It can't teach a puppy how to behave in all rooms of the house.

But puppies are puppies and they simply can't have unsupervised household freedom. Your house will be trashed, your puppy will be wild, and you will be *really* sorry. Obviously, some structure is in order here, but what can work as well as a crate?

I found an alternative.

THE TEACHING LEAD

I call the alternative the Teaching Lead. It is a leash designed to communicate your control and condition appropriate household behavior *passively*. Use it to limit freedom and structure situations so your puppy will develop good habits through positive reinforcement.

It's a fast, easy, economical way to teach your puppy how to behave in every room of your house. Anyone can do it—with little or no discipline. Best of all, you get to keep your sanity. Have I got your attention?

I began to develop this concept after discovering a training method called *umbilical cording*. Its proponents, trainers Job Michael Evans and Carol Lea Benjamin, suggested that you tie your dog around your waist when you can't give her your undivided attention at home. You're free to move around the house, she's not isolated, and everybody's happy!

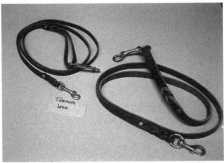

The Teaching Lead is designed to communicate control and to condition appropriate behavior passively.

Over the years, I've expanded that idea to bring about a whole new approach to raising and training both puppies and delinquent dogs. In this chapter I will explain how I use the Teaching Lead to:

- take the place of a crate when you're at home;
- housebreak your puppy;
- eliminate excessive jumping;
- encourage good chewing;
- discourage nipping;
- calm your puppy around company.

The Teaching Lead can't be bought in stores, but it is patented and available from me. You can make your own by buying a sturdy six-foot lead and a double-headed clip from the hardware store. Place one end of the clip on the handle of the leash as shown in the photograph. I suggest you buy a leather lead, as it provides much greater leverage when trying to control an excited puppy. To protect the leash from your pup's teeth, cover it with Bitter Apple Paste, which can be bought at a local pet store.

A Little Preview

The Teaching Lead has two applications: *leading* and *stationing*. Once you understand both methods you can use them interchangeably. The next chapter outlines both in detail, but here's a preview.

Stationing

You'll select a special spot for your puppy in each room she'll be permitted in as an adult. At first she'll be secured to the area on the lead, but eventually, you'll be able to send her there off leash, using a special command like Settle Down.

Leading

You'll secure your puppy to your side and lead him around using specific commands. Eventually, he'll respond to these commands off leash. Leading makes you look like a competent leader!

Until your puppy is behaving reliably, don't give her freedom in any other room but her original gated area. When introducing her to the house, use the teaching lead with one of the two applications.

In the next chapter I expand the discussion of the Teaching Lead and give you examples of how you can use it to teach your puppy how to behave in your home.

TRAINING COLLARS

The Right Collar

Various training collars.

Until your puppy is 16 weeks old, use a regular buckle collar. Until this age the tissues are still forming around your puppy's neck; an improperly used training collar can strain this area and cause permanent damage to the trachea. Once your puppy hits four months, she's ready for a necklace!

- *The Training Collar:* This collar is effective in most cases. Improperly called a "choke" collar, it is often misused. Worn and used properly, it is the sound of the collar that reinforces a correction. Choking and restraint aggravate behavior problems. This collar must be placed over your pup's head in the proper direction and must ride high on your puppy's neck.
  NOTE: When instructed to snap the leash, keep your knuckles facing the ceiling and your thumb wrapped underneath the leash.

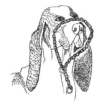

To place the training collar on your puppy correctly, face him and create the letter *P* with the chain. After slipping it over his head, slide the loops between his ears and bring the collar high on his neck. (Tina Engle-Balch)

Extending your arm behind you, snap backwards quickly from your elbow. Release the pressure on the leash immediately. Repeat if necessary. You do not want to jerk back and hold your pup in place, as this will choke him (it's the sound, not the restraint). You want to avoid holding the leash improperly and jerking up, as this will frighten your pup and cause him to pull away from you.

- *The "Self-Correcting" Collar:* It looks barbaric, but it isn't. Developed by the Germans for many of their bull-necked breeds, it offers control for dogs and pups that are pain-insensitive and too powerful to persuade on the chain collar. I call it the "self-correcting" collar because it requires little strength by the handler; by simply locking your arm into one place, the pulling pup will feel a pinch and slow down.
  NOTE: Very occasionally, these collars pop and fall off. To prevent a possible emergency, buy an oversized training collar and attach your leash to both when walking in an unconfined area.

- *The Halti/Gentle Leader:* Whenever I meet a particularly dominant, excitable, or mouthy puppy, I recommend this device. It looks like a muzzle but it's not; dogs can eat, chew, and play without any difficulty. It works on the "mommy" principle: When puppies act up, mother dog puts pressure on the wild one's muzzle. You can do the same thing with a Halti. It works wonders in these situations. It's also useful for people who are unable to use neck collars. It requires minimal physical strength, so anyone can use it.

THE FLEXI-LEASH

No, you don't have to take up jogging to exercise your puppy! The Flexi-Leash is a retractable cord that looks and works much like a fishing reel. It comes in lengths of 16 feet or 26 feet and is an invaluable exercise tool because it allows your puppy to race around while you stand still or walk at a normal pace.

Until you are very comfortable and familiar with its use, don't take it near a road or use it in a heavy-trafficked area. It takes some practice, and you don't want to put your puppy in danger!

Some puppies love to chew their Flexi. Soaking the cord in liquid Bitter Apple overnight is a good deterrent. If this is ineffective, you can try snapping the cord *into* her mouth or spiriting her nose with a diluted Bitter Apple spray mixture as she goes for the lead.

THE SHORT LEAD

Clients often tell me that their puppies jump or nip during free time in their enclosed area. If this is happening with your puppy, attach a short leash and grab it to correct your puppy when she plays too rough. Pushing her away physically encourages dominance play, but a sharp tug of the short leash is unpleasant. Encourage more appropriate play with a kickball or bottle (*see* index).

THE CAR LEAD

Driving a car is a job in itself—you shouldn't be wrestling with your dog while doing it. It's a safety hazard for you, your dog, and other motorists. To remedy this situation, I suggest you make a car lead by tying a hardware store clip to a piece of rope and then fasten it to a seat belt or hook in the backseat or cargo area of your car. Here's how it works:

- Create an area in your car for your dog. Middle seats or back compartments are ideal.
- Lay down a blanket and put in a favorite chew toy to help her recognize her spot.

A car "station" in the backseat, using a short car lead. (Debbie Miller)

- Tie the rope or slide the short lead through the seat belt. If the area is in the back compartment, tie the rope onto a hook.
- Tell her cheerfully, "Go to your spot," as you place her and offer a treat for cooperating. Hook her to her area and ignore all protests. Praise her vocally when she's calm.

Remember—it's safest to confine your puppy while driving. It protects her like a seat belt protects you. Crates are cumbersome but can also be used to secure your puppy while you drive. Be sure the station rope or lead is short enough so your pup can't jump over the backseat. It is very unsafe to you and distracting to other motorists to have your dog in the front seat. And never let your puppy ride in your lap.

PLEASE NOTE: It is unsafe to allow your puppy to hang its head from the window or ride in the back of open pickup trucks. Dogs are exposed to flying pebbles or other objects that could permanently damage eyes and are at great risk if you should have an accident.

5

The Teaching Lead

Okay, I'm going to come right out and say it. Your puppy doesn't know too much. Oh, he's intelligent all right, but he's just a baby. Motivated by needs, he isn't sitting around having complex thoughts. In time he'll know plenty, but right now things are pretty simple in puppyland. Here's what it's like from both your perspective and your puppy's.

Owner: My puppy peed on the rug. He *knows* he's not supposed to do that!
Puppy: Pee. Here. Now.
Owner: I bend over, clap my hands, and call his name and he runs away! He's teasing me!
Puppy: Play! Fun! Run!
Owner: My puppy gives me such sad eyes when I leave. He's trying to make me feel guilty.
Puppy: Change. Confusion. Anxiety.
Owner: He knows when he's been naughty. When I yell at him, he slinks away on his belly.
Puppy: Shouting. Scary. Hide.

So you see, your puppy doesn't really "know" things, you have to teach him. I designed the Teaching Lead method to simplify this step for both of you.

What Is It?

The Teaching Lead is a leash. As described in the previous chapter, you can make your own by attaching the handle end of a regular six-foot leash to a double-headed clip.

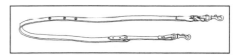

The Teaching Lead is used to lead your dog (while freeing your hands) and to station it in a particular spot. (Tina Engle-Balch)

23

The Teaching Lead shows your puppy how to behave in your house and around company. It reduces the problems associated with excessive isolation as well as those associated with unlimited household freedom. It also lays the groundwork for further off-leash training. It's a fast, easy, economical way to teach your puppy good habits with little or no discipline. Just about anyone can do it.

Oh, Sure

Honestly! It's not too good to be true. The Teaching Lead has two applications: leading and stationing. You'll be using them interchangeably, so before you start it's best to understand them both. Some days you will do more leading than stationing, and other days you may find that your puppy is stationed a large percentage of the time.

NOTE: When introducing your puppy or older adolescent dog to the house, keep him on the Teaching Lead by using one of the two applications. Until he behaves, give him freedom only in a gated puppy-proofed room or in a fenced enclosure.

Before you begin, please go down this checklist. You must be able to answer yes to each question:

- Is your puppy at least 12 weeks old?
- Are you able to read your puppy elimination signs?
- Can you tell when your puppy is too excited to sit still?
- Do you have a planned feeding schedule?
- Have you puppy-proofed your house?

Even at 12 weeks old puppies have a lot of needs that override the Teaching Lead. Please be attentive to them. If he's hungry, needs to eliminate, or is wild with energy, you need to take a break and provide for his needs.

Okay! You're ready to begin!

LEADING

Before you begin, remember:

- Your puppy must be at least 12 weeks old to begin this process.
- Your puppy must be used to his leash (*see* Chapter 8).
- Do not practice when your pup needs exercise. Leading does not take the place of a run.

Leading is a good word to describe the process of connecting your dog to your side because it communicates leadership to your puppy. It's a passive and fun way to show your puppy around and let him know who's the boss. In a big family everyone can take turns.

The Dog Belt

Slide the leash around your waist like a belt. Put it around your left side if you want your dog on the left, or around your right side if you want him on your right. Everyone must keep the pup on the same side. Connect the end loop to the appropriate waist hole, and you're ready to go!

The Right Collar

Until your puppy is 16 weeks old, use the regular buckle collar. If your

With the Teaching Lead, your puppy will be connected to you during training.

puppy is older than 16 weeks, he's ready for a training collar. In the last chapter we discussed the various collars available to you. Please review this section if necessary and find the collar best suited for you and your puppy.

Follow the Leader

Where you go, puppy goes. All household decisions begin with you—this is your chance! It may seem awkward at first, but soon you won't even know he's there. It might even be fun! Remember you're teaching him to follow *you*, so if there is a conflict of interest (he wants to go left when you're going right), go *your* way and encourage him along.

Giving Direction

While connected, use the following commands conversationally. Encourage everyone handling him to use them as well. Speak clearly and enunciate your syllables—dogs understand sounds, not words!

1. *"(Your Dog's Name), Let's Go!"* Give this command whenever you start walking or changing direction.

2. *"Sit."* Use this command whenever you offer your dog something positive like food, praise, a toy, or a pat. Say the command once, positioning if the dog doesn't respond. Remember—dogs understand sounds. "Sit-sit-sit" sounds much different from "Sit."

3. *"Name."* A few times each day, stand in front of your dog (back straight!) and call out his name. If he doesn't look to you, direct his eyes toward you with a finger and a clucking sound.

Hold the lead properly, knuckles up, so you can snap straight back behind your thigh to correct.

4. *"Wait and Okay."* Use this command to stop your dog at doors, stairs, and other important thresholds such as the car and the veterinarian's office. Command "Wait" and bring your dog behind you. He may get excited, but wait until he settles down to command "Okay." Make sure *your* feet cross the threshold first. Leaders must lead!

5. *"Excuse Me."* Say this whenever your dog crosses in front of or behind you. Also say this if your dog presses against you or blocks your path. Remember, this is a hierarchy and you're a leader, not a leaning post.

Sitting Still

Whenever you sit (to talk on the phone, do homework, or watch TV), slide the end clip around to your tailbone and sit on the remaining slack of the leash.

Leave enough room for your puppy to lie comfortably *behind* your feet. Give your puppy a bone and encourage her to lie still by petting her when she does so.

Taking a Break

If you feel like taking a break, you can do two things: have interactive playtime off leash in a fenced enclosure or gated area, or take her out on a Flexi-Leash; or station her (make sure her bladder is empty). There will be days when you station much more than lead—that's okay. Use both methods interchangeably, but keep that puppy with you when you're home!

It's important to take breaks, too.

Don't be alarmed by your puppy's energy spurts. They're normal—and usually very cute. If your puppy gets too riled up and starts to jump at you, attach a short leash to her buckle collar. Correct her by grabbing it and snapping it to one side. Pushing or hitting will only be interpreted as rough play, and things could get wilder.

How Leading Can Work for You

Murphy is a sweet-natured, 8-month-old Golden Retriever/Doberman Pinscher mix. His family loves him tremendously, but they're not sure how to discipline him. Left free, he prances about nervously. When he can't get anyone's attention, he urinates on the rug or steals things off the counter. They try yelling and hitting, but it leaves them feeling guilty and frustrated. It doesn't solve his housebreaking and stealing problems, either. Both actions get him attention, and he repeats what works. Until I met him, Murphy had only been on a leash to go the veterinarian's office. Although his owners wanted to take him when they went for their daily walk, he pulled too hard and had to be left behind.

When I first put Murphy on the Teaching Lead, he was a little nervous. His hyperactivity was a sign of his internal anxiety—he wasn't sure how to behave. I led him around gently saying his name before each turn. He soon caught on to the idea and swung his head to me each time I said his name. By the end of the first hour, he had calmed down considerably. Everyone in the family successfully repeated the sequence as I had done—Murphy was thrilled to be getting a little direction! For the first week he was kept stationed near his family or led around by them. Someone was in charge finally, and Murphy reacted very positively. I taught them other skills to control the housebreaking and stealing, and soon both difficulties were only a memory.

Henry is a roly-poly jet black 3½-month-old Cocker Spaniel. His devoted owners found that when they couldn't be 100 percent attentive to him, he would pee on the furniture or mouth their young son, so they were forced to crate him quite a bit. Henry barked in his crate. That made the family feel guilty because they knew he wanted to be with them. They wanted a way to train him quickly.

They called me just six days after they brought him home. I introduced them to the Teaching Lead and demonstrated its techniques. The leading technique taught Henry to watch his owners for direction. His young master also was able to lead Henry by wearing the leash around his chest like a banner. Henry quickly understood that in his house the two-legged dogs are the leaders!

Common Questions About Leading

Can everyone belt around?

Yes! You don't want your hierarchy to become a dictatorship. The only unacceptable combination is small children and big puppies. Other than that, everyone should take part. If the lead is too long for a child, it can be worn like a banner.

What if my dog grabs the leash?

Puppies love to walk their owners. It's enormous fun and reminds them of all those tug-of-war games you play together. The first step in correcting this problem is eliminating the game. When your pup takes the leash in his mouth, snap it back *into* his mouth very sharply and say *No* firmly. Pulling it out encourages a rougher reaction.

NOTE: Rub Bitter Apple paste on the leash, a vile-tasting but completely harmless substance found at any pet store. This substance will not harm the lead and will discourage mouthing.

What if my dog won't move?

Have you got a mule wannabe? This is a very common resistance ploy. Your puppy is hoping that you will rush back and give him lots of attention, but please avoid this! I use two approaches, depending on the pup and the situation.

The first is just keep walking. Don't turn around! Praise the air in front of you and walk a little faster. When your puppy catches up, praise him happily and continue. This method works well with large breeds who have a record of being stubborn.

If your puppy grabs the lead, snap it up into her mouth.

If you have a more delicate breed, kneel down in front of him when he puts on the brakes. Tap the floor and encourage him to come to you. When he does, praise him warmly, then go out to the end of the leash again and repeat yourself. He'll catch on soon. Remember: No attention for stubborn stopping and absolutely no pickups!

STATIONING

Before you begin, it's important to remember:

- Your puppy must be at least 12 weeks old before you begin this process.

- Make sure the station is away from stairs, electrical cords and outlets, or entanglements like posts.
- Be sure the object is immovable, sturdy, and unable to tip.
- When securing your puppy, make sure he's wearing a buckle or tag collar, *never a training collar.*

Stationing lets you take your puppy into every room he's permitted in and shows him how to behave there. Here's how it works.

Pick an Area

Select a small area or corner in each room he'll be allowed in. This will be his *station*, and eventually, he'll go there automatically. Right now, you must secure him in his area with the lead.

Secure Your Puppy

Secure your puppy at his station. Wrap the leash around an immovable object and attach the double-headed clip to the opposite end of the leash (*see* picture). Alternatively, you can screw an eye bolt into the wall and clip the leash through it. When stationed, your puppy should have no more than three feet of freedom; given too much room, he may piddle or pace.

Select a small area in each room where your dog will be allowed and secure him there with the lead.

When first practicing this procedure, stay with your pup. Make him feel comfortable in the area and encourage him to chew his bone. Leave only when he's busy with a chew toy or resting. Bravely ignore whining or barking (unless he's communicating a need to go out), and return to him when he's settled down. Soon you'll be able to hook him up and leave immediately.

Whenever possible, reinforce good behavior at a station by praising or petting your puppy.

Keeping Close

Remember, your puppy wants to be with you or another family member whenever you're around. The point of stationing is to teach your puppy how to behave in social situations, so make sure you station him in a room with people.

Giving Direction

Whenever you lead your puppy to his area, command "Settle Down" and point to his spot.

Station Goodies

A comfy cushion or blanket and a favorite chew toy will help your puppy identify his space. Ask your veterinarian for suggestions. Avoid rawhide bones with big knots—they can cause indigestion and other problems. Remove end fragments of hoofs or rawhide to discourage gulping.

Giving Attention

An unsupervised puppy often gets attention for being naughty. On the other hand, a stationed puppy can't cause too much trouble. Instead of having to run around scolding him, you can love and praise him warmly whenever he is calm or chewing a bone.

Stationing Can Work for You

Fred is an adorable 8-month-old Beagle. Although he is given a high-quality puppy food (which he eats with gusto), he hangs around the kitchen table looking soulful and starved. This technique usually pays off with a few pats and an occasional tidbit, although both owners would prefer he lay in the corner. Fred also enjoys begging during formal dinner parties. His owners would like to take him along when they visit family and friends, but Fred's food manners have placed him on the "B" list for most social affairs.

When I met Fred, I discovered a very happy fellow who thought begging was just the right thing to do. How could something that resulted
in attention and treats be wrong? I suggested that his owners create a
station in the kitchen at least 10 feet from the table. As I predicted, Fred
barked during the first few meals, but his determined owners ignored
him. Soon after, he began to settle down and chew his bone. Within a
month he was staying in his area off leash. The Teaching Lead has
helped Fred to make a successful transition from a social outcast to a
welcomed guest.

Lucky is a rough-and-tumble 3½-month-old Irish Setter puppy who
shares his home with four children. After school, Lucky is let out of his
gated area to play with the kids. It's exciting for everyone, but before
long Lucky starts to nip and pull at their clothing. The children try to
stop him by pushing him away, and the parents try to correct him by
shouting. He interprets this increased activity as an invitation to play
harder. Lucky quickly reaches the overstimulation point and has to be
isolated. End of playtime.

Lucky learns nothing about good behavior by being isolated. This
overstimulation/isolation cycle would have continued, but his family
took the time to train him. We will go over methods on how to discourage chewing and rough play later, but part of the solution for Lucky and
his family was a station on the edge of the kid's play area. When Lucky
is calm or chewing a bone, the kids pet him and give unlimited love and
attention. When they play, Lucky observes them happily. Lucky feels
good because he doesn't have to be isolated all the time, and he has his
own space in the children's world.

Common Questions About Stationing

How many stations will I have?

You can have two stations or twenty. Create a station in every room your dog
will be welcome. You can also have outside stations and one in the car. Here is a
rundown of my dog Calvin's stations:

- **Family room:** This one is near the couch, so we can pet him while
  we watch television.
- **Dining room:** While we're eating, he relaxes across the room so he
  won't be tempted to disturb us.
- **Kitchen:** Our kitchen is small, so Calvin's station is just outside the
  door. He can watch the preparation, but he can't get underfoot in his

unending quests for floor goodies. Since there was nothing to station him onto, we originally screwed a large eye hook in the base of the wall.

- **Greeting room/front hall:** Calvin used to get somewhat overexcited when company arrived, so we created a station 10 feet behind the door. Now he knows he'll be greeted after he settles down.
- **Bedrooms:** We gave Calvin his own dog bed next to the dresser. Confining him initially helped with housebreaking and also taught him to sleep quietly through the night. Dogs older than four months can be stationed at night rather than crated, provided they are reliably housebroken. Keeping them close to you makes them feel more secure and calm.
- **Office:** When I go to my office, Calvin usually accompanies me. To help him learn how to settle down, I gave him a special corner with a great big dog bed.
- **Outside:** We have a badminton net in the backyard. Neighborhood kids like to use it sometimes. Left free, Calvin would love to retrieve the birdie and lead a spirited chase around the block. But what Calvin *wants* to do and what Calvin *should* do are sometimes two very different things. We created a tree station on the side of the court. He now knows to watch the kids and play with them off leash after their game.

Do I have to leash him forever?

No! The leash is only temporary; for now you are using it to create good habits that will eventually apply off leash when he's housebroken and in control of his chewing habits.

How long can a puppy be stationed?

That will depend on your puppy. A sleepy puppy of any age can handle an hour or more. An older pup can handle more extended periods. The best gauge is your puppy—keep him stationed near you, and be aware of his signals. If your pup has been napping at his station for an hour and suddenly gets up and starts acting restless, it's probably time to go to his bathroom spot (see the House-breaking section in the Etiquette chapter). If your puppy chews on a bone for 15 minutes and then starts acting like a jumping bean, it's probably an energy spurt and time for a little play.

What if he panics?

First you must determine if his reaction was really panic or simply a persuasive protest. Ignore the protest. If he is truly panicked, initially station him only when you can sit with him. Encourage bone chewing and begin to leave his side only when he's sleeping. Pretty soon he'll get the hang of it.

What if my dog chews the leash?

Rub Bitter Apple paste on the leash. Bitter Apple can be used on many household objects. If Bitter Apple is not effective, try mixing some red pepper juice with a little garlic and spreading it on. You may also try soaking the leash overnight in liquid Bitter Apple. This is a good deterrent, although it may discolor the leather.

If all else fails, get a chain lead and temporarily station him on that.

What if my dog barks?

Does he need to eliminate, or does he have some other pressing need? If not, ignore him. If he's persistent, buy ear plugs or try distracting him by using a fancy long-distance squirt gun. (I found the Super Soaker to be very effective—long range and accurate, too!) But you must be very sneaky—he can't know where the water is coming from. Only release a dog from a station once he's calm and quiet.

My puppy is 13 weeks old. What do I do when he gets too excited?

Your puppy may be cycling into a high-energy mode, or he may need to eliminate. If he needs to exercise, take a time-out and play with him in his gated area, a fenced yard, or on his Flexi-Leash.

Do I need to unstation him if I'm just running out of the room for a few minutes?

No. Short departures are good because they get your puppy used to being left alone and show him that you won't desert him. Tell him "Wait" as you leave, and go calmly. If he's very theatrical when you return, ignore him. You'd reinforce his anxiety. Wait until he's calm and then go over to reassure him.

Wrapping Up

As you can see, the Teaching Lead encourages a lot more participation than the crate. Remember, it doesn't replace the crate, it simply encourages you to keep your puppy with you when you're home. It lets you communicate your control passively, spend time with your puppy, and quickly train him how to behave in the house. In short, it helps you create a four-footed family member!

6

Special Considerations

Your puppy is a very special creature. Like us, she loves affection, company, treats, and play. But she's not completely like us. She doesn't want her own room. She won't deliberate over three balanced meals a day, and she won't put her toys away when she's through playing with them. She needs a few special considerations.

SLEEPING ARRANGEMENTS

There is no way around it. Your puppy will feel a lot safer if she's near someone at night. She'll sleep better. You'll sleep longer. She won't cry, and she'll be less hyperactive in the morning. Your puppy is a social gal and doesn't like being alone! Bunking together also enhances your training. If she wakes up during the night and is frightened, she'll look to you. When she sees you sleeping quietly—her fearless leader—she'll feel reassured. While she's a young pup, you'll need to crate her or keep her in a large open-topped box by your bedside. As she grows up, you can give her her own bed and station her on her teaching lead. Before you know it she'll be tucking herself in at night!

If she can't sleep near a family member, put her in an enclosed area, play some soft music, and turn off the lights. When you come in in the morning, wait until her excitement has tempered down to greet her.

NOTE: Few things in life are as tempting as a big cuddle on the bed with a puppy, but think to the future. Big dog. Shedding dog. Muddy dog. Fleas. If you do not want your adult dog on the bed later, don't confuse your puppy now. On the other hand, if you're not adverse to sharing your sanctuary, I suggest you teach your puppy that she may come up with your permission *only.* When you

Your puppy doesn't have to sleep on your bed with you, but she does like to be close to you at night.

If your puppy is normally too distracted to eat, put him in his crate at dinnertime.

want to bring pup up, say "Sit" (helping him if necessary), then lift her up. If she jumps up on her own, either ignore her or command "Off." Soon she'll catch on and sit for permission.

THE FOOD

Puppies aren't really picky about what goes into the dinner bowl. Though some very fancy gourmet dog food commercials might lead you to believe otherwise, dogs don't have the discriminating palate we humans enjoy. A high-quality dry food is your best bet. Your veterinarian can suggest a good brand and answer questions about how much and how often you should feed your puppy. Watch her weight! Since all puppies are individuals, they will have different requirements.

Some puppies are just too distracted when you put their food down. Who wants to eat when we could play? You have two choices: Place your puppy in her crate while you eat, or create a food station.

How about table scraps? I don't recommend giving any table treats to your dog because it encourages begging, stealing, and lap drooling. Bad table manners aside, it's unhealthy to give your puppy a wide range of human goodies. Her digestive tract is much simpler than ours, and she can't break down all those yummy chemicals we enjoy so much!

CHEW TOY

Keep your puppy's toy box simple. Filling it with a variety of shaped and textured objects only confuses her. She'll be unable to identify what belongs to her and what is yours. Consider your puppy's rather simple worldview when choosing a toy: Does the fringe on that rope toy look like the fringe on your living room rug? Does that stuffed toy look too much like a throw pillow or stuffed animal?

Find a chew toy your puppy likes. Choose from pressed rawhide, cow hooves, pig knuckles or ears, Nylabones, or a Puppy Pacifier. Buy several and place one at all her stations. Let her chew whenever she wants and give her plenty of attention for good chewing habits! Throughout her first year, your puppy will be overflowing with nervous energy, and since she can't chew her finger nails, she needs an acceptable alternative.

THE SCHEDULE

Your puppy will spend almost all her time doing these four things:

- eating
- eliminating
- exercising and playing
- sleeping

You might find it helpful to create a schedule to organize these activities. Here is an example of a schedule for a 12-week-old pup:

Morning	Afternoon	Evening
6:30 Outside	12:00–12:15 Second feeding	5:00–7:30 Stationing or isolation
6:45–7:30 Back to bed!	12:15–12:30 Outside and play	7:30–8:00 Outside play and exercise

Morning	Afternoon	Evening
7:30 First feeding	12:30–4:00 Stationing or isolation	8:00–10:45 Stationing or isolation
7:45 Out again!	4:00 Out again please!	10:45–11:00 One last trip outside
7:50–8:15 Play and exercise	4:00–4:30 Exercise and play	11:15 Bedtime. Whew!
8:15–11:30 Stationing or isolation	4:30 Last feeding	
11:30 Outside		
11:30–12:00 Exercise and playtime		

DESIGNATING RESPONSIBILITY

If you have kids, I encourage you to have a short meeting before the puppy arrives. Everyone should get involved in care and training. Make a schedule like the one above, writing in the names for who does what. Have a pen handy so everyone can check off when their assignment was completed. If everyone takes part, your puppy will quickly get accustomed to all her new pack members. Providing care raises your pack status!

Notice that many blocks of time suggested either keeping your puppy on her teaching lead or isolating her. Try to make isolation the exception rather than the rule. Your puppy is a social critter, and too much isolation creates what I call "hyper isolation anxiety." She's so overwhelmed to see you, so she acts confused, hyperactive, and very crazy when greeted. A well-socialized puppy is a happy puppy! And a happy, relaxed puppy is easier to train.

Remember

Your puppy cannot read your mind! She can't tell you audibly what she needs, though her needs are many. She relies on you to provide her with food that's easy to digest, chew toys that she enjoys chomping on, and sleeping quarters that make her feel safe. Your special considerations will add up to a calm, well-cared-for puppy who'll be more at ease and open to your direction!

7

Starting Off on the Right Paw

Your mother was right—first impressions count! If you bring your new puppy into confusion and chaos, he may act accordingly. To make him feel as welcome as possible, follow these suggestions.

The House

Clean up! Make sure nothing is on the floor but furniture. Your puppy is like those toddlers you see in the grocery store, grabbing everything in sight. For more on this subject, please refer to the "Puppy Proofing" section in Chapter 17.

The Family

Have a puppy pow-wow. Everyone sit in a circle on the floor with the puppy in the center. Let him approach each person on his own. No bribery or unfair attention-getting ploys are allowed.

To help your puppy feel welcome, have a puppy pow-wow, with the family in a circle and the puppy in the middle. Let the puppy come to people as he chooses.

Special Rules for Kids

It's a big day. The kids will be bubbling with excitement. However, the puppy will be startled if he comes into a house of squealing children. Explain to them that the puppy needs help in getting used to his new house, and he'll be homesick for his mom for a couple of days. Encourage them to speak softly and kindly to him. Let them follow him around, but discourage

41

all roughhousing and shouting. This is a very exciting time, but your puppy might be frightened by the extraordinary energy level generated by your kids.

Other Dogs

Don't expect an older dog to jump with joy at the prospect of sharing his space with a new puppy. The concept may take some getting used to. When introducing the pup to an older dog, don't interfere unless you see an unusually aggressive response. Some older dogs will growl or paw at a new puppy—this is a good sign. Big dog is showing little dog who's the boss. Sometimes a small puppy will shriek if the big dog even comes near; again, don't interfere! If you comfort the puppy, it may alienate the older dog and make the puppy more fearful. To keep the hierarchy harmonious, pay more attention to the older dog, greeting and feeding him first. As long as he feels like he's still number

When introducing the pup to an older dog, don't interfere unless you see an unusually aggressive response.

one in your heart, he should cope just fine. It's hard not to meddle and feel protective of a puppy, but remember—these are dog pack rules!

The Resident Cats

Cats have mixed feelings about new puppies. Some cats head for the highest object in the house and stare at you reproachfully. Some wait confidently for the curious puppy to get close enough for a good, solid bat on the nose. In either case, keep your response low-key. Overreacting will make both of them nervous. If your cat can't cope with the puppy, keep them in separate areas and bring them together when your puppy is old enough to be stationed.

If you own any caged animals, don't bring them out immediately. Let the puppy get used to you, then show him the cages when he's sleepy. Acclimate him to the caged creatures slowly and positively.

Friends and Guests

Encourage any visitors to get down on the floor when greeting your puppy. Of course, use common sense when suggesting this idea; not everyone can or will want to romp around with the pup. If possible, cradle your puppy into a sitting position when they approach. You'll be getting a head start on good adult manners!

People with Special Needs

If your puppy is going to be around someone who's frail or physically challenged, help encourage calmness from the start. Use common sense—if you have a big breed, don't allow him to get on anyone's lap. Your puppy may be small now, but nobody needs a 140-pound Great Dane sitting on him. If there is a wheelchair involved, teach the puppy to walk behind it and to lie down when it's stationary. When first introducing your puppy, bring him over when he's calm. Offer him a toy (treats are too exciting) and a few pats.

THE FIRST 24 HOURS

During the Day

The first day can be a little strange. After all the anticipation and preparation, the little creature is finally in your home. Some puppies jump right into the swing of things, others have a more reserved approach. Don't compare him with other puppies you've known, and don't worry if he seems too rambunctious, too cautious, or too anything! This is all very new, and he's trying to figure out what's going on. If he wants to sleep, let him sleep; put him in his crate with the door open. At mealtime, put his food in or near his crate and leave him alone for 15 minutes. If he doesn't touch his food, that's okay. It's probably just his nerves! After the meal, give him some water, then walk him outside or to the papers (see "Housebreaking," Chapter 13).

Have an easy day. Don't overstimulate him with 300 toys and millions of people running in and out. Give him some adjustment time. If he is enthusiastic and wants to explore everything, go with him. If he wants to sit in a corner all day, just mill around the room, petting him for venturing out. Don't pet him if he's cowering in a corner—you'll reinforce that behavior. If you pay attention to a timid puppy, you'll have a timid dog. If your puppy has an accident or grabs something inappropriate, don't correct him. He's too small and disorganized to retain anything, and you'll just frighten him. Relax! You're doing fine. This is just the beginning.

During the Night

Ideally, the puppy should sleep near you at night, in a large box or crate by your bedside. He may whine the first few nights, but he'll feel a lot safer here than if he's alone in another room. He will probably need to get up one to three times during the night to eliminate. Quietly take him to his spot and then back to his enclosure. Don't start playing games at three o'clock in the morning. We'll cover this topic in more detail in the "House-breaking" section.

As your puppy adjusts, don't compare him with any other puppies you've known. Let him take his own time to develop.

If sleeping in your bedroom is out of the question, crate or enclose your puppy in a small area like a bathroom or kitchen. Turn off the lights, leave on some classical music, and be ready to come down and walk him if he cries. Ahhh, the joys of puppy parenthood!

8

The Infant: 8 to 12 Weeks

L et the fun begin! Training a young puppy can be one of life's most rewarding experiences. You're giving your puppy a head start on life and avoiding a lot of frustrations that result when training is postponed.

Even though your puppy is capable of learning at this age, don't expect too
much, and avoid harsh corrective techniques completely. Your puppy will learn
best when training is incorporated into her playtime. Hang around with her, use
her name, introduce her to a leash—pretty basic stuff. Begin housebreaking, but
please don't expect a totally housebroken puppy in four weeks. Forget discipline
right now because she's just too young to understand it. You'll only succeed in
frightening your puppy and eroding your relationship.

At this point in your pup's development, her life is centered around satisfying
one of four basic needs: sleeping, eating, eliminating and playing. You should be
feeding her three to four times a day, taking her out constantly, and letting her
sleep when she wants. You'll begin to witness "the wild puppy energy spurt."
It's something to behold! Several times a day, you'll notice a crazed look in your
puppy's eyes. Suddenly, she'll dash around the house or yard completely out of
control. If she were a cartoon, all four legs would be in the air, and she'd be leaving a trail of smoke. There isn't much you can do to influence her behavior at
this time; the best thing I've found is to redirect her energy with an empty plastic soda bottle or soccer ball. *Always remove plastic objects after play. Never play with
a damaged bottle, and place it out of reach when leaving your puppy unattended.*

Here's a list of simple, interactive puppy play-lessons. These will let you get
to know your puppy and help her become the well-behaved, well-adjusted dog
you've been dreaming about.

The Name

Pick a short name or nickname and use it each time you offer her something positive like food or praise. Speak in a warm, happy tone. Watch that squealing!

Leash Training

Put a collar on your puppy immediately. Remember that puppies grow fast, so keep an eye on the collar size and loosen it when necessary. It's okay if she fusses at first. Next, attach a light leash and let her drag it around. After a day, pick up the leash and follow her around. As she gets used to this, start to call out her name and encourage her to follow you. Do any number of foolish things to pique her interest (like the "wild walk" game explained later in this chapter.) When she starts following you, praise her generously! Say "Let's go!" and kneel often to hug her. If she resists strongly, don't run over to her—you'd be reinforcing the resistance. Instead, tug the leash gently and lower yourself to the floor while you praise her.

Pick a short name and use it whenever you offer something positive.

"Sit"

Use this command frequently throughout the day. Whenever your puppy is calm enough to sit still, command "Sit" and position her. Just before

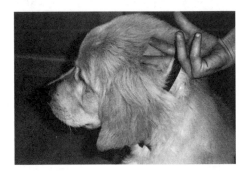

Put a collar on your puppy right away, but check it often to make sure it's not too tight.

you offer her something like a toy, treat, food, or pat, command "Sit" and position her. Remember—puppies understand sounds not words, so don't get in the habit of repeating yourself. "Sit-sit-sit" sounds different from "Sit."

"Okay"

This is a release word; it gives permission to go forward or eat food. It's a happy command and something that a well-trained puppy looks forward to hearing. Follow each "Okay" with praise and say "Good girl!" Use it in the following situations:

- Putting down the food bowl or offering a treat.
- Leading your puppy out the door.
- Letting your puppy out of the car.
- Releasing her from a Sit command.

We'll use this command more in the future, but you can start making your puppy feel good about it now. It's the happiest of all commands!

Walking the Stairs

Stairs can be a very formidable obstacle. Some small breeds are just too little to negotiate the stairs and must be carried. That's okay—in time they'll be scampering up and down like the big guys. Some large-breed puppies are big enough, but they're afraid because their depth perception isn't completely developed. If you've got a puppy with stair phobia, help her walk the stairs by cradling her belly and guiding her paws. If possible, have someone crouch a few stairs away to cheer her on!

Handling

When you're calmly petting your puppy, occasionally play veterinarian. Peek into your puppy's ears, check out what's going on in her mouth and eyes. Press her belly gently and handle the base of the tail. Handle the paws like you're trimming her nails. Praise your puppy gently as you do this, or give her a treat so she won't get scared. You'll be helping yourself and your veterinarian, who always appreciates a good patient!

Handle your puppy gently all over and praise while you're doing so. Your veterinarian will thank you later!

Every other day go to your puppy during one of her meals. Offer her a biscuit and a pat and say "Good girl!" Once she anticipates your offering, remove her bowl while she eats the treat, then return the bowl and leave. At this point, if you have children in the house, bring them with you and start the process from the beginning. Early food bowl conditioning prevents food guarding later in her development.

Socialization

Puppies at this age are too young to be taken out on the town, but this is the best age to socialize your puppy with new people and other dogs. Puppies who are not socialized often develop a fear of new situations and people. Invite your neighbors and friends over, borrow a group of active kids, have a puppy playdate with another healthy canine, and socialize that puppy!

Rig situations to introduce your puppy to unusual objects. Praise while the pup investigates.

Your Puppy's Fears

This age is ideal to introduce your puppy to household appliances and potentially scary stuff. Remember, your puppy has only been on the planet a couple of months, so everything is very new to her, and she'll startle easily. In people and in pooches, fear can be a very debilitating emotion. Puppies can be afraid of anything, including vacuums, hairdryers, food processors, umbrellas, lawn mowers, cars, and floor grates. Left unchecked, these fears can last a lifetime. To prevent this, try these simple steps:

- Never race after your puppy or poke her with an unfamiliar object. It will only increase her fear.
- If your puppy is experiencing fear, don't bend over to soothe her. Your puppy will think you're afraid, too.
  It's best to calmly investigate the object of your puppy's fear and to ignore her until she follows your lead.
- Rig situations to introduce your puppy to noisy appliances and unusual objects. Show your puppy the object by placing it in the center of the floor. If it's a machine, don't turn it on. Let her sniff the object while you investigate it together. Feed her treats and praise her lovingly during this initial introduction.

Once she seems comfortable, pretend to use the object. Sing a happy song and toss treats. If your puppy shows fear, stop and investigate the object as if you're curious but unafraid. You're helping your puppy not only to overcome her fears, but also to build confidence in you. Progress slowly. As your puppy's confidence grows, turn on machines at a distance. Ignore her fear response. Toss treats for your puppy when she approaches.

Your puppy may show sudden fear when out for a walk or when meeting a new person. The startle response is due to the novelty of the situation. Remember—your reaction counts for everything. If you pet your puppy or soothingly tell her "It's okay," you're actually reinforcing the fear. It's better to ignore your pup. Act brave and approach the scary object—what a courageous leader you are!

PROBLEM SOLVING

NOTE: Please refer to Chapter 13 for a more expanded discussion on these issues.

Initiate Housetraining

You can start conditioning good elimination habits by taking your puppy outside or to her papers every hour or two, depending on your puppy's needs. Follow the same route to the bathroom area giving a command like "Outside," and give her a short command like "Get busy" *every time* she goes. Don't expect miracles, but early preparation helps speed this very important process along.

Discourage Nipping

At this age, your puppy might be pretty wild. She's fresh from the litter, where biting games were acceptable and fun. Corrections are often interpreted as rough play, so the nipping gets worse. Here are a few suggestions to get you through this stage:

- Puppies often nip when they have a pressing need. Does your pup need to eliminate, eat, sleep, or exercise? Take care of her needs, and she'll calm down immediately. Say "Kisses, good girl," every time she licks you.
- If your puppy has a lot of energy, don't play hand games like tug-of-war or fetch. I've found playing soccer with a plastic water or soda

bottle (paper and cap removed) keeps the little jaws at bay. You can also try the hi-ho squeak toy mentioned later in this chapter.

- Keep a bottle of vinegar and water mixture on hand to spray your puppy when she leaps for your clothing. Make this experience unpleasant, and she'll avoid it in the future.
- Avoid corrections. She's too young! Your tactics will change as she gets older, but for now, spray without verbal or physical reprimand.

Discourage Jumping

Nobody *plans* to have a jumping dog, but so many people do! If you're determined to avoid the jumping bean syndrome, let me give you one piece of advice: Ignore all forms of airborne activity. It's not easy, but it works! If your puppy is jumping on you to greet you or jumping on the couch to get attention, ignore her. As soon as she stops, command and position a sit. Pretty soon, you're dog will begin to learn that *sitting* gets attention, not jumping.

Discourage Chewing

Your puppy probably won't start chewing things for real until she's a bit older, but at this age, curiosity overtakes her. She'll begin investigating everything with her mouth. Provide her with a good chew bone.

Discourage jumping by ignoring your puppy when he jumps on you, then praising him to sit when commanded.

Catch me if you can!

Each time you see a wandering mouth situation, startle her with "Eh, Eh" or a loud "Sssst," and refocus her attention on her bone by saying "Where's your bone?" Eventually, she'll go and find her bone without prompting.

Good Games

The best way to teach your young puppy to watch you for direction is by playing organized games. Here are some of my favorites:

- *Puppy Ping Pong:* Stand 6–10 feet apart from another person. Call your puppy's name and praise her when she gets to you. Withdraw your attention as your partner begins to call her name. Send her back and forth a few times, then quit while it's still fun!
- *The Wild Walk:* This is especially important for young puppies and great fun for people of all ages. At various times during the day, enthusiastically call your puppy's name and back away from her in a kooky, erratic pattern. Kick up your heels, take giant steps, bend over, tap the floor, make funny sounds! Do whatever it takes to get her to follow you with a wagging tail!
- *Hi-Ho Squeak Toy:* Tie a squeak toy to the end of a four-foot string and bring it out when your puppy has lots of energy to burn. Bounce it along in front of her and command "Let's go" as you walk about. She'll have a ball pouncing and playing with the toy and will be diverted from nipping and pouncing on you or the children.
- *Hide and Seek:* You can play this game inside or out. While your puppy is off investigating, hide around a tree or a corner and call out her name. Keep calling out her name until she finds you, then celebrate your togetherness. In the beginning, make your hiding places pretty obvious. You don't want a panicking puppy!
- *Catch Me if You Can!:* When playing with your puppy, grab her toy and race away as you call out her name. Run away for 10 seconds, then stop and turn to her. Instruct "Sit" as you place her and give her the toy immediately. Do this once or twice when playing with her. Stop if she gets overexcited.
- *Snoopy Soccer:* When your puppy's engines are revving, place a plastic soda bottle on the floor and let her kick it around. If you want to play, tap the bottle along gently with your feet. This helps divert the puppy from excited nipping. Use two bottles if necessary.

Common Questions

Sometimes my puppy plays very rough. She mouths hard and leaps at me. I've tried correcting her, but then she gets worse. What can I do?
Your puppy is going wild! A few times a day she'll overflow with energy and needs to expel it by racing around for a few minutes. There is nothing you can do to discipline her. Her need to exercise is as strong as her other needs. The best thing to do is to place a plastic milk bottle on the floor (no paper wrapping or caps), and let her play herself out. Avoid playing fetch games or tug-of-war.

Sometimes my puppy gets very mouthy out of the blue. Why?
In most cases, puppies get very mouthy when one of their four needs is not being met. Ask yourself: Does she need to eliminate? Could she be hungry, tired, or need exercise?

My puppy is leash trained, but occasionally, she'll stop in her tracks and refuse to move.
A mule puppy! Even at this young age your puppy is testing certain routines to determine their attention-getting potential. If you race over to plead with your puppy, uh-oh!, you're encouraging her to repeat that behavior. The best tactic is to praise the air in front of you and skip forward happily. You may be dragging your pup for a second or two, but once she sees you won't cave in, she'll race forward to see what all the fun is about. Praise her whenever she walks with you.

When company comes, my puppy gets so excited I can't control her.
Train your company! Don't allow your guests to reward an overstimulated puppy with kisses and pats. Ask your guests to ignore her. If the situation doesn't improve, crate or isolate your puppy (not your guests, no matter how tempting) until she calms down. Bring your puppy back and cradle her into a sit as they greet her calmly.

How about a training collar?
No! Your puppy is too young. The tissues in her neck are still developing. You can read about training collars in Chapter 9, but don't plan on using one until your puppy is four months old.

Wrapping Up

At this age, your puppy will learn best if her new words are part of the fun. Keep your expectations low; she's got so much new information pouring in she might not remember a new command from one day to the next. That's okay—she's just a baby. Her brain is still developing. Avoid any sort of physical discipline or shouting because it teaches her nothing but fear. Enjoy this stage!

9

The Terrible Twos: 12 to 16 Weeks

As your puppy matures, you'll notice his personality developing. He'll get a bit bolder, braver, harder to impress. He'll march right up to company and demand attention. He'll insist on being at the center of all household activities. Your position as all-knowing leader won't impress him as much. He's growing up.

By 12 weeks, your puppy's brain is fully developed, and he's ready to learn! This is the best age to begin training because your puppy is old enough to understand and remember your direction but still a little young to take matters into his own paws. Remember, your puppy is starting to learn things whether or not you train him. If you don't train him, he'll train you!

Has your puppy begun a training program for you? Here's how to tell:

- He solicits (and *gets!*) your attention by jumping, nipping, whining, and barking.

It's hard to be upset with your puppy when he's so adorable! (Tina Engle-Balch)

- He has taught you how to wrestle and play tug-of-war during walks.
- He grabs your clothing and tries to carry it around the house (while you're still in it!).
- When he wants a biscuit or part of your lunch, he expresses this desire by barking in your face. Advanced dogs-as-trainers may simply help themselves.

If any of these scenarios sound a little too familiar, don't despair! Help is on the way!

UNDERSTANDING THIS STAGE

Sometimes I think puppies were made so cute because they can be so annoying! And sometimes I think they know it—"How can you *possibly* get mad at me when I'm so completely *precious?*" It's a good system, but you must remember, this darling little bundle is keeping score. He's starting to know what behaviors will get attention, what games last the longest, and who wins. Your puppy may be acting bold, but he's still unsure about his world and needs direction from you now more than ever. Keep these points in mind while you're working with him during this important developmental stage:

- **Attention Is Key:** Attention is the key in training your puppy at this age. He wants it, he needs it, and he'll do *anything* to get it. Remember the canine credo: All attention is good; positive or negative doesn't matter.
- **Eye Contact:** At this age, your puppy is learning about eye contact. If you watch him more than he watches you, he thinks you're looking for direction.
- **A Dog House or People House?:** This is the age to tighten up the rules on housebreaking, chewing, nipping, and jumping. If your puppy is making the decisions on these things, you're living in *his* house. That's one expensive dog house!

What to do? Let's begin by reviewing the concepts we've learned so far. Please become completely familiar with these concepts before you begin working with your puppy. Review Chapter 5 if necessary.

THE TEACHING LEAD

Stationing

Create a place for your puppy in each room he'll be permitted in as an adult. Choose a location that is free from entanglements, stairs, electrical outlets, and other dangers. Select an immovable object or use an eye hook (from a hardware store) to secure the Teaching Lead and allow no more than three feet of freedom. Help him identify the area by decorating it with a towel or dog bed and a chew toy. Whenever you're going to spend time in one room, bring your puppy and station him, telling him "Settle Down" as you hook him up. Keep him with you at all times; do not station him alone. If he gets fidgety, he may need to eliminate or exercise. If he starts to protest-bark, just ignore him.

This technique helps your puppy create good habits and teaches him that he has a special place in every room. At this point the command "Settle Down" needs to be reinforced with the leash, but before long he'll go to his area automatically or when you send him. You can avoid isolation and keep him with you, which will make both of you feel better! When your puppy is calm or chewing a bone, give him lots of love and attention—you'll be helping him learn how good dogs behave!

Leading

When you have the time, remove your puppy from his station and wrap his leash around you like a belt. Walk around the house, doing whatever you need to do. Ignore your puppy's directional requests. If he wants to go left, go right. If he wants to go faster, change direction. Don't be angry, just call out his name happily and go your way. When you sit down, slide the end clip around to your backbone and sit on the leash.

Walk around the house doing whatever you need to do.

Puppy on the Loose!

Your puppy can and should have free time in the house in an enclosed area. Just make sure he has eliminated recently, and you can watch him. It's best to enclose a "free time" area in some place like the kitchen by shutting doors or erecting gates. Play ball, sit on the floor if he's not too nippy or kick an empty soda bottle around (removing it after the play session), and play. Then put him back on the teaching lead or in his crate if you're leaving when playtime is over.

If your puppy is rough or jumpy during playtime, attach a short leash onto his collar. If he starts misbehaving, take the leash and snap him away or off. If you use your hands, the behavior may escalate because hands are interactive. *And in your puppy's mind, interactive is good, good, good!*

Correcting the Pushy Pup

When your puppy is attached to the leash, you can correct any mischief without physical interaction. If Mini the Mastiff put her front paw in my lap and I pushed her away with my hands, I've actually encouraged her to do it again because, in her mind, pushing is interactive. If, instead of pushing, I grabbed the leash, tugged her off, and ignored her until she was calm, she'd learn that calm puppies get petted. You can refer to Chapter 13 for other hints on handling misbehaving pups.

TEACHING YOUR YOUNG PUP

Your puppy is still very young, and although he can learn a lot, he's still very sensitive and vulnerable to your impressions. So stay cool! Getting frustrated or impatient will only frighten him and make him less responsive to you.

Keep your lessons short and snappy, no more than a couple of minutes. Speak your commands clearly and enunciate your syllables. Repeated commands sound different from commands given once (the indecipherable "sitsitsitcomeonplease sitdown"). Continue to use your commands during playtime!

I encourage hand signals even at this age because they help you get visual attention. I also use treats with some of the commands, but you'll completely fade off your food dependence before this stage is through. Here we go! Your puppy can have a 10-word vocabulary by the time he's four months old.

Up Here

You need to teach your puppy the importance of alerting to his name. Follow this sequence twice a day:

- Place your puppy in a sit position.
- Pivot six inches in front of him (standing or kneeling) so that your feet are facing his paws.

- Keeping your back straight, snap your finger above his nose.
- Call his name as you rapidly draw your finger to your eyes.
- When he looks up, freeze! Look away *after* your puppy breaks the stare.
- Try to get at least three seconds of eye contact.

"Let's Go"

Continue to use this command whenever you're walking your puppy on his leash. Remember, "Let's go" is not optional! If your puppy doesn't want to go and you stop to cajole him, you're reinforcing his resistance. Say the command happily, then skip, bounce, or dart ahead—whatever you can do to encourage his quick and willing participation.

"Sit"

Twice a day for four days, take your puppy aside with a handful of small treats. Place a treat between your index finger and thumb and say "Sit" as you bring the treat slightly above your puppy's nose. When he sits, give him the treat, say "Okay" and praise him. Repeat this no more than five times per session. The hand signal will become lifting your index finger above his nose. As the days progress and your puppy seems to catch on, try giving the command and signal outside of a lesson time without a treat. After four days, fade off the treat and stop using *this* command in lessons. Continue to use the command and signal throughout the day.

Give the command "Sit" only once. Hold the treat just above the nose.

"Down"

Once your puppy has mastered sit, you can work this command. Twice a day for four days, take your puppy aside with some treats. Placing them between your fingers as above, instruct "Sit," but before you let go of the treat, drop your hand between your puppy's paws and say "Down." Your puppy may not know what to do, so as he looks down, cradle his shoulders with your left hand and press him gently into position. Let go of the treat when his elbows hit the floor, praise him and say "Okay" to release. Repeat this five times. The eventual hand signal is a pointing to the ground. As the days progress, try this command out of lesson time without a treat. After four days, fade off the treat and stop using *this* command in lessons. Continue to use the command and signal throughout the day.

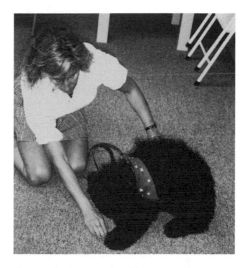

From a sit, drop your hand between your puppy's paws and say "Down."

"Stand"

This command is handy for cleaning muddy paws and general grooming sessions. Twice a day for four days, take your puppy aside with some treats. Place one between your fingers and give the command as you pull an imaginary string from your puppy's nose forward. When your puppy stands, stop your fingers and cradle his belly as you repeat "Stand." Pause and then release with "Okay" as you allow your puppy to have the treat. Your pup may try to snatch the treat, but hold it firmly and don't release it until he's standing. Repeat this five

As you command "Stand," bring the treat straight forward from your pup's nose.

times. The eventual hand signal is a short point forward from his nose. As the days progress, try this command out of lesson time without a treat. After four days fade off the treat and stop using *this* command in lessons. Continue to use the command and signal throughout the day.

"Bring and Out"

Most puppies enjoy this game. Try it first with your puppy on a leash and some treats in your pocket. Take your puppy into a small, quiet room with a favorite ball or squeak toy. Kneel on the floor and praise your puppy happily for nearly a minute before you bring out the toy. When you bring it out, toss it in the air to encourage his interest. Then give it a short toss. If he takes the toy, go to him and say "Good Boy—Out" as you offer him a treat. Continue this until you notice that he looks to you as soon as he picks the toy up. Then gradually encourage him to walk toward you with the toy as you command "Bring."

He should release the toy quickly, but if he doesn't, you can encourage him by squeezing his upper muzzle just behind his canines. Praise him for releasing and repeat five times. Praise him profusely when the game is over. Practice these commands in the confines of a small room for five days, then bring the command into normally populated areas, fading off the treats gradually.

NOTE: Most puppies like this game, but some have no interest in it whatsoever. If you have a puppy who couldn't care less, don't frustrate yourself with this game. There are plenty of others to choose from.

"Settle Down"

You first read about this command in Chapter 5. In each room, your puppy should have a special corner or area equipped with a bed and a chew bone. In the long run you want to be able to send your puppy to this area on command; this tactic is especially useful during mealtime or when you have company. To teach him this principle, select areas in each room. With your puppy on leash, command "Settle Down" and point to the area with a free hand. He will probably need an escort, so take him there, then hook him to his area with the lead (*see* illustration). Soon you'll notice that your puppy leads you over and lies down quickly. He may start to take himself to the area when he's tired. What a good puppy!

A puppy in his "Settle Down" spot.

NOTE: Please read and understand the stationing concept (Chapter 9) before you begin.

"Wait and Okay"

When approaching doors or stairs, command "Wait" and bring your puppy behind your feet. This maneuver is best accomplished by bringing the leash behind your back. Pause a couple of seconds, then command "Okay" as you step out first. The leader must always lead!

"Excuse Me"

Puppies like to get in the way. It gets them attention! But it makes you look subservient, and it can be dangerous as they get older. Whenever your puppy trips you up, gets on the wrong side of the leash, or just basically gets in your way, command "Excuse Me" and move him out of your way with the leash or by shuffling your feet under his body. Don't yell or kick your puppy. Thank him for respecting you; soon he'll move with his tail wagging.

"Leave It"

Teach "Leave It" by setting up a tempting situation, then refocusing the puppy's attention and praising when he looks at you. (Debbie Miller)

This is a discipline command. Eventually you will be able to use it to curb your dog from chasing small animals or from approaching food or strangers. But first you must teach him what you mean.

- Place your puppy on a leash.
- With your puppy stationed in the next room, prepare a plate of crackers and place it on the floor.
- Go get your puppy and take him toward the setup.
- When your puppy starts to sniff and approach the food, pull back sharply on his leash and command "Leave It" in a stern, disciplining tone.
- Say "Leave It" as you snap back on the leash.
- Release the pressure immediately and continue walking. If he lunges again, repeat the correction but continue walking.
- Praise your puppy when he refocuses his attention on you.
- Walk by as often as necessary until he avoids the setup altogether. Don't forget to praise him when he does!

More Good Games

Games are still a very important part of the learning process. You can continue to play the ones from the Infant chapter, and add these to your fun.

Four-Footed Fax: Once your puppy has mastered Puppy Ping Pong (from chapter 8), you can teach him this fun little exercise. The only prerequisite is the "Bring and Out" exercise. Stand 6–10 feet apart from another person. Call your puppy to you and encourage him to take his toy. When he does, say "Bring It to Bob," then withdraw your attention as Bob calls the pup. Bob can give a treat for a speedy delivery, then send him back to you, using your name in the same way. Use treats at first, but fade off in a week or so, continuing with lots of praise.

Call your puppy back and forth four times, and then quit while it's still fun. As your puppy catches on, increase the distance between you and your partner. Before long you can exchange the toy for a note paper, and you can send messages all over the house!

Snoopy Soccer: Buy a nondestructable ball from the pet store or use an empty plastic soda bottle. Put it on the ground and kick it gently with your feet until your puppy shows interest. After finishing your play session, put it away so your puppy can't hurt himself. This game is great for kids because it doesn't encourage nipping or jumping.

Catch Me If You Can!: Your puppy loves a chase, and if you don't get him to chase you, he'll get you to chase him. The one who starts the chase is the leader, so you decide! Once a day take one of your puppy's favorite toys, dangle it in front of his nose, then call out "Let's Go!" Race off to the next room or around a tree. Praise him for following, and dart around four times, requesting a quick "Sit" before giving him his toy!

NOTE: This game is not for children; the puppy may jump or nip at them in the excitement of play. If your puppy gets too frantic, try playing at a lower energy time, or drop this from your list.

HANDLING

As first addressed in the Infant chapter, early handling benefits both you and your veterinarian. Continue to manipulate his paws, ears, eyes, belly, and tail as you would if you were grooming or medicating him.

If your puppy will be around children, be sure he can handle it. Act like a kid! Pull his coat gently, squeal, make sudden movements. Praise your puppy and give him treats during your performance.

If your puppy will be around children, be sure he can handle it by praising him while you gently pull his coat or make sudden movements.

SOCIALIZATION

Your puppy loves to party. He loves friends with four legs and friends with two legs. If he's too young to be taken out (ask your veterinarian), invite people in— kids included. If you don't have kids, borrow some! Once your veterinarian has completed your puppy's shots, start taking him out on the town, and introduce him to everyone you meet. Take him to three new areas a week.

Ask your veterinarian if there is a well-managed puppy kindergarten class in your town. Joining a class is a fun way to meet other puppies and people.

Lots of socialization won't create a dog who won't protect his home or his people. Socialization will encourage your dog to trust your judgment where people are concerned. Lack of socialization may create a dog who is overbonded to his family and intolerant of visitors. Depending on his breed and temperament, this dog will become fearful or defensive of other people on or off your property. Such dogs are difficult to manage and are a constant concern around people. Spare yourself the agony and socialize that puppy!

Common Questions

What do I do when my puppy is outside and ignores "Come"? Shouting seems to make it worse.
You must limit your puppy's freedom to confined areas only. He is simply too curious and full of fire to run free without restrictions. Don't take it personally. He's just responding to his genetic instinct to be young, wild, and free. Disciplining your puppy for this behavior will make matters much worse. He'll want to avoid correction and prolong the fun as long as possible.

If you get into this situation, avoid shouting because your pup interprets your shouts as barks. This only fuels his enthusiasm. You can try joining in the game by running in crazy circles then running out of sight or dropping face down on the ground. Yes, this sounds far-fetched, but your puppy will often be fascinated by your unusual behavior and come running. If this doesn't work, you can try getting in the car—lots of puppies adore car rides and don't want to be left behind. If all else fails, simply follow your puppy quietly until he tires out.

Can I still let my puppy off leash to play outside?
I would not suggest it unless the area is confined and safe. Your puppy is finally feeling secure about his world and wants to go exploring. It's not that he doesn't want to listen, it's just hard to hear over all the delightful new sounds filling his head! Buy a Flexi-Leash and go exploring with him.

Is my puppy too young for a training collar?
Wait until your puppy is four months old before fitting him with a training collar.

How long and how often should training sessions last?
Have two to three training sessions a day. Sessions should last no more than one to two minutes.

When practicing the "Sit" command my puppy often jumps up at my treat/signaling hand.

You're probably lifting your signal hand too far above your puppy's head. When signaling with a treat, lift it only an inch out of your pup's reach and then release it with praise once he responds.

My puppy often stands up when I give the command and signal for "Down."

When you signal, make sure you're placing your treat hand between your puppy's paws, not in front of them. If he still gets up, place your free hand on his waist to hold him in a sit.

Often when we play fetching games it turns into a tug-of-war match.

Avoid reaching into your puppy's mouth to retrieve an object. Persuade your puppy to release by squeezing his muzzle behind his canine teeth or pinching his back jaw hinges. Force him to release it instead of wrestling him for it. As you do command "Out. Good dog."

Wrapping Up

You've entered the train-or-be-trained zone with your puppy. It is hoped that the tools and suggestions found in this chapter help you sway the odds in your favor! When you begin training at this age, keep the lessons short and simple and your frustration level under the boiling point. Your little darling is still discovering his world. He wants to please you, but there are a lot of new and interesting things to investigate.

10

The Budding Adolescent: 16 to 24 Weeks

U h-oh, there's a very naughty stranger in your house, and she looks just like your puppy! Defiant as a devil, she's taken the place of that sweet, compliant puppy you had just days ago. Be prepared. You're about to enter the bratty zone. But don't panic. It's normal. It's even survivable! And it won't last forever if you train her through it.

Here are some surefire signs that your puppy has become a brat:

- You call her. She looks at you. She pauses. She bolts.
- She grabs, jumps, and nips relentlessly.
- She barks in your face and whines incessantly.
- She grabs the leash and jumps on you when you correct her.
- She begins mounting everyone in sight. (Ignore the derisive comments from your friends. This is a sign of dominance, not sexual interest.)
- She insists on being the center of attention every moment of every day.
- Corrections make her behavior worse.
- She is driving you crazy.

Look out! Your once-compliant puppy is turning into a bratty adolescent!

Remember, this stage is normal. As much as you might want to hide in a box for the next three months, don't! This is the best time to start training. Since this stage lasts about eight weeks, lessons will be broken down week by week. Avoid jumping ahead because each week builds on the next. Keep your lessons short, and use each new command during lesson time only for the first week. This process allows your puppy to feel successful, mastering each word before you apply it in her day-to-day world—similar to letting children master their addition skills in school before asking them to balance your checkbook.

A FEW THINGS FIRST

All the Right Stuff!

Here is a rundown of all the training equipment you'll need.

- A training collar.
- The Teaching Lead.
- Create or buy a short (12- to 36-inch) lead.
- Buy a Flexi-Leash—the longer the better.
- Have plenty of tantalizing chew toys and bones on hand.
- A ball or Frisbee fetch toy.

Keeping Control

When you're home, you should always know where your puppy is. If you give your puppy complete freedom, she *will* misbehave, and you'll end up paying a lot of attention to naughty behavior. Unsupervised, she'll rearrange your closets, eat garbage, and chew the couch. Remember, you're dealing with a puppy! Keep her nearby you in one of three ways:

- on the Teaching Lead
- under complete observation in an enclosed area
- on the short lead (attached to the buckle collar)

Restrained, she'll get attention for *good* behavior. Continue to organize her free time in the house with the Teaching Lead unless you're able to give her your complete attention in an enclosed area. If she's beginning to respond well on her own, attach the short lead and give her some freedom in the house. Don't rush it though! If she does well for the most part but falls apart when company comes, put her on the Teaching Lead when you have visitors.

Continued Politeness

Continue to use the command "Sit" throughout the day. Use it before you pet her, put her food down, or offer a treat, when you let her out of the car or house, and before her admirers approach. Remember—give the command *once*, correcting her with "No" and a leash tug (position her if it's a new distraction).

Praise vs. Petting

When your puppy learns something new, it's very exciting for everyone! Please try, though, to control yourself. If you get fired up, your puppy will too. Learning takes a lot of concentration, and an excited pup can't learn much. As you practice your exercises remember, there's a difference between praise and petting. Petting comes from your hand; it excites your puppy and communicates play intentions. Praise comes from your voice and eyes and is given from an upright position; it calms your puppy and communicates your leadership. Remember this handy phrase: *Praise between exercises; pet to end them.*

WEEK ONE

Her Name

Your first goal is to teach your puppy to alert to her name. If she's in an unsafe situation or getting too rambunctious, she must stop quickly when you call to her. To encourage a positive and immediate response, practice these two exercises this week:

1. Up Here!

You may have already started this exercise in the last chapter. If you have, great! Continue. If you haven't—start practicing.

- Place your puppy in a sit position.

Encourage your puppy to focus up when you call her name.

- Pivot six inches in front of her (standing or kneeling) so your feet are facing her paws.
- Snap your finger above her nose.
- Call her name as you rapidly draw your finger to your eyes.
- When she looks up, freeze! Look away *after* your puppy breaks the stare.
- Try to get at least three seconds of eye contact.

Total time commitment: Five seconds, twice daily. Don't overdo it!

2. The Darting Game

Your little darling must learn that the leash was invented *by* humans *for* humans. Ground rules include: no pulling, biting, or jumping at the hand that walks you. The first word your puppy must learn to follow is her name. No matter what fascinating distractions may come her way, she must alert to her name and come to you when you call. Try this exercise:

No matter what fascinating distractions come your puppy's way, he must alert to his name and come to you when you call.

- Wrap the Teaching Lead around your waist.
- In a long hallway, walk forward with your pup on your left.
- Do not hold the leash or try to control your puppy's speed.
- The minute she darts ahead, call out her name and dart away from her. Be realistic with the intensity of your motions. Larger dogs will need more momentum; smaller dogs, just a hop.
- If she looks, super! If not, she'll be tugged toward you; praise her anyway.
- The second she turns toward you, resume walking.
- Continue this little game until she happily trots behind.

Once your puppy has caught onto the darting game and is paying more attention to you when you walk, practice this same exercise around everyday distractions. Here are two examples:

The Indoor Distraction

Every puppy lives to hear the doorbell ring. A new admirer could be calling! It's okay to be excited, but throwing yourself all over every visitor is totally unacceptable. To teach your pup better manners, rig a situation where you have a friend or family member sneak to the front door and ring the bell while you practice the above exercise. Ask them to ring the bell at 20-second intervals until you have enough control to open the door. Remember—every time your puppy darts out, call her name and run in the other direction.

The Outdoor Distraction

Garbage men, squirrels, and neighborhood joggers can be quite irresistible temptations. Let's pretend that you're out on a walk, and suddenly your puppy notices two gray, bushy-tailed tidbits playing near a tree. Every muscle reacts, and she crouches for the pounce. You no longer exist. The leash no longer exists. It is just she . . . and the tidbits. You must take action immediately! Call her name and dart in the opposite direction. She'll probably get a leash tug, but that's okay. Try again. Walk her back to the scene, and when you notice the radar picking up, repeat the process. Keep doing this until she follows you when you call to her. Don't expect her to ignore the temptation, but do expect her to turn her attention back to you.

Your long-term goal is to get your puppy's attention when you call out her name—on or off leash.

Total time commitment: At first, practice this exercise in five-minute sets. Once she catches on, expect her attention whenever you call her name.

Week One Questions: NAME

When I practice the eye contact exercise she won't look at me.
Your puppy isn't taking you seriously. Don't bend over. Speak her name clearly. Snap the leash if she continues to ignore you and persist, persist, persist.

When my puppy looks up, she barks or jumps at me.
Your puppy is a little comedian. She is trying to turn this serious exercise into a game. Stay relaxed. Snap her to the side, say "No" and repeat the process. If you give in and laugh, you're following your leader (your dog). This reaction would be enormously satisfying to Ms. Funny, but it's detrimental to your authority. Be serious!

My puppy growls at me when I do this exercise.
Call a professional. Your puppy is very dominant and will need firmness to avoid aggressive behavior.

When practicing the darting game, my puppy wrestles the leash and jumps at my clothing.
Don't face off and correct her. She'll interpret this as a challenge. Ignore your puppy when she does this and snap the leash straight into her mouth. You can also spritz her mouth with diluted vinegar spray.

WEEK TWO

The Heel Command

Your goal will be to teach the command Heel. Heel will communicate good walking control. It's also a position your puppy should return to when you call her. When she hears this command, you want her to rush back to your side. Always the same side, always the same spot. I call this the directional position.

Though your long-range goals are quite high, you must start small. At first, you want to make your puppy feel like a genius every time she hears this command. That way, she'll always enjoy responding to you when you give it.

Twice a day, take her aside and practice the following exercise for two to three minutes. Keeping your lessons short ensures success!

Days One to Four

Merry-Go-Round
Clear an area and pattern a circle. You can practice outside on pavement (grass is too distracting) or inside around the furniture. Following this sequence, practice just a couple of minutes twice daily:

- Face in a counterclockwise direction; your puppy must be on the inside of the circle.
- Sit your puppy in the directional position. This is your starting position.
- Keeping your arms straight, hold the end of the leash so that no slack remains, but the training collar is loose.

- Hold the leash *behind* your thigh. If it's in front of your thigh, your pup will be too.
- Standing very tall, face forward and command "(Name), Heel" as you begin circling.
- Walk in a forthright manner, keeping your puppy at a trot.
- Praise your puppy for watching you, or snap the leash to encourage focus.
- Stop after each circle by slowing your pace and reminding "Heel" as you place your puppy in a sit position at your side.
- To place your puppy in a sit, grasp the base of the leash with your right hand and with your left hand free, position your pup in the directional position.

Walk five circles and quit with tremendous praise!

Days Five Through Seven

Merry-Go-Round with a Twist

Warm up with three normal circles. Next when circling, change your pace. Go a little faster by trotting (not sprinting!). Slow your pace gradually by lengthening your stride. Stop. Praise. For your next and last circle, change your direction. Start forward in a normal pace, command heel, and pivot slowly to the right. Walk in the other direction for six paces and pivot again. To help your pup stay with you, slow down as you pivot and slap your leg, cluck, or bend your knees. Stop. Hug that pup!

As the Weeks Continue

Once your pup gets the hang of this command, you'll notice that she responds without any pressure to her collar. Now is the time to begin encouraging her to focus outside of lesson time. Encourage her to Heel by guiding her on her Teaching Lead or short lead as you walk around the house. Once she gets the hang of that, practice outside in low-distraction environments.

Remember—if she gets wild, don't start shouting "Heel! Heel! Heel!" She'll just get more excited. Maybe she has too much energy to concentrate; she's still young, so be forgiving. Practice only when she is calm, and there are few distractions.

Total time commitment: Two or three minutes, twice a day.

Week Two Questions: HEEL

My puppy gets very distracted when practicing the Merry-Go-Round exercise.
Is your puppy on the inside of the circle? Make sure you are walking in a counterclockwise direction and keeping your left hand behind your back.

My puppy turns to face me when I stop.
She's facing off to you. Another attempt for control! To discourage this activity, grab the base of the leash with your right hand and hold it against your left leg as you stop. Use your left hand to position your puppy in the directional position.

My pup is constantly pulling ahead.
Are you keeping your left hand behind your back? If your left hand is parallel with or ahead of your thigh, your puppy will have an advantage. If you're still having trouble, perhaps you might try another collar. Check your choices by referring to pages 19–20.

WEEK THREE

The Sit-Stay

Your goal this week is to teach your puppy the meaning of "Sit-Stay." This command has a lot to do with eye contact and self-control. When told "Stay" you want your puppy to think "Okay, though I'd like to run like a crazy dog and jump all over that person and chase that cat and meet that dog, I can't right now because my leader (that's you!) thinks it is in my best interest to be still. So I'll just wait until it is safe to move."

Once again we face lofty, long-range goals! And once again we must start with small steps. When first practicing these exercises, go into a quiet room and keep the lesson short. No more than two to three minutes. When you go into the room, follow these preliminary steps:

- Fold the leash neatly in your left hand.
- Position the collar between her ears, high on the neck.
- Begin and end each exercise with your pup in the directional position.

- After you command "Stay" look at your puppy's ears, not her eyes. Staring will make her nervous.
- The word *Okay* is your release word. Use it to end all exercises.

Use your hand signals to encourage visual attention. All are given with a quick flick of the index finger from your pup's nose.

- Sit: A sweeping motion from her nose to your chest.
- Stay: An abrupt point above the nose.
- Okay!: A sweeping motion away from the nose as you step forward.

Use a quick point from your index finger to indicate "Stay."

Days One Through Four

Let's begin! You'll practice five quick exercises.
After you command "Stay":

- Pause at her side for five seconds. Release with "Okay" and praise.
- Pivot six inches in front of her (holding the leash up)—and pause five seconds. Return to her side, release and praise.
- Pivot six inches in front of her and march in place slowly for three seconds. Return to her side, release and praise.
- Pivot six inches in front of her and make animal sounds (dog, cat, sheep—whatever your specialty). Return to her side, release and praise. *Do not stare at your puppy. Look at her ears.*
- Pivot and stand still for 15 seconds. Return to her side, release and give her a hug.

Days Four Through Seven

If all is going well, spice things up a bit.

As your pup improves, increase the distance (and the distractions).

1. *Extend your distance.* Do this slowly. Up until now you've been pivoting directly in front of your pup. If she holds still, try pivoting one foot in front, then increasing one foot at a time. If she fumbles at five feet, go back to three feet. No big deal—it's not the Super Bowl. Go easy on her. After all, she's just a pup.

2. *Act like a nut.* If your puppy has handled your motion and sound distractions well, increase them. You're doing this to encourage her focus in distracting situations, so cry like your friend's baby, meow like the neighbor's cat, and throw a tantrum like your three year old. Increase your distractions slowly—too much crying and tantrum throwing can be nerve wracking (for both of you). If your pup can't be still, it means you're going too fast, you're staring into her eyes, or you're being too annoying. Check yourself.

Do not correct a young puppy for breaking a command. Just reposition and slow it down! *Total time commitment:* Two to three minutes, twice a day.

As the Weeks Continue

If you spend a good solid week practicing this command, you'll notice that your puppy's eye contact with you increases overall. As the weeks progress, begin to use these commands around commonplace distractions when she's on the leash. If it's a new situation, stay at her side and hold her still if she gets too excited.

Do not correct her for breaking a command yet! She's still too young, and you could frighten her.

Week Three Questions: SIT-STAY

My puppy jumps at me when I turn in front of her.
Are you standing tall? Stand tall and hold the leash above her head. If she jumps, snap her to the side and back into place quickly as you say "Off!"

My puppy gets up when I return to her.
You're probably releasing her as soon as you return to her side. Avoid this because she'll come forward in anticipation of her release. Return to her side and pause for varying lengths of time (3 seconds, 10 seconds, 30 seconds, 60 seconds).

My puppy gets up to follow me when I go out to the end of the leash.
Slow down! Go back to pivoting six feet in front. Leave your puppy with a firm "Stay" as you step forward and hold the collar above her head to enable a quick correction.

My puppy jumps at my finger as I give her signals.
Your finger looks awfully tempting as it looms above your puppy's head. Give all signals quickly and remove your finger promptly.

WEEK FOUR

Down

Your goal this week is to teach your puppy the command "Down." This command has a lot to do with trust and submission. Some pups flop right down, but most don't. At this age your puppy may be a know-it-all with little interest in submitting to you. But submit she must. By teaching this command, you're showing her who's the boss. She must trust in your protection when she's in a vulnerable position.

Hit the Dirt

Start your lessons in a quiet room when your puppy is in a calm or sleepy mood. How you teach this command will depend on your pup's willingness to participate. I use three techniques for three different types of puppies:

1. Low-Key Learner

The easy-going gal. During practice time, kneel next to her and command "Down" as you hit the floor with your right hand. As she follows your hand, praise her while gently pressing your left thumb between her shoulders. If needed, gently lift out her right paw with your right hand. Praise and pet her for five seconds, then release.

Encourage the low-key learner to Down by gently lifting out her right paw to help her down. (Debbie Gorirn)

2. No Thanks

The not-so-easily-impressed one. After you command and signal, take each paw at the elbow with your corresponding hand, lay your left arm across her shoulders and position her swiftly. Pet and release.

3. Jaws Junior

This pup thinks "Down" is a call to battle. To teach this one, stand up tall and put the leash beneath your foot. Point at the ground without bending over and command "Down." Pull up on the leash so your puppy's head is bent toward the ground. If she doesn't lie down at this point, position her by pressing between her shoulders. Stand up and praise her, but don't pet. Release after a few seconds. Work on this command and don't give in. Avoid corrections because this will strengthen her resolve to ignore the command.

Note: Few pups pick up this command in one week. Don't give corrections or get frustrated—you'll convince your puppy that Down is indeed an unsafe idea.

The Finale

Once your puppy agrees to go down, you can start the next step:

- Standing straight at your puppy's side command "Sit" and slide the leash under your foot.
- Point to the ground and command "Down" once.

Once your puppy agrees to go down, start to work with the lead. (Debbie Gorirn)

- If she doesn't respond, pull the leash up to position her. Praise her as you position. If necessary, push between her shoulder blades.
- Pause, release, and praise.

As the Weeks Continue

Once your pup has gotten the hang of Down, practice using it throughout the day in all situations. If she doesn't respond, position her with your foot. Avoid bending over her, correcting her, or repeating yourself.

Week Four Questions: DOWN

My puppy rolls over when I get her down.
Your puppy is trying to deal with the stress of submitting and wants the focus back on her. Sweet thing. She figures if she gets a belly rub, then no loss of face, right? Wrong. But don't correct her. Just ignore her and wait until she's upright to release.

My puppy is mouthy after I position her.
Another stress reaction. No corrections, as they reinforce the intensity of this command. Ignore her without withdrawing your hands. She'll stop. Release when she rights herself. If this is ineffective, please refer to the "Junior Jaws" paragraph in this section.

My pup gets nasty when I try to position her.
Don't give up. Position your puppy as explained in the "Junior Jaws" paragraph of this section. If the aggression doesn't wane, call in a professional.

WEEK FIVE

The Come Command

Come is a pretty big concept. Imagine leaving something you're enjoying just to go stand next to somebody! Like Heel, Come must be taught as a position as well as an exercise. "Come" must mean stop what you're doing and run toward me, then stop when you get to me, and sit still. Whew! This command asks a lot!

There are a few rules to follow when teaching the "Come" command:

- Never call your puppy for negatives such as punishing, isolating, or medicating.
- Don't repeat yourself or use multiword variations like "Come on" or "Come here."
- Don't chase your puppy if she doesn't respond.
- If you must retrieve her for being naughty, don't get angry. It'll only frighten her.

Encourage your puppy to come by playing hide-and-seek.

Days One to Four

Inside

Take your pup into a quiet area and practice teaching this command from a Sit-Stay.

- Command "Stay" and walk out to the end of the leash.
- Standing tall, sweep your arm across your chest and command "(Name), Come" in a clear commanding tone.
- Immediately run backward, slapping your legs and cheering your pup on.
- When she reaches you, encourage her into a sit position as you repeat "Come," then release and praise.

Practice two "Sit-Stays" in between each "Come." Repeat three times only.

Outside

When your puppy is on leash, hide behind a tree or house corner, then call out "(Name), Come!" Praise her as she looks, and hug her into a sit position when she finds you!

Days Four Through Seven

Inside
Repeat the above exercise from a Sit-Stay in a quiet area. When she reaches you, encourage a straight Sit by pulling the leash underneath her chin and signaling from her eyes to yours.

Outside
If you have a Flexi-Leash, use it to extend your distance in the hiding exercise described above. (*See* "Puppy Ping Pong" in the Directed Play session.)

As the Weeks Continue

Once you've mastered the Come on the six-foot leash, begin practicing on the Flexi-Lead to encourage distance control. If you want to try the Sit-Stay exercise outdoors, begin on the six-foot lead, then continue on the Flexi-Lead.

Don't call her out of *every* Sit-Stay, or she'll anticipate your call and break too soon. Use this practice time to hone your Sit-Stay exercise, releasing her from the directional position.

Total time commitment: Five minutes, twice daily and during walks.

Week Five Questions: COME

My puppy gets overexcited as she comes and runs right into me.
Ms. Momentum! Practice on your six-foot leash. As she races toward you, lean forward and grasp the leash as you bring her to halt in front of you. Praise generously and release as normal.

My puppy veers to one side as she gets close to me.
Are you standing upright? If you're bent over, your puppy won't come to you because you're in her way. If she continues, let her run by, then snap the leash as you bring her into position. Praise and release.

When she reaches me she jumps.
Stand tall. Check your tone; if it's high pitched and excited, she'll think play. Praise in a calm fashion and snap her to one side if she gets too excited. Bring her to sit in front, release and praise.

WEEK SIX

The Wait Command

Your goal this week is to extend your puppy's understanding of the command "Wait." Not to be confused with the command "Stay," "Wait" instructs a pup to freeze quickly and focus on you for permission. Stay is formal, whereas "Wait" is more sudden and impulsive.

The command "Wait" has been introduced in previous chapters. If you've already started using it, good for you! If not, it's time to begin. This command requires that your puppy be leashed and under your control.

Days One Through Four

Before going up stairs or across the street, bring your puppy to your side and ask her to "Wait."

At first, use this command in three controlled situations.

At Doors and Curbs

Before you go through a door or across a curb, bring your puppy to your side by holding the leash behind your back. Command "Wait." Give the leash a sharp tug if she lunges and say "No." When she settles down, say "Okay" as you lead her forward. Always remember, the leader leads.

At Stairs

Your puppy must learn to wait until the stairs are clear before charging up or down. Take her on leash to the top of the stairs and command "Wait." Pull her behind you using "No" if she strains to pull ahead. Step forward when she looks to you saying "Okay—Easy." If she throws herself ahead, stop, snap back, and say "No" disapprovingly.

Around Food

Break a biscuit into five pieces and follow this sequence:

- Stand next to your puppy holding the end of the leash in your left hand.
- Give your puppy the first two biscuits with the command "Okay!"
- Offer the next biscuit, but tell your puppy "Wait."
- If she starts forward, pull her head back and say "No."
- When she pauses say "Okay!" Repeat three times.

Days Five Through Seven

Continue to extend your control at doors, at stairs, and with food. Begin to introduce the command outside during walks. Using your six-foot leash, stop two or three times during your walk and command "Wait." Freeze as you give the command, tugging your puppy if she doesn't stop with you. Pause a few seconds and release with "Okay." As she improves, use it on the Flexi-Leash to perfect her distance control.

Teach her to "Wait" when a treat is offered by another family member.

As the Weeks Continue

Extend your control. Once she really gets into the swing of things, try using it off leash in the house. For a big challenge, have her Wait when company or kids hand her a treat!

Total time commitment: Five minutes twice daily.

For a big challenge, ask your puppy to "Wait" while a child offers a treat.

Week Six Questions: WAIT

My puppy leaps forward or jumps at the treat.
Are you pulling your treat hand away? If so, you're inviting trouble! Hold the treat still and pull your puppy's head back.

My puppy jumps out of the car. Can I use "Wait" here?
Yes! Great application of your new-found control.

WEEK SEVEN

The Stand Command

Your goal this week is to teach the command "Stand." This is the hardest position for a puppy to understand becasue she thinks, "As long as I'm up, let's move!" But "Stand" means stand still. It's great for cleaning muddy paws and grooming, and veterinarians love a dog who stands calmly on the examining table.

Days One Through Four

Your long-range goal is a pup who stands still when you say "Stand."

Command "Stand" as you prop your puppy into position

- Kneel on the floor next to your pup.
- Place her into a sit position.
- Slide your right hand beneath her collar and your left against her tummy.
- Command "Stand" as you prop her into a comfortable standing position.
- Pause, sliding your left hand to rest on her right thigh. Release in five seconds and praise.
- Repeat four times, twice daily.

Days Five Through Seven

Begin to command from an upright posture as you prop her into position. If she seems to get it, resist propping her belly and just pull forward on the collar. Extend the duration of still time and always release with "Okay" and praise.

Use this command whenever you need it. If you have to brush or bathe your pup, tell her "Stand." Wow your veterinarian by using it on the exam table!

Total time commitment: Two to three minutes, twice daily.

Begin to command "Stand" from an upright position, slowly asking your puppy to hold the position longer.

Week Seven Questions: STAND

My dog snaps when I touch her belly.

Some dogs are very testy down there. Condition your puppy to accept handling during playtime or while offering treats. Otherwise, call a professional.

My dog collapses in a funny wiggling heap when we practice this command.

The comedian strikes again. Ignore your puppy's attempts to make you laugh. Start again, perhaps from a standing position yourself.

WEEK EIGHT

A Chain of Commands

Now that you've taught your puppy all the essentials, practice using any five of your seven commands in a varying five-minute pattern each day. Blend the commands smoothly from one to the next so you don't confuse your dear puppy. Speak clearly and stand tall. If she's not paying attention to you, snap the leash, but be sure to encourage her warmly when she responds.

Continue to use your commands and signals when interacting with your pup throughout the day. They are your communication link!

Fun Adolescent Activities

It's important to provide a structured environment for your puppy and implement a sensible, responsible training program. These are the tools you use to create a happy, well-adjusted pet. That, and the ability to cut loose, roll on the carpet, make silly noises, and play doggy games! Do bear in mind, however, that your puppy is still very impressionable. Rivalry games like tug-of-war and all-out gladiator matches will undermine your Top Dog status. Avoid them! Instead of rivalry, you want to communicate direction and fun. Yes, games can be educational *and* fun. Read them over and take your pick.

Directed Play: Your puppy learned three stationary commands: Sit, Down, and Stand. These commands can be tedious for pups on the go. Hasten her understanding by using these commands while playing with her favorite toy or giving her a treat:

Sit: Hold a toy or treat to your puppy's nose. Then bring it back just above and between her ears as you command "Sit."

Down: Hold the toy or treat to your puppy's nose. Command "Down" while you drop the treat to the floor in between her paws.

Stand: From her nose, bring the toy or treat straight out 6 to 12 inches as you command "Stand."

Hide-and-Seek: When your puppy is least expecting it, call her name and the command "Come" and race into the next room! Praise as you run to encourage her to follow. Kneel down to accept her enthusiastically.

Fido, Fetch!: When your puppy was younger, we encourage fetching. Now you can take a crack at teaching her this game! Be a patient teacher remember this is supposed to be fun!

Playing "Fido, Fetch" is fun for you and your puppy.

- Place a lead on your puppy and let her drag it around.
- Introduce a ball with praise. Get your puppy excited, but don't tease her.

- As soon as she shows interest, praise and toss the ball a short distance while holding the end of the leash.
- When she takes it in her mouth, tell her to "Bring It."
- If your enthusiasm cannot reel her in, use the leash. Tell her "Out" and immediately toss the toy again. If she doesn't release the ball promptly, squeeze behind her canine teeth as you repeat "Out" and continue praising.

Repeat this exercise three to four times, then remove the object quietly, without saying anything. When the game is over, put the toy away.

If your puppy taunts you with a toy or stays just out of reach, walk away or ignore her.

"Over!" Puppies love to jump! Since she can't jump on you or the furniture, set up a jumping arena in your living room to give her an outlet for all that enthusiasm:

- Lay a broomstick on a carpeted floor. Let her sniff it. Next, command "Over" as you walk your puppy over the stick.
- Balance the stick over two objects of equal height (paper cups, toilet or paper towels).
- Lead your puppy over and let her sniff the setup. Praise her.
- Walk her back, run happily to the jump and command "Over!" as you both jump together.
- When she's confident, command "Over" as you let her jump go first.
- Repeat the last step. Once she's over the jump, stop, bend down, and tap it to encourage her to jump back.

Do not encourage your puppy to jump any higher than her elbow—she could get hurt.

Sniff-n-Snarf: The last hurrah! This is one of my dog's favorite games, probably because a biscuit is involved. Break a biscuit into five pieces and follow this format:
- Sit your puppy and tell her to "Sniff" the treat (no snatching!).
- Instruct "Stay," holding the leash above her head.
- Toss the treat out three feet and pause.
- Command "Okay—Go Find!" as you release your puppy to snarf up the treat!
- As your puppy improves her stay control, you can walk forward and hide the treat around the corner or even a kid! If she acts confused, get down on all fours and show her how to use her sniffer!

Game Questions

My puppy runs around the jump when we play the "Over" game.
Lay the stick across a threshold. When guiding your puppy over the jump, hold the leash closer to her head. Don't drag her over the jump, though. Let her do it herself.

My puppy's favorite game is Sniff-n-Snarf, but after I hide it she antic-ipates the release and darts forward.
When you return to your puppy, vary the amount of time she must hold her stay before you release her to find it.

Other Common Questions

Sometimes I get so frustrated that I yell at my puppy—I've even thought of hitting her. And the madder I get, the worse she gets! What am I doing wrong?
In the wild world of dogs, the top dog calls the shots, and the lesser dogs get frazzled keeping up. Do you see a parallel here? You're acting like a lesser dog! Rise above the situation by restricting your errant puppy. Use your Teaching Lead and do not allow off-leash freedom outdoors. This tactic will get your dog back on track in a jiffy. Give small doses of freedom as she proves herself worthy.

My puppy is great when it's just the family, but she loses it around company!
Continue to use your Teaching Lead around company. Don't let guests pay attention to her until she's settled down.

Sometimes when I praise my puppy she gets overexcited and starts to mouth.
Are you petting your puppy? Petting is very exciting! The object of praise is not to stimulate your dog, but to make her feel accomplished and proud. Tone down your praise.

Wrapping Up

I call this stage the "rude awakening." When confronted with the sometimes aggravating budding adolescent, all dog owners think wistfully of the endearing infant stage. But please try to understand it from your puppy's point of view: she's getting bigger, the world is less scary, and she's aching to find out just how much she can get away with. Teach her your expectations patiently, be persistent with your training, and take a deep breath, because it's not over yet!

11

Puppy Puberty: 6 to 9 Months

If you've just begun this book, please go through the training program outlined in Chapter 10. Your dog is a little older than the recommended starting age, but that's okay. It's never too late to train your dog!

RAGING HORMONES

Your puppy is about to go through a major transformation. She's growing up! Remember growing up? Hormones, rebellion, confusion, curiosity . . . puberty. An exciting time, but not always pretty. Well, it's no different for your puppy.

At about six months, those hormones start coursing through her veins, and she'll begin to experience a jumbled mix of internal signals: Dominate! Submit! Explore! Hide! Approach! Retreat! If she were a child, she'd get an unusual haircut and laugh at your clothes but still be a little nervous when you're not home.

On top of these typical growing pains, add the awakening of breed-specific instincts telling herders to herd, hunters to hunt, guarders to guard, pullers to pull . . . it's utter canine chaos, and she's still cutting her baby teeth!

So here we have this puppy/dog, pumped full of hormones, high spirits, and anxiety. It's no wonder she may give you the puppy equivalent of a teenage eye roll when you give her a command.

You may wonder if you'll be able to tell when your puppy is shifting into this stage. You will. Trust me. The most telling sign is unpredictability. It's like having two different dogs—the precious angel who gazes up at you with adoring eyes and the wild-eyed demon dancing just out of reach with your shoe in her mouth. The one you show off during walks through the park and the one you say belongs to your brother. The one who makes you smile and the one who makes you cringe. The ease and speed with which she can transform herself is truly amazing.

Puberty is further characterized by these behaviors:

Puberty is characterized by a recurrence of jumping up.

- She'll know all her commands, but she'll be selective in her response.
- Reccurrence of jumping, nipping, and leash pulling.
- Destructive chewing or housesoiling when left alone.
- Excessive whining and bossiness.

As if the bratty stage wasn't fun enough!

Now that she's in training, your eager little student will try to use all her hard-earned knowledge to train *you*. On the leash, your puppy may be a real crowd pleaser, but off leash . . . that's another story. You'll find yourself shouting, repeating commands, pleading, offering bribes, giving in. Ah, puberty—such a joy. Call your parents right now and apologize for yours.

Training is critical now. Without it, dogs may not outgrow this stage, condemning you to life with an eternally pubescent dog. Surely you've met adult dogs who jump, mouth, mount, and generally misbehave at every opportunity. These dogs are "stage stuck." Don't let this happen to you!

FIRST OF ALL

Let's review the cardinal rules of dog training:

- Speak in your dog's language (Doglish).
- Don't repeat yourself.
- No shouting, pleading, or giving in.
- No bribery!

Though you may be using the Teaching Lead less, I do recommend its use for the following situations:

- If your dog has ignored a correction more than twice. Station her quietly away from you for 15 minutes. Never station in anger. Allow the two of you to cool off.
- If the environment is over stimulating (company, kids playing, etc.). Station or lead her at your side to maintain verbal control.

If the environment is overstimulating, keep your dog on lead at your side to maintain verbal control.

- If you're leaving a room temporarily and you want your dog secured from mischief. As you leave, tell her to "Wait."

Never station a dog near entanglements, outlets, or ledges and do not station her on the training collar. Please review Chapter 9 if the teaching lead principles are unclear.

THE RIGHT ATTITUDE

The toughest thing to control during this stage isn't your dog, it's your temper. We humans are a control-oriented bunch, and we want our dogs to come when called, stay calm in exciting situations, and control their game-y impulses. But these young dogs want to play! Have fun! Chase a butterfly! They are often unimpressed by your frustration. Some may show fear, but most think a shouting, foot-stamping Top Dog is inviting play, and the game accelerates—as does your blood pressure.

Five Steps to Successful Communication

1. **Detach:** This is more a meditation exercise than a dog-training technique. Breathe in—breathe out. Detach yourself from your puppy. Avoid taking her behavior personally. Though you may think all your training has been a waste of time, it hasn't. Remember this equation: Puppyhood equals Patience plus Persistence.

2. **Stay Centered.** When your puppy is acting up, use all your energy to stay cool. If you get angry or tense, she'll know she got to you. You'd be playing her game and following her lead.

3. **Watch that Eye Contact!** Puppies are very concerned with status at this age: "Am I a leader or a follower?" If your puppy can get you to look to her more than you can get her to look to you, you're the follower. Ignore your puppy's attempts to get your attention. Pet and gaze at her when she is in a calm state of mind. Give her eye contact when directing her behavior.

4. **Fall Back:** Even if you've successfully weaned your puppy from the teaching lead, you'll probably need it during this stage. When your puppy is overstimulated and unable to focus, connect her to your side or station her for a while with a bone.

5. **Have Three Plans:** During behavior emergencies, for example, door greetings, article stealing, runaway dog, and so forth, use your commands if they work. Most dogs, however, become temporarily deaf during these situations, so it's best to have alternative plans. Here is an example for the above-mentioned situations:

   - *Door Greetings:* Always ask guests to ignore your dog until she has settled down. Your three options might include: stationing her to a far corner of the greeting room; connecting her around your waist to maintain leash control; or if all

else fails, crating or confining her with a favorite toy. Bring
her out when she has calmed down.

- *Article Stealing:* When your puppy steals an article of clothing, leave the area and shut the door behind you. At this
age, most puppies are more concerned with playing than
with chewing. If you ignore her, she'll lose interest in the
game. Another option would be leaving the house. Put on
your coat, grab your keys . . . that should be enough to distract her. Take your pup out for a minute or two if you try
this trick, or she'll start to see through it. As a last recourse,
follow her around without eye contact or corrections,
slowly cornering her in a small area. Calmly remove the
object by squeezing her muzzle and commanding "Out."
Never correct a puppy while you're doing this, or she'll
quickly distrust you.

- *Runaway Puppy:* This is not just frustrating, but dangerous.
You should never let your puppy off leash unless the area
is confined; if she does sneak off, have your plans well
thought out. Try a command or two. If they don't work,
stop. Don't panic. Try running around like a lunatic (without
eye contact), screaming, and waving your arms. Drop to
the ground in a heap and see if this strange and interesting
behavior brings her running. Try getting in the car—many
dogs can't bear the thought of missing out on a car trip. If
nothing works, follow her quietly to make sure she stays
out of danger. Yelling will only make matters worse.

Avoid getting angry at your puppy after the fact. She'll learn to be
more wary of your ploys. Never use treats as bribery. Used in this way,
treats actually reinforce the naughty behavior.

CONTINUED TRAINING

In the last chapter we went over leash-training techniques. Please make sure
you've mastered them before you begin the exercises outlined below. In this

section we'll be working on advanced training techniques—but don't attempt them in an unconfined area. Puppies are extremely curious and easily distracted. Your puppy may dart away and disobey you not out of spite but excitement. If you fall into the trap of disciplining your dog off leash, she'll remain skeptical of off-leash commands forever.

Before we begin, I suggest you add the following items to your equipment collection. Please be sure you have the right training collar. (If you're unsure about what collar is right for your dog, please refer to pages 19–20.)

Flexi-Leash
This retractable leash is an invaluable prerequisite for off-leash work. The longer the better.

30-Foot Line
You will be using this for advanced training techniques. Buy either a canvas leash from a pet store, or create your own using lightweight clothesline and a clip.

10-Foot Line
Again, use lightweight clothesline and a clip or a canvas leash. You'll use this line for indoor distance control and to correct your delinquent pup.

The Short Leash
An additional training and problem-solving tool. It should be long enough to grab, but it should not touch the floor.

THE TOP FIVE COMMANDS

We will be extending your control on all the commands learned in the last chapter. These are the top five that I encourage you to use most often:

Heel
Continue using this command to encourage good walking control. In addition, use this command to call your dog to your side. To teach your dog this concept, place her on a leash and let her walk ahead of you. Suddenly call her name and

command "Heel" as you slap your left thigh. Lead her to your side by reeling in the leash. Lead her around your left side in a "U" or to your right around your back. When she reaches your side, make sure she sits before you release her. Once she gets the hang of this "Heel" (thigh-slap) begin to encourage her to come to your side around distractions (on-leash at first) and when you're sitting down. Always give the command positively, enforce a proper sit, and praise her warmly before you release her with "Okay."

Heel!

Sit

Continue to ask her to "Sit" in all situations. Give the command once; if she doesn't respond, give her collar or leash a tug that says "No" and ask her again. Position her sharply if she doesn't listen.

Sit!

Down

Continue to work on this command even if your puppy doesn't want to cooperate. Slide your left foot under the leash, point to the ground and command down as you pull the leash upward under your foot. Press on her back if necessary. Ignore her if she rolls around wildly on the floor or nips your shoelaces. Release her only after she's calmed down.

Down!

Wait.

Wait

Continue to use this command to catch your dog's attention at doorways, cars, stairs, or before entering an area of high stimulation (e.g., the veterinarians, a room full of children, dog-training class).

You'll recall from the last chapter that this command means stop dead in your tracks and look to me immediately. If you're successful using this command in the above situations, begin to practice it when walking your dog on her regular or flexi-leash. Stop in your tracks as you command "Wait." Pull back on the leash if your pup doesn't stop with you. Release with "Okay."

Leave It

You worked on this correction in previous chapters. If you haven't learned it, please review pages 61–62. Once your dog understands that when you say "Leave It" you mean it, begin to practice this outside when passing squirrels, dogs, bikers, and other temptations. Tug the leash sharply as you say "Leave It" in your sternest correction tone.

USING YOUR NEW EQUIPMENT

You'll be using your new equipment to increase your command control. Each piece will be explained separately, but you can use them interchangeably.

The Flexi-Leash

This leash is great to use when exercising your puppy. It allows plenty of freedom to romp while giving you complete control. As a training tool, you can use it informally during a walk to reinforce the following commands:

Name
When you call your puppy's name, she should look to you promptly. When she's distracted, call her name. If she looks, praise her and let her get back to whatever she was doing. If she ignores you, press the stop button on the Flexi and give her a sharp tug, praising her when you've got her attention.

Wait
Begin to use this command when your dog is 3 feet in front of you. Increase your distance to 6, 8, 10, 15, and 26 feet in front of you. Command, then tug if she ignores you. Pause for several seconds, then release with "Okay."

Heel
When you give her this command she must return to your side. As explained above, this command communicates position as well as good walking etiquette. When your puppy understands the basic concepts, repeat it outside on the flexi-leash. Call her name (tugging the leash if she ignores you) then "Heel" as you slap your leg. Reel her in if necessary.

Sit-Stay
You can use the Flexi both inside and out to increase your distance control on this command. The Flexi adds resistance to your pup's collar, so she may get confused and follow you. To help her understand, practice the following exercise:

- Leave your puppy in a stay and pivot in front of her.
- Remind "Stay" as you gently pull forward on the leash. You should see her actively resisting the pressure to obey the command.
- Return to her side and release with "Okay!"

Come
Remember the structure of this command—your puppy must return to you and sit down in front. If you fudge on the last part, she may come to you but run right by. Practice the structured exercise from the Sit-Stay. Increase your distance as her focus improves.

Emergency Down
This exercise can be a real lifesaver, but don't try it until your dog has mastered the down command. Once a day, when she least expects it, give the command with dramatic urgency in your voice. If she ignores you, position her quickly. At first, give the command when she is close at your side, extending your distance as her responsiveness improves.

Leave It!
As described earlier, this is a correction not a command. As soon as your dog comprehends that "Leave It" means just that, extend your control with the Flexi. If your dog ignores you, snap the leash sharply as you repeat the correction.

30-Foot Line

Make or buy a 30-foot line. Tie it to a tree or post in your yard. Please make all knots secure. Leave the line on the ground and follow this sequence:

- Warm up with five minutes of regular leash work. Stop your dog next to the long line. Attach the line, then detach your regular lead.

- Fold the six-foot leash and place it in front of your dog. Your hands are free.
- Command "Stay," leave your dog and walk out at a comfortable distance.
- Run your fingers through your hair and swing your arms to show her that no lead exists.
- If your pup falls for this and tries to make a getaway, wait until she hits the end of the line, then give a firm "No." Return her to position and repeat at a shorter distance.

The command "Come" can also be practiced on your long line, but never call at a distance greater than the line will reach.

Practice "Stay" on a 30-foot lead.

The Short Lead

Use this lead inside to encourage off-leash control. Attach it to your dog's training collar. Go into a small, quiet area and practice your commands as you did on leash, initially holding the lead to enforce control. Once warmed up, begin to drop the lead. Slap your leg and use peppy body language to encourage your dog's focus.

Even if she disobeys, avoid strict corrections as they will create fear of off-leash responses. At first, do simple exercises to build her success rate. Keep the lessons short (about two to four minutes), and end with a game.

SOCIALIZATION

Your puppy's curiosity is peeking at this age, and she needs to make her debut! If you don't introduce her to the outside world, she may try to go out and do it herself. If you don't introduce her to the outside world and she *can't*

Obedience classes help socialize your puppy and refine your training.

get out, she may develop a mistrust of anyone and anything that is outside of her territory. It's easy to socialize your puppy—just take her along when you go places! Puppies hate to be left behind and love to watch the trees whiz by from the back seat of a car. And she won't care what kind of music you like or how badly you sing. Please see page 21 for suggestions on safe car confinements.

This is the best age to consider enrolling your dog in a well-managed and structured obedience class. Meet or speak to your instructor ahead of time to be sure you're comfortable with her style. Typically, classes are held once a week—and the smaller the class the better. My classes have a six-dog limit, which guarantees plenty of individual attention and gives the classes a nice social feeling. If you have a family, ask if more than one handler is welcome. Although I discourage handling by children under five (they're just pups themselves), I encourage complete family participation. Training your puppy should be a family affair!

YOUR PROBLEM CHILD

Your puppy can be quite a frustrating little creature during this stage. Everything she does is for the pure sport of it, and she'll rarely show remorse. Often, discipline is interpreted as play—she just won't take you seriously!

To borrow a saying from an old Chinese prophet, hang on and let go. Hang on to your ideal of a well-behaved dog. Let go of the hope that your puppy will become Lassie overnight. Persist, train, have patience—you'll get through.

Please have the following equipment ready to help you through some of the common behavior problems of this stage:

- *The Teaching Lead:* You will use this to station and lead your pup when her behavior calls for it.
- *Short Lead:* To be left on your puppy when you're home with her. This give you something to grasp when correction or guidance is needed.
- *10-Foot Line:* Useful in long-distance corrections.

Barking

This is the age when most pups begin to bark at unfamiliar sounds and movements. You may want your dog to do this, but if overly encouraged, you may end up with a barking machine. A good watchdog quiets down when you tell her to and lets people enter the house if you think it's a good idea. You need to teach your dog to be "Quiet." Place her on the 10-foot line and rig a situation to encourage barking. Let her bark a few times then correct her with "Quiet" and a leash tug. Next tell her to "Heel" and bring her behind you if she won't respond. Tell her she's a "Good Girl." Use the lead only when necessary.

Another effective long-distance correction tool is the long-distance water pistol (I use something called a Super Soaker, available in toy stores). When your pup begins to bark, spray her from behind (don't let her see you) as you correct with "Quiet." Encourage her back to your side with "Heel." Eventually she will alert to the noise and run to find you automatically.

Jumping Up

Your puppy may be very body assertive at this age. She may paw you or throw her body weight against you. She may fight you for the leash or plant her paws on your chest. This is not acceptable. It's annoying. It's insulting. It's puberty, puppy style. I'll list several corrective techniques. They are all safe and humane, so try them and see what works for you:

- Ignoring your dog when she jumps up can be the best plan of attack. It is denying the one thing she is seeking: attention.
- Snap the leash firmly down and forward. Ignore her until she is calm.
- Fill a plant mister with a water and lemon juice or vinegar mixture. When your pup jumps up, mist her indiscreetly as you continue with whatever you're doing.
- Fill an empty soda can with 10 pennies and shake it (out of her sight) when she jumps up. Do not look at her until she is calm. If this works, make more and have them handy around the house and during walks.
- For jumping up on company, please refer to page 92 under Three Alternative Plans.

Ignoring your dog when she jumps up can be the best plan of attack.

Praise her when she sits to be petted.

Do not stare at her or push her away when trying to correct jumping behaviors. She'll take it as an invitation to play rougher. Avoid using verbal corrections for the bratty jumper because this can sometimes be enough to excite your pup. Please refer to Chapter 13 for other suggestions on jumping behavior.

Nipping

If your puppy is still nipping at this age, you're not the leader. You must climb back to the top of the doggy hierarchy immediately! The new rule is *no nipping.* Your attitude is very important in solving this problem. Be stern! To correct your puppy, leave your hand in her mouth (yanking it away is too funlike) and do one of the following:

- Pinch her tongue and lower jaw between your index finger and thumb and hold on for 10 seconds as you correct her with your eyes and sternly say "Shame On You!"
- With your free hand, spritz her muzzle indiscreetly with a diluted vinegar spray mix (50/50) as you shame her.
- Tug her sharply from your body with your free hand as you shame her (she must be on her teaching lead or short lead; tugging the collar is not as effective).

Mounting

Your puppy is not trying to embarrass you with this behavior (although he's doing an excellent job), she's trying to assert her dominance. Mounting is a big no-no, both socially and politically. Children are often the targets because their puppy-like behaviors communicate submission. Whether it's you, your kids, or visitors, it is completely unacceptable! If your pup is prone to mounting, keep her on a short leash. When she gets that look in her eye, snap her off, push her onto the floor, step on the lead, stand up, and correct her harshly saying "Don't You Ever Try That Again." A good correction won't be questioned!

Marking/Housesoiling

Marking is popular with dominant pups: As soon as those hormones start flowing, they want to spread the message to the world. This is an ideal neutering time. To discourage marking in the house, you must discourage marking outside. Pick one area for your pup to relieve herself and don't let her mark during your walks. For this and other housebreaking problems, please refer to Chapter 13.

Though she may look grown up, she's still experiencing the pains of puppyhood. Keep those chew toys handy!

Chewing

At six months pups cut some of their more painful teeth. Though she may look grown up, she's still experiencing the pains of puppyhood. Keep those chew bones handy! If she goes after something unacceptable, correct her with "Leave It" and a snap. Encourage her to find her own bone. Always praise her when she chews on her toy.

Stop, Thief!

Puppies are quick to recognize the benefits of stealing. Everyone looks. Someone gives chase. Victory! Puppy plans to repeat this game very soon. To prevent this battle of wits, learn to anticipate it. When you sense your puppy's energy level is rising, take her out for some exercise before she turns that energy against you. If you can't exercise her at that moment, station or lead her. For more ideas please refer to Chapter 17.

Separation Anxiety

Though it can develop at any age, many puppies develop separation anxiety during this stage. It can result in destructive chewing, housesoiling, or excessive barking. Despite your puppy's growing up, she's more confused about herself than ever. She depends on your presence to reassure her. She may also be over-bonded to you, feeling lost if you're not there to direct her.

This issue can be solved, but there are a few ground rules:

- Avoid overemotional good-byes. Lavishing your puppy with kisses, biscuits, and drawn-out declarations of devotion do not reassure her. They're stressful. Stay cool when you come home too. Ignore her until she settles down. Flying through the door and hurling yourself on the floor before you've even removed your coat may assuage your guilt, but you're reinforcing very bad greeting manners.
- Leave a radio playing classical music to cover unfamiliar sounds.
- Place your dog in a dimly lit area to encourage sleep.
- Leave a favorite chew toy (rub it between your palms).
- *Never* correct your dog after the fact. Corrections only intensify her anxiety, which leads to more destruction.
- If you're leaving your puppy for over six hours, try to find someone to walk her. Otherwise, proof the house against her destruction by buying an indoor pen. Such pens fold nicely to store when your

home and can be set up before you leave to give you puppy space when you are gone for extended periods. Puppies get cramped when left in small kennels for over six hours and develop "hyper isolation anxiety."

- When home with your puppy, temporarily decrease your physical attention by 50 percent. Do not give in to her solicitations. Although it relieves your guilt feelings, it is too sharp a contrast from being left alone all day. When alone, your puppy will pine for companionship, and since chewing finger nails or watching the soaps isn't an option, she'll settle for your couch.

- If possible, buy a kitten for your dog. Kittens are super companions, and they are great company for dogs if raised with them. Getting another dog is also an option, though it's better to wait until you've raised this one successfully.

The next step to remedy her anxiety is a series of practice departures. Station your dog in a familiar spot. Instruct her to "Wait." Leave the room for 15 seconds. Return. Ignore her until she's settled, then praise her lovingly. Repeat this 10 times or until she's picking up the routine. Continue these short separations until she shows no anxiety. Double the separation time and repeat the procedure. Continue until you're able to leave the room for 30 minutes.

Once she's comfortable at 30 minutes, go back to short separations, but this time leave the house. Gradually work your way up to 30 minutes out of the house. Start over, this time getting into and starting your car. With patience, you'll be able to build her confidence and leave her for longer and longer periods.

Common Questions

What is a good age to spay or neuter my dog?
Speak to your veterinarian. Any time after six months is safe.

Is spaying or neutering really necessary?
Unless you're breeding your dog, I strongly suggest it. Neutered dogs stay closer to home and don't experience the mating tensions and aggressive instincts of their unaltered counterparts.

My dog is jabbing me with her chew bone. What should I do?
Say "Excuse Me" and shove her off you with your knee. Do not look at her, withdraw your body, or pet her because that will encourage pushy behavior. If you choose, you can go to her when she's calm and hold the bone so she can reach her back molars for a good chew.

When I correct my puppy she slinks away and looks as though she knows she did something wrong, but she doesn't retain the correction. Why?
Because she didn't know what you were correcting her for. Unclear corrections will frighten her and cause her to retreat from you. Good corrections encourage her to find an appropriate alternative. Reread the problem-solving section of this chapter and Chapter 17.

When I call my puppy she looks afraid and stays out of reach. Why?
She may associate the "Come" with something negative. Avoid calling her inside or to crate, medicate, or discipline her. Refer to the previous chapter on how to introduce this command. Practice this command on leash until your pup trusts your positive response.

How do I get her to come inside if I can't call her?
If you use "Come" to call your dog inside she'll start avoiding the command because it ends her playtime. Instead teach her "Inside" when she's on leash, give her the command, then go inside and play a game or give her a treat. If she likes the Sniff-n-Snarf game (page 86), you can play it by putting your dog in a Sit-Stay outdoors, hiding the treat just inside the front door and command "Inside-Find It!" Always make coming inside a plus, but avoid the command "Come" because there's no way to hide that it ends their outdoor adventures!

When I call my dog she runs away!
This dog associates "Come" with play. If you've unsuccessfully tried this command off leash and have been forced to chase her down, you've inadvertently created a game. Avoid using this command off leash until you're very experienced.

What's the difference between "Wait" and "Stay"?
Stay is formal, following one of the stationary commands (Sit, Down, Stand). Wait is impulsive. It means stop short and focus on me.

My dog is addicted to tissues. She'll steal them out of the garbage, off the counter—even out of my pocket.

This is a very common problem. You can try several things:

- Prevention—put wastebaskets off the floor or in a cabinet until she's a bit older.
- Teach your puppy to retrieve tissues. (*See* the "Chewing" section of Chapter 13.)
- Keep a bottle of Bitter Apple by the waste cans and spritz after you toss until your pup no longer shows interest.
- Rig a situation to correct the tissue as explained in the "Chewing" section of Chapter 13.
- Ignore your pup. Many do this for attention. They may swallow a few, but puppies often drop this behavior if it no longer gets the recognition they seek.

Tissue stealing is a very common problem.

Wrapping Up

Remember—don't take your dog's actions personally. Your puppy is going through some radical internal transformations, and she can barely sit still to relieve herself! Once those crazy hormones start to balance, you'll notice that her concentration improves, and she's more willing to obey. But it won't happen overnight. Be patient in your training and persistent when she struggles to get her own way. Correct her firmly when her behavior demands it—this is almost a teenager you're dealing with!

12

The Trying Teen: 9 to 12 Months

No, it's not over. Almost, but not yet. By now, your puppy is starting to calm down. He manages better on his own. He chews his bone. He responds immediately to your commands. He doesn't assault your visitors. Why, he's almost perfect!

Okay, sometimes he ignores you. Every now and then he runs right by you when he's called to come. Occasionally, he'll fidget himself out of a Sit-Stay or face you when he ought to be at your side. Please understand: He *wants* to behave, but his teenage genes are relentlessly telling him to make one more glorious attempt for Top Dog status. To that end, he begins a subtle campaign of defiance. You might not think a sloppy, sideways sit is a very big deal but your dog makes a little mental check mark every time you let him get away with it. It's one small step up the Top Dog ladder. Here are a few more signs he is making his ascent:

You might not think a sideways sit is a big deal, but your dog remembers what he's allowed to get away with.

- Does your dog shift positions before responding to a Sit or Down command?
- Does he face away or pivot in front of you during a Heel command?
- Does he slam into your leg on the Come command?

These little acts of defiance are more of those I talked about before. Nothing earth-shattering, but not acceptable!

FIRST OF ALL

At this stage, your puppy's world is being shaped by two conflicting forces: the desire to please you, and the urge to test his leaders once more just to make sure they can walk their talk. Don't take it personally! Once your puppy understands that you most certainly *do* mean what you say, you'll be in the driver's seat. Here are a few rules of thumb:

- Remain calm. Don't let your dog see that you're angry or frustrated. All teens, regardless of species, derive perverse pleasure out of your discomfort.
- Never lose. If your dog is challenging you on a command and he is on leash, argue your point to the bitter end (as instructed later in this chapter). If your dog is off leash and he ignores or defies a command, ignore *him* and withdraw from the situation. A graceful retreat is not a failure.
- Raise his consciousness. Teach him the meaning of "*No.*"

CANINE CONSCIOUSNESS-RAISINGS

During the last stage (puppy puberty) I discouraged all but the mildest corrective techniques during training. Now that your dog has become a teen, however, he's emotionally ready to learn that not everything he does pleases you.

It's natural for your dog to test your flexibility on the commands he's learned. He wonders if perhaps the "Sit" in front of company means something *juuuuust* a little different than the "Sit" in front of you.

In previous stages you labored over the teaching process. You showed your dog exactly what each command meant. Now he knows. Every time he doesn't respond or responds in *his* fashion, he's questioning you. If you repeat yourself or position him, he'll never learn to respond on his own. Not unlike teaching a child to tie shoelaces. Eventually it must be done independently.

To develop the all-important canine consciousness you must do two things:

- Decide what you want when you give a command.
- Follow through. If your expectations are unclear, his reaction will be, too.

It's time to teach your pal *"No."*

CONSCIOUSNESS-RAISING WITH COMMANDS

On Leash

When practicing your commands, avoid repeating yourself or positioning your dog. If he doesn't respond, snap the leash as firmly as required and say "No" in a corrective tone. If he still doesn't respond, review your tone (stern enough?) and your snap (firm enough?). Make adjustments as needed. If your dog still ignores you, position him without praise.

If your dog pivots out of position when you stop in Heel, inches forward on the Stay commands, or moves in front of you during stationary commands, he's testing you! If you position him sweetly, you're actually giving him attention for his defiance.

When practicing commands, avoid repeating yourself or positioning your dog.

In these situations, snap the leash firmly as you say "No" and position him by maneuvering him into place with the leash. This may take several tries and a temper tantrum from your beloved pet, but if you let the structure slide, you'll never have a reliable off-leash dog.

Off Leash

For starters, you need the following equipment:

- 30-foot lightweight clothesline
- 10-foot lightweight clothesline
- short lead

Never place these lines on the training collar or leave your dog attached in an unconfined area. Use them only when you know where he is—even in the house.

30-Foot Line

In an enclosed outdoor area, attach the line to your dog's buckle collar and allow him to roam freely under your supervision. Play with him by engaging him with a stick or ball. Avoid over-commanding. Just hang around together.

Every 5 to 10 minutes, position yourself near the rope and call him to you using "Come" or "Heel." If he races over, help him into the proper sit position and give him a hug! Release him immediately. If he ignores your command, quickly step on the line and say "No." Don't scream, just speak sternly. After the correction, give your dog the opportunity to make amends by re-commanding. If he doesn't respond, correct him again and reel him in.

You can also reinforce other commands (Wait, Leave It, Sit, Down And Stay) using the long line. But before issuing any command, position yourself within stepping distance of the line to enable a quick correction.

When it's time to go inside, instruct him in by pointing to the door and saying "Inside." (Avoid using "Come" or "Heel" because going inside may not be the highlight of his day, and you don't want any unfun ideas associated with these

Practice "Wait" on a 30-foot lead in an enclosed outdoor area.

commands.) If he gives you that "I Don't Think So" look, step on the line and say (what else?) "No." Point to the door and repeat "Inside," reeling him if necessary. Make going inside a good time, even if you have to drag him in. Pet or play with him for a few minutes or give him a treat.

10-Foot Line

Continue to strive for long-distance control in the house. Let your dog wear the 10-foot when you're paying attention to him. Every 5 or 10 minutes, go up to him and give him any command. If he doesn't listen, say "No." Re-command him. If he still ignores you, correct him with the lead and reel him in. Always praise him for a proper response.

If you give your dog a command and he gives you some canine back talk (a bark or dodge), step on the lead, snap it firmly saying "No," and station him in one of his areas for 15 minutes. Ignore him during this time and remove his chew objects. He's been grounded without TV.

Short Lead

When your dog is in the house with you, place him on a short leash unless you're working with him on the 10-foot line. Use it to reinforce stationary commands, proper sits for Heel and Come, and for a correction when needed. If you give your dog a command and he doesn't respond, pick the lead up calmly and correct him with a snap and "No."

Heeling inside on a short lead.

DEVELOPING A CONSCIENCE WITH NAUGHTY BEHAVIOR

This is where the phrase "No—Shame On You" comes in very handy. It's intended to embarrass your dog, and it really works! Use the 10-foot and 30-foot lines.

Here's a rundown of common problem areas encountered with this age. If you can't find your answers here, please refer to Chapter 13.

Counter Cruising

What do you think is going through your dog's mind when he's sniffing around the stove? He's probably not thinking much about behaving. More likely, he's thinking "opportunity." To rehabilitate the compulsive eater, snap him away firmly when he's doing a counter survey (i.e., when you catch him thinking about what's on the counters!). In your best corrective tone say "No. Shame On You."

Next, place your dog on his long line and set up a situation by leaving him alone with an irresistible temptation perched tantalizingly close to the edge of your counter. Drape the long line into the next room. Before you depart tell your dog "No" as you point to the object. Instruct "Wait" as you leave. Don't go far—you must be able to sense his actions (mirrors are helpful) and correct him with the long line. When your dog shows *any* interest in the forbidden treat, pull the line sharply. Don't verbally correct your dog, just snap him quickly and sharply. Pause for a few seconds, and then return to the room. Praise him if there is still food on your counter! Eventually, you can be really brave and practice this off leash.

Dog Dodging

Does your dog have a favorite hideout under a table or bed? A place where you're unable to reach him and will always fail in your attempts to shame him? If this behavior is associated with a particular time of day (when you're leaving for work or when the kids get home from school), attach the 10-foot lead ahead of time. When your dog dives for cover, stay calm. Quietly pick up the lead, snap it firmly saying "No" and expose him. Correct him once more with "Shame On You," then station him for 15 minutes.

Goodie Grabbing

A popular favorite at any age. With more freedom your dog may feel he has gained the upper paw in this little battle of wits. Not so! Especially if he's on his 10-foot line! Once he's grabbed a forbidden object, casually stroll by without looking at him. Once you're close enough to step on the line, turn toward him and tell him to "Bring It" to you. If your request is greeted with the blank stare or the guilty dart-away, snap the leash and tell him "No—Shame On You." Reel him in if necessary and station him alone without chew toys for 20 minutes.

Power Chewing

If your dog chews when you're away from the house, please refer to the section "Separation Anxiety" in the last chapter. If your dog is chewing in your presence, act *very* ashamed of him. Look as depressed as you probably feel. If, for example, you walk into the living room and find your dog munching on a couch pillow, go over quietly, pick up the pillow, stare at it mournfully, and say how disappointed you are. Station your dog and withdraw your attention for 20 minutes. Act very happy when you find him chewing his toy!

Scary Barking

This is the age when dogs begin to get protective. You may want a protective dog, but you certainly don't want a threatening one. When your four-legged alarm goes off, thank him for barking as you check to see who's calling. Once you've determined that all is safe, tell your dog "Quiet" and direct him behind you with the command "Heel," bringing him there with whatever lead he's wearing at the time.

If you can't cope with handling your dog and greeting your visitors all at once, put your dog at a designated station in or near the greeting room. Release him after he calms down.

Cat Chasing

Fun, fun, fun! To curb this age-old game, put your dog on either long line. Anchor the line to the ground with your foot. Let him give chase. Just as he gets to the end of the rope (and gets corrected) say "No."

The long line can help correct cat chasing, too.

Slam Dancing

This dog likes to race at you full speed and slam into your body. Dogs love it; people hate it. And it can be extremely dangerous. It's very bossy behavior. This dog has a real identity problem.

It may sound a little medieval, but get a steel garbage can lid to shield yourself. Attach your dog to his long line. When he circles by with that crazed look in his eye, get ready. Your feet must be quicker than his eye. Stand your ground as your dog races toward you. Deflect him with your garbage can shield. Step on the line and shout "No" as your dog hits the end of his line. While he's still trying to figure out exactly what happened, put him in a down and say "Shame On You." Give him a good, menacing glare.

Car Chasing

A big scary animal approaches your dog's territory. Your brave dog gives chase. The scary animal runs away like a coward! Victorious, your brave dog awaits the next interloper. Your dog may think he's doing everyone a big favor, but car chasing can be a lethal habit. And not just for your dog—motorists have been killed swerving to avoid a dog.

Take your dog for a walk on his six-foot leash. Any time a car approaches, tell him "Leave It." If he moves an eyeball, say "No" and repeat your request. Repeat over and over and over. Once that sinks in, take your dog out on his 30-foot line or Flexi-Lead. When he shows interest, step on the leash or press the Flexi's stop button. When he hits the end of the line shout "No—Leave It!"

Dominant Nipping

If your dog is challenging you for the leash or nipping you for attention, get your hands on Bitter Apple spray in a pump bottle. When he starts with the mouth, spritz his muzzle as discreetly as possible with the liquid and tell him "No."

If he continues, step on the leash, pinning him in a down position for a few minutes and withdraw your attention. Call a professional if the problem escalates.

SOCIALIZATION

Come up with new adventures for you and your dog. If there's an obedience class, join it. It is a great way to socialize, train, and expose your dog to new people, dogs, and situations. A training class will create a well-rounded, polite, and gentile dog who will always be welcome around company or crowds.

If you're heading to town on a quick errand, bring your pal. New experiences may make him feel a little unsure and (best of all) make you look confident and brave! He'll depend on you for direction. And a little of that will rub off at home! Use simple commands when out and about and help him into position if he's too distracted to listen. A nice "Heel" for walking and "Stay" for when people want to approach are staples for town escapades. And don't forget "Good Dog!"—lots of those to keep his confidence high!

If you're heading to town on a quick errand, bring your pup for socialization and for working around distractions.

Common Questions

My dog is good most of the time, so I pet him like crazy, but when he misbehaves, he ignores me.
If you smother the little darling with too much affection, he'll think he's the lord of the manor, and you're his dedicated servant. Mix your love and affection with commands. Before you pet him, give the "Sit" command. Before a biscuit, give the "Wait" command.

How can I remain calm when my dog is actively defying me? I want to hit something!
Wanting to hit something is fine, just don't hit your dog. It erodes your relationship. If you're really angry, walk away. A graceful retreat is not a failure.

I've heard the slogan "Train only with love, praise, and reward—not discipline."
Many training programs use food as an incentive. My dog would do anything for food, but if that's all I used to train him, he'd have no conscience, and that's one of the things I love about him. It makes him *almost* human.

When I shout "No" my dog barks at me. What am I doing wrong?
You're barking! At least that's what your dog thinks. Speak in a stern, low tone and reinforce your correction with the leash. Check your body language too—are you bending over? That's a confrontation or play posture. Stand tall!

I'm worried about the long lines getting caught in the door.
There is good reason to worry, because they do. Make sure you clip the long line onto your dog's buckle or tag collar, and never leave him unattended.

How do I correct my dog after he has stolen something?
If your dog has a pot roast halfway down his throat, there isn't a correction in the world that can stop him. Sorry.

When people come to the door, my dog gets aggressive.
Call a professional. Canine aggression is a serious problem and beyond the scope of this book.

Wrapping Up

This stage means different things for different people. Some dogs become more aware of your weaknesses and continue to highlight them in a last attempt to lead the pack. Others have exhausted all options and are content to follow your lead. If your dog remains skeptical of your leadership, hang tough! Persist in making your point clear. Consider an investment in group or personal dog training. Don't quit!

Now think a moment. If you asked your dog to describe you, what would he bark out? "Fun to be around, confident and in control," or would he wag his tail nervously and say, "Impatient, easily fooled and unsure." Don't think for a minute that your dog has no opinion—during your training time together, he's learned to read you well. Make a good impression! Stand tall, be patient but firm, and don't be afraid to have fun!

Part 3

Mister or Miss Manners

13

The Encyclopedia of Canine Etiquette

> **House Rules 101.** As you read through this section, remember that you are *teaching* your puppy. He wasn't born knowing where to eliminate or what to chew. Be patient, communicate in Doglish, and bear in mind that frustration and harsh punishment will create fear, not respect or understanding.

THE BLOODCURDLING BARKER

Puppies bark for different reasons at different ages. Young puppies bark because they're uncomfortable, scared, or feeling playful. Older puppies bark at sounds or visual distractions. They also bratty-bark to establish top dog status or bark to protect their territory.

Following is a rundown of different scenarios and suggestions on how to handle them.

Protest Barking

If your puppy barks when isolated and you rush to respond to him, he'll bark every time he's left alone. To avoid this headache, try to ignore him when he begins to bark. Remove him from his station or isolation area when he's calm.

If ignoring him fails, there are a few other options you can try. Try to startle him out of a barking fit by discretely tossing a ring of keys or a soda can containing a few pennies *near but not at* your puppy. A long-distance water pistol might work too (unless you have a water lover). Whatever startle method you choose, remember this rule: He must *not* know you did it. He needs to think the reaction came from the environment, so he'll think that if he's quiet, that annoying can full of pennies will stop rolling around his area.

For the true diehard barker, you'll have to be a little more clever. Buy a Halti Gentle Leader (explained on page 20) and accustom your puppy to wearing it. Attach it to a long line and drape the line out of the isolation area where you leave your puppy. Isolate your puppy as usual and wait for his response. When he begins to bark, pull the line (this will close his mouth), and say "Shhh!" in a very dramatic tone. A few of these setups should remedy the problem.

If all else fails, seek outside help!

Play Barking

If your puppy starts to bark at you when you're playing with him, refocus his attention on a toy or end the session. Do not encourage this behavior because it may lead to heightened dominance play or aggression.

Sound and Motion Stimulus

Some puppies are more reactive to unfamiliar sounds and motions than others are. This situation can get out of hand, resulting in a chronic barking problem. To prevent this, teach your puppy to "Speak" and be "Quiet" on command.

- "Speak." Whenever your puppy starts to bark, use this command and a snappy hand signal (you can make up one) to egg him on.
- "Quiet." After four or five barks, stand tall and in a low, flat voice say "Quiet." Give the leash a tug and encourage your puppy to follow you using "Let's Go" or "Heel." Praise him when he does and refocus him on a treat or toy. Soon you'll be able to get your dog to bark on cue, and more important, quiet down on command.

Don't yell at a barking puppy. When you yell, it sounds like you're barking, too! You're having a bark-along, and he won't want it to end!

Bratty Barking

One day, your darling puppy will look at you, his owner, protector, and caretaker, and bark right in your face. He wants attention, a biscuit or a game, and *he wants it now!* This is bratty barking, and it's typical adolescent behavior. I hate to sound like a broken record, but if give in to his demands, he'll do it again. Ignore him. He's trying to train you.

Protective Barking

You probably want your dog to bark at strangers, but you certainly don't want him to threaten your houseguests. When your puppy responds to a knock at the door, don't shout at him or egg him on. Keep him on his leash and say "Good Dog, Quiet!" Then offer him a toy to redirect his energy. Bring him behind you with the leash as you open the door. Ignore him until he is completely settled down. You're letting your puppy know that barking is okay in this instance, but the Top Dog (that's you!) ultimately controls the situation. If it escalates, leave the room.

Please refer to the section on stationing in Chapter 5 for alternative ideas on controlling your puppy when people visit.

Common Questions

I'm ignoring him, but he won't stop barking!
You have three options:

- Buy wax ear plugs.
- Leave the room.
- Connect him to your side and walk around the house using the foundation commands.

Some dogs and certain breeds (especially the smaller ones) are very dedicated barkers. It's a test of wills. Be strong!

My puppy whines excessively and makes other vocalizations. Can I stop him?
Most pups start this as an attention ploy. If you cave in and pet your puppy, I don't have to tell you what you're teaching him to do. Whiners need to be

ignored. If the action can't get your attention, it won't be repeated. If your puppy has been successful in the past, it may take him some time to get the message. Be patient.

My puppy carries on when I leave him outside.
He may be too young to be left alone, or you're leaving him outside too long. Remember, your dog wants to be part of the action! Reread Chapter 5 and make an effort to organize your household so he can be indoors when you're home. As he matures, he should feel more secure and able to be left alone more often.

Dogs are social animals. They thrive on group interaction. Prolonged isolation will result in "hyper isolation anxiety," which causes behaviors from barking to digging to other destructive behaviors like chewing or digging.

THE CHAMPION CHEWER

Just like children, puppies are enormously curious about the world around them, and they love to explore. Kids use their hands, puppies use their mouths. Both are capable of going to great lengths to satisfy that curiosity. At around 14 weeks, puppies begin to teethe. Teething children may keep you up at night, but they will not chew your furniture to alleviate their discomfort—your puppy might. It is your task to supply and encourage the use of proper chewing substitutes to carry both of you through this challenging time. Here are a few other suggestions.

Keep your puppy on his Teaching Lead.
If you haven't read Chapter 9, read it! It describes how to socialize your puppy to new areas of the house using the teaching lead. This leash enables you to control your puppy's actions while keeping him with you.

Provide one chewing object.
Giving your dog many different toys will confuse him. He'll assume everything on the floor is his to play with. Providing just one *type* of chew object will make things clear. Place a replica of that toy at each station, and offer one to your puppy if you're talking on the phone or reading the paper.

Teach your puppy to find his bone.

In the beginning, command "Where's Your Bone?" whenever you give your puppy his bone. Any time your puppy is looking mischievous, clap your hands and ask him "Where Is Your Bone?" then help him find it. In a few weeks you'll notice that he seeks it out on his own.

Correct the object, not the dog.

Read carefully! At first, puppy must be on leash to use this technique properly. If you notice your puppy showing interest in something he shouldn't (like your shoe, a garbage can, or the ever-popular used tissue), startle him by tugging his leash and say "Leave It" in a disciplinary tone, then pick up the object and correct it. "Bad Tissue! Bad! Bad!" Speak angrily and stare furiously *at the object* not at your puppy. You can also rig the following situation:

Make a game out of your puppy's finding his bone.

- Place a tempting object on the floor. A crumpled paper towel can be quite irresistible.
- Bring him to it on his leash.
- When he approaches, tug back and say "Leave It!"
- Pick up the object, shake it, and speak harshly to it. "Shame On You. Bad Paper Towel!"

Correct the object, not the dog. Don't look at your dog while you're correcting the object.

Look at the object, not the puppy.

- Toss the object on the ground! Vent your frustrations. Correct it again. It's a very naughty object. Then, calmly look to your puppy and command, "Let's Go."
- Walk by the setup until your puppy is avoiding contact.

You can correct dishwashers, refrigerators, garbage cans, and so forth. If you can't lift the object, kick it. But be careful!

Once He's Got It

If your puppy already has something in his mouth, you'll need to change your tactics. Never correct a puppy once he's gotten something in his mouth. Corrections encourage destructive chewing or even swallowing the evidence. When you see something in your puppy's mouth, kneel down and enthusiastically command "Bring It," praising him even if you're less than thrilled with his choice. If he won't come to you, reel him in on his leash or run into the next room. He'll follow you if he thinks there's something more fun around the corner. Praise him when he gets to you. Remember, your puppy doesn't yet know good from bad; he just want to have fun and get your attention. If you get angry, he'll learn to hide from you when he finds something. If you encourage him to show you what he's found, he'll bring you all his treasures to share.

Common Questions

My puppy specializes in the "Grab 'n' Go."
This is a fun game that many dogs teach their owners. Here is your dog's strategy: Grab a forbidden object; make sure your people see you; act as if you might give it back to them … let them get pretty close; then, quickly turn and run! Pivot! Dart! Fake left! Points are awarded based on how long the game continues, how many people chase you and how much attention you get.

This is a dog's game, but you can win! Here is your strategy: Keep your puppy on his lead when you're home. When he grabs something, tell him to "Bring It," reel him in, and praise him when you get it back.

If he steals something off leash, don't look at him. Simply ignore the situation or walk out of the room. The game usually loses its appeal at this point. If he continues, wait 20 seconds and *calmly* go after him. Don't discipline—if you do, he'll improve his avoidance skills. Remove the object from his mouth, then station or crate him with a bone.

My puppy can't resist clothes from the laundry basket.
Are you giving your puppy clothing to play with? If you let him have old shoes or knotted socks, he'll think that all shoes and clothing are fair game. Corrections will really confuse him! Make sure that you only provide dog toys. You can also correct the laundry basket as described earlier in this section, or teach him a good habit by stationing him to a corner of the laundry room with his chew toy.

My puppy chews while I'm out.
It can be scary for a puppy to be left home alone. Your puppy gets anxious when he feels deserted, and since he can't nibble on his fingernails, he nibbles on whatever is handy. If you have an anxiety chewer, don't get angry. He's not being spiteful, he's nervous! Corrections will only increase his stress. To help your puppy feel safer when you're gone, try the following:

- Keep him in a crate or small enclosure if you are gone less than six hours. This helps him learn to sleep when you're gone.
- Leave one chew toy, scenting it with your palms.
- Leave him in a dark room to help him nap.
- Leave a radio on with soft music playing.
- Avoid emotional hellos and good-byes.

If you're still having difficulties, please refer to the separation anxiety section on pages 103–104.

Should I shower my puppy with gifts?
Your puppy should only have access to one chew toy at a time! If your puppy has hundreds of toys, he'll think everything on the floor is his. Buy several of the same toy to keep around the house, but avoid getting an array of objects.

My puppy has a thing for garbage.
Are you feeding your puppy people food? If you are, stop. Puppies can't distinguish between a dog bowl and a garbage can, so all those table scrapings look like fair game. And garbage cans contain a veritable cornucopia of other canine delights too: spoiled food, tissues, worn-out gym socks. Add to this the almost guaranteed attention-getting properties of garbage raiding, and you've got doggy heaven in a can!

To get this behavior under control:

- Until he's clear on the garbage rules, don't give your puppy freedom in the kitchen unless the garbage is off the floor.
- Put your puppy on a leash and have someone put the pleasantly filled can in the center of the floor.
- Walk your puppy by it and watch for his reaction.
- The second he looks at it or sniffs toward it, pull back on the leash and say "Leave It!"
- Correct the garbage can harshly without looking to your puppy. "Bad Can!"
- If it's large, kick it. Once your can correction is complete, turn to your puppy and cheerfully command "Let's Go." Continue to walk by the can until your puppy is visually avoiding it.

My puppy puts everything in his mouth. Sometimes he swallows inedible objects. Is this unsafe?

Yes! It's common for puppies to mouth objects and eat twigs and grass, but it's unsafe for puppies to eat anything inedible (plastic, rocks, metal, coins, etc.). If you own a pup with this problem, keep a close eye on him and check to see if his bowels are regular. If you think your puppy has eaten something large (a sock or the dreaded pantyhose), call your veterinarian immediately. These items block the intestines and, left untreated, can kill your pup.

To control this problem, take the following preventative measures:

- Do not correct your puppy when he has something in his mouth. It may cause a gulping response.
- Condition your puppy to alert to the sound of a box of biscuits. Shake the box and offer him some; repeat this process until he looks up when you shake the box. Put boxes around the house.
- When your puppy grabs something inedible, grab a box and in a happy tone tell him to "Bring It!" as you shake the biscuits. You want to condition your puppy to show you every new thing he's found rather than to eat it.
- If you see something potentially tempting in your puppy's path, don't dive for it. Remember, you're setting an example. Try to distract your puppy and remove it calmly.

This is not a problem to be taken lightly. If it continues, question your veterinarian or seek professional help.

THE HORRENDOUS HOUSESOILER

You should begin to housetrain immediately, but don't expect miracles before your puppy is 12 weeks old. Take your 8- to 12-week-old-pup out every one to two hours. In general, puppies are very neat, clean little creatures. They choose nice, absorbent surfaces to pee on, and they don't like to stick around after they've gone. Their fastidiousness makes housetraining easier.

Here are some housetraining guidelines:

The Outside Routine

Your pup will need to go after feeding, exercising, napping, and isolation. Use the following chart as a guide.

Age	Trips to the Spot
6 to 14 weeks	8 to 10
14 to 20 week	6 to 8
20 to 30 weeks	4 to 6
30 weeks to adulthood	3 to 4

Confinement

The fastest way to housetrain your puppy is to keep an eye on him. Use the teaching lead as you learned in Chapter 5 (your puppy must be 12 weeks old to begin this process), crate or isolate him or take some time for interactive play. You may allow short periods of freedom if he has relieved himself, and you have the time to play.

Food

Ask your veterinarian to help you select a high-quality puppy food. Refer to Chapter 6 for a feeding

Confining or stationing your puppy allows you to keep an eye on him and know when he'll need to go to the bathroom.

schedule. When feeding time arrives, put the bowl down for 15 minutes, then remove it. If your puppy can't stay still for the allotted time, station him with his bowls or feed him in his crate. If he doesn't eat, don't worry! He can skip a meal or two, and then he'll get in the habit of eating at mealtimes. It is easier to housebreak a puppy on a consistent feeding schedule. His last feeding should be between 4:00 P.M. and 6:00 P.M. because it takes about six hours for his bowels to cycle.

Water

Make water available during feedings. Before you take him to his spot, let him have a sip. Don't give him free access to water yet, or he'll turn into a fountain. Remove all water after 7:30 P.M. If you think he's thirsty later in the evening, give him an ice cube.

Create a Routine

Puppies are very habitual. Create a routine when taking him outside. Use the same pathway to the same place, using the commands described below.

Create a routine when taking your puppy out. Use the same pathway to the same place every time.
(Tina Engle-Balch)

- *Pick "The Door":* Be consistent. Use one door and follow the same path to the door when you take him out. Each time you lead your puppy, command "Outside!"
- *Pick "The Spot":* Designate a five-by-five-foot area in your yard or house as "The Spot." If you're training the puppy to go outside, find an area close by the door. If you're paper training, cover a large area, slowly decreasing its size until it's appropriate for your puppy's needs.
- *Pick "The Word":* Use a short, snappy command like "Get Busy" or "Do It" when your puppy squats to eliminate. Say it once or twice and praise him calmly when he finishes. You'll appreciate this command when he wants to go out in the pouring rain at four o'clock in the morning.

No Free Rides

Avoid carrying your puppy to his spot. This is something he must learn to do himself!

First Things First

When you first wake in the morning or come home at night, don't greet your puppy until after he has eliminated. Put on his leash and walk him to his spot, commanding "Outside!" As he goes, command "Get Busy," *then* greet him and play or go for a walk.

Corrections

Do not hit or yell at your puppy if he makes a mistake because you will only frighten him. If you catch him in the act, startle him by making a guttural "Eh, Eh, Eh!" sound or clapping your hands, then command "Outside!" If you find a mess after the fact, don't punish your puppy. Remove him from the room and clean up. Do not clean up in front of him because this is a sign of approval (his mother did the same thing!). You are actually reinforcing the indoor housesoiling as appropriate and pleasing—which it is not.

Decipher His Signal

Before you take this step, make sure your puppy is clear on the "Outside" system (*see* "The Door" step). One morning, take him to the door quietly without saying your Outside direction. No pats or eye contact, just walk him to the door. Stand still and pay attention. He's accustomed to going to the door and marching right out, so he'll probably start whining or pulling. When he does, he's giving you a signal. Say "Outside!" and get him to come and tell you, rather than jump at the door. Praise him and take him to his spot immediately. As he starts catching on that he must give you a sign before you go outside, use this system in rooms farther away from the door.

Common Questions

Where should I put the crate?
The closer to you the better. Puppies like to sleep with their group. If you can keep him in your bedroom at night, he'll be much calmer.

My puppy wakes up in the middle of the night.
Many young puppies can't make it through the night. If your pup wakes and appears restless, quietly take him to his spot. Not that you'd want to, but don't play games in the middle of the night.

My puppy eliminates in her crate at night or when I go out.
Your crate is probably too big. Your puppy should be able to comfortably stand, turn around, and lay down. That's all! Any extra space is used as a toilet area. To make the crate smaller, you can use crate dividers (available at pet stores) or make your own, using a metal object or wooden board. No plastic or toxic materials, please.

Until what age do I keep him in the crate?
Until you trust him. Use your crate when you go out for up to four hours or when you sleep. To encourage good household behavior when home, use the stationing or leading techniques outlined in Chapter 9. These methods of handling will help him habituate good household manners and speed up the crate-weaning process.

Once he makes it through the night, you can station him with a bed and a blanket and a good chew toy. This is the first step toward giving your puppy freedom at night. Make sure your station is not near a ledge, electrical outlet, or entanglements and remove anything that might interest a young mouth! *Never station on a training collar.*

My puppy is peeing outside but pooping inside.
When you know your puppy needs to eliminate, take him to the door, but before you go out insert a paper (not wooden) match. No, I'm not kidding. The

sulfur serves as a suppository. Cradle his body backward between your legs and give him a treat to occupy the front end. Gently insert the matchstick end into his bottom, then move quickly to your spot!

My puppy associates outside with play and inside with elimination.
Make sure you take your puppy to his spot before you go for a walk or give him attention. Stand quietly for 5 minutes. If he shows no interest, bring him in. Crate or station him for 15 minutes and try again. If you're having no luck, use the matchstick technique described above.

Yuck! My puppy eats other creatures' poop!
Unfortunately this is normal and quite a delight for young pups. Corrections will aggravate the problem because he will try to eat it faster while you're not looking. Luckily, the problem generally fades as he gets older. If you're puppy is eating from your cat's litter box, put it in an inaccessible area, or correct the box as outlined in the chewing section of this chapter. There's only one thing to be happy about in this situation—and that is that you're not a dog!

Double yuck! My puppy licks or eats his own feces!
Yes, this is quite disgusting to you and me, but in the dog world, it's just a handy way to keep the den clean. He watched his mother do it, and when he sees you, the pack leader, pick up his excrement, he thinks you're going to . . . well, never mind. Let's just say he thinks he's copying you. To stop this impolite social habit:

- Do not correct the interest. Just refocus. If you fuss, they gulp. Yuk!
- Ask your veterinarian to give you a food additive that will make his feces distasteful. I know, what's more distasteful than dog poop? Such things do exist.
- After he has eliminated, get him focused on a toy by saying "Where's your ball?"
- Squirt something on the pile like Bitter Apple, Tabasco sauce, or vinegar.

My puppy plays with me when I clean his mess.
For this reason, don't clean up in front of him.

What if my puppy piddles when he's overstimulated?
This is very normal. If you correct your puppy, it will make matters worse. To solve this problem:

- When you come in, ignore your puppy until he has calmed down.
- Teach him to "Sit."
- Kneel down to pet him, rather than bend over him.
- If your puppy is timid with new people, encourage everyone to ignore him, yourself included. If you try to soothe him, it will make him more nervous. When your puppy approaches the new person, let them kneel, pet his chest, and offer him a treat.
- If your puppy piddles during an all-out play session, cool off wild play until your puppy has a better grip on his bladder.

What if we work all day?

You must not leave a puppy crated for more than six hours at a time. If you can't get someone to walk your pup, buy a playpen specially designed for dogs (found at a pet store) or gate off an area. Place paper in one section of the enclosure, food, water, and a bed in another. At first, cover most of the enclosure with paper, decreasing the coverage as your puppy gets the idea. Some dogs can hold it eight hours, others less. If you want your puppy to go outside when you're home, remove the paper when you come in and spray the area with a vinegar mixture.

Ever considered a cat?

Many puppies don't respond well to long hours of isolation. They get lonely. Wouldn't you? Maybe your puppy needs a companion! But two puppies can be double trouble. Why not consider a kitten? Energetic and curious, a kitten about the same age as your puppy would make a great friend. Pick a bold kitten who won't be intimidated by your pup.

Kittens and puppies can be great friends.
(Diana Postel)

THE JOYFUL JUMPER

Everybody knows a joyful jumper: little jumpers and big jumpers; wild, knock-over-the-furniture jumpers and the muddy-paw-print-on-your-pants jumpers. The most popular excuse for this behavior is "he's just saying hello." Not true!

He's saying, "Thank you for teaching me this excellent way of getting attention. I'll do this again and again and again!"

Let's take a closer look. All dogs start out as attention-seeking puppies. Your puppy is irresistible, and when he jumps, he probably gets kissed, petted, or picked up. Puppy lesson number one: Jumping is an interactive behavior, certainly worth repeating. As he grows bigger, the charm wears off. You push him away to discourage a behavior he was once rewarded for. Puppy lesson number two: Jumping is still interactive, still worth repeating. He continues to jump, you continue to push. Jump, push. Jump, push. Help!

To bring your Jumper back to earth, follow these suggestions.

- Whenever your puppy jumps, either ignore him or correct him with the leash, not your body.
- Whenever you're home with your puppy (12 weeks old or older), keep him with you on his Teaching Lead, as described in Chapter 9. If you need some off-leash time, attach a short leash so you have the ability to correct him (without physically interacting) when he jumps.
- Use the command "Sit" every time you stop or sit down. Position him if he doesn't respond. Praise him warmly. This creates good habits.

Your puppy is irresistible, and when he jumps up he probably gets petted or kissed. No wonder he jumps up!

Puppies jump for different reasons at different times and require different corrections for each situation.

Attention Jumpers

If your puppy jumps up for attention, try to ignore him. Look at the ceiling and keep quiet. If he's unbearable, grab his lead or collar and snap down saying firmly, "Off." Continue what you're doing and ignore your puppy until he sits calmly or chews on a bone.

Greeting Jumpers

When you greet your puppy after an absence, *stay calm!* If you go nuts, you're teaching him to be hog wild when the door opens. Mom's right again—good manners do start at home. Ignore your puppy until he settles down. If he's banging around in his crate, don't open it until he's quiet. Instruct "Sit" when he gets a grip and pet him gently. Reinforce calmness, and you'll be doing both of you (not to mention your guests) a favor!

Company Jumpers

When company arrives, station your puppy 6 to 10 feet from the door. Tell your puppy "Wait" and give him a special toy (one he only gets when company comes in). You'll need to do some company training too—insist that they ignore your puppy, even if he barks. When he settles down, bring him and his toy over to your company. Hold him in a sit position while they pet him. Correct jumping with "Off" and a leash snap. As you visit with your guests, sit on his lead and give your puppy his special toy.

Furniture Fanatics

Decide right now if you really want a furniture dog. Do you want your full-grown dog jumping on the couch, sitting in your favorite chair, hogging the bed? If that sounds like your plan, read no further. If you'd rather have a floor dog, read on.

Create a place for your puppy near the furniture. Encourage your puppy to lie there by sitting with him and offering a toy or a treat when he does. Whenever your puppy leaps up at the furniture, snap the leash sharply and say "Off." Repeat if necessary. Once your puppy has calmed down, point to his special place and command "Settle Down." Once your pup is calm, pet him. Soon he'll be going to his place automatically.

A Final Hint

Control yourself! Puppies are just so cute and small, it's almost impossible to resist the temptation to drag them up on the couch and let them jump all over you. Fight this urge! It's hard, but you can do it.

THE COUNTER CONSPIRATORS

Not all dogs choose human targets. Some find the defrosting chicken on your kitchen counter far more interesting and will perform mind-boggling gymnastic feats to get it. If you have a counter culprit, put your puppy on a leash and set up a tempting situation. If he considers what is on the counter, tell him "Leave It!" firmly, and snap back on the lead. Quickly turn to the subject of interest and correct it (not your puppy) firmly. "Bad Chicken! Bad! Bad!" Slap the counter viciously!

Next place a long line on your puppy and drape it out of the room. Leave a tantalizing object on a nearby counter and tell your puppy "Leave It" as you bang the counter and correct the food. Walk out of the room, but listen for your pups next try. If he goes to jump, pull the long line and march in to correct the object. Repeat the sequence. Your next step is to practice it off leash!

Common Questions

My puppy jumps on me when I walk him on the leash.
Don't face your puppy when he acts this way. When you do, you're accepting his challenge! Take a spray pump filled with a diluted vinegar mixture. When your puppy starts leaping, spray his mug with your mixture. If your puppy is sound-sensitive, you can achieve the same effect with a soda can filled with a few pennies.

If you're still having difficulty, check to see if you're holding the leash too tightly. If possible, buy a Flexi-Leash that extends up to 26 feet to give your puppy some extra freedom. Bring out your kickball or plastic jug to kick around to divert his attention.

My puppy jumps on the furniture or counter when I leave the room.
He's an opportunist! You need to station him more often and to correct the things he jumps on. For a while you must suspend all furniture privileges.

Sometimes when I correct my puppy he gets wilder!
He's not taking you seriously. Are you bending over to correct him, holding the leash too tightly, or pushing him away? If you've exhausted all other options, he

is probably experiencing wild energy spurts and the only options are to take him out to play soccer or crate or isolate him with a bone for half an hour. If he is over 16 weeks old, you can also place him into a down position by stepping on the leash until he's calm (30 seconds to 3 minutes).

Should my puppy sleep on my bed?
No, he should not. If he does, he'll think of you as a playmate. Remember—dogs do not live in a democratic society. If they sleep on your level, they will see you as an equal. If possible, however, keep your puppy in your bedroom at night. He'll feel secure in knowing his leader is close by.

Can I let my puppy jump sometimes?
Believe it or not, yes! But not now. First you must teach him *not* to jump, following the above instructions. Once he's mastered that, you can instruct "Okay—Up!" and let him jump on you or the couch with permission. If he does it without invitation, however, correct "Off," then ignore him.

I have a toy breed. He only reaches my ankles!
Small dogs have a very high cute factor and are often treated like toys instead of dogs. Carried from place to place, allowed on all the furniture, and generally treated like royalty, this puppy may develop what I call the **Small Dog Syndrome**. An intelligent little creature, he knows a good thing when he sees it—people are servants, and he is Top Dog. Therefore, he is in charge of all household activities (the chronic yapper), doesn't like to be disturbed when eating or resting (the nipper), and will not be denied his way (the growler). Basically, these dogs are brats! Treat him like a dog, not a toy. Remember—a well-trained dog can be selectively spoiled.

THE NAUGHTY NIPPER

As they wean from nursing and begin hierarchy play with their littermates, young puppies start to mouth. Older puppies take nipping more seriously, often using it to clarify their position as top dog. As you know, your puppy cannot be Top Dog. That job is taken—by you.

The best way to deal with nipping depends on the age of your pup.

Young Puppies (8 to 14 weeks)

These little creatures are just naturally oral. They nip their mother softly when weaned (when she isn't letting them nurse anymore). She tolerates soft mouthing without recognition, but if they nip too hard she gives them a clear message to back off. When puppy siblings play, they nip each other. Rough play and hard nipping elevates a puppy's position in the group hierarchy. When you bring your puppy home, he wants to know if these new group members are mother figures or littermates. Mother figures get respect, littermates get nipped. Here are some tips to help you communicate your status to your young pup:

Any time your puppy licks you, command "Kisses," and praise him.

- Any time your puppy licks you, command "Kisses" and praise him.
- If he mouths or nips you softly, ignore him, leaving your hand in his mouth. Remember, this is what his mother would do.
- If he bites down too hard, glare at him and make a sharp, low-sounding "Eh," but leave your hand in his mouth. If he doesn't let up, tug his head from you hand with your leash or collar and repeat "Eh."
- Do not yank your hand out of your pup's mouth because he'll think "Hmmm . . . potential game here" and do it again.
- Once your puppy has learned how to behave with you, he must learn to respect the rest of the family, especially the children. Sit with each child, holding the leash in one hand. Hold the child's hand in yours and together pet your puppy. If he nips, snap back on the leash and together say "Eh." Eventually fade off the vocalization, then the snap.

Note: At this age, puppies like to interact around your face. Yes, it is a sign of affection, but they also bite faces in play. Don't let an excited puppy near your face. Puppy play bites can hurt!

Older Puppies (past 14 weeks)

If your puppy doesn't know the command "Kisses" for licking, teach him. Every time he licks, use this command; soon you'll be able to request a kiss whenever you'd like!

By this age, your puppy should not place his mouth on your skin. Correct any and all mouthing by snapping his head away firmly with the lead or collar and saying "Eh." Remember: Do not pull your hand out of his mouth because it will encourage rougher play. Act indignant and yank that mouth away.

Common Questions

Help! It's the Bathrobe Assault!

Your puppy may find it exhilarating to attack your clothing. Many puppies think that first thing in the morning is a good time for this activity. Others like to wait until you've got a cup of hot coffee in your hand. Prevention is the best solution to this situation:

- Tie a plastic milk jug, soda bottle, or squeaky toy to a four-foot string.
- Just before the assault begins, pull out the string toy and bounce it along in front of your puppy.
- Once his energy dissipates or he finds something new to do, put it away until next time.

What if he starts to wrestle or chase the children?

They're small. They're energetic. They love to play games and get riled up. And I'm not talking about your puppy! It's easy for your puppy to mistake these little creatures for littermates, and that can lead to some pretty wild behavior (on both their parts). You're faced with a double whammy: training the puppy and training the kids.

- Any time your children can't seem to slow down, put the puppy in his crate, station him, or lead him away. Avoid getting angry! Help your children see that overenthusiasm ends playtime.
- Put your puppy on a leash and bring him to your side. Encourage the kids to run and play in front of you, but don't let them taunt the pup. When he begins to charge, snap the leash and say "No!" Repeat this until your puppy watches them calmly.
- Small children may pull on your puppy's coat or explore around his face. Condition your puppy to accept this handling by praising him while you gently pull his coat and handle his face. He'll be more accepting of children if you accustom him to this type of handling first.
- Encourage your children to play with the puppy when he's calm or chewing a bone. Make this a special time with you and your kids. Reward both for being calm!

Sometimes corrections make him more wild. What then?
Your puppy has entered the wild zone. No miracle cures for this one. Simply put, your puppy has too much energy to be good. He needs to go crazy! It's a tail-chasing, play-bowing, run-in-circles burst of energy that just can't be stopped. Corrections will fall on deaf ears, so don't get frustrated trying to reason with him. It won't work. The best thing to do is go with the flow. Play soccer with a ball or a plastic soda bottle. Soccer lets you stand tall in a dignified, top-dog fashion, unlike fetch, which may encourage mouthing. If you don't have time to play, put your puppy in his crate with a bone to chew.

Is tug-of-war a good game?
No! Puppies love this game because they almost always win, but tug-of-war encourages nipping and aggressive play. Please see "Good Games" in Chapter 9 for a list of less-competitive games.

14

Beyond the Cooperative Canine

Wow! What a year! You've worked hard. You've learned to be patient and tolerant. You've developed willpower. You've grown right alongside that pup of yours. You're a Top Dog!

And your beloved friend has grown too. She has stretched his skin, lost some teeth, gained some weight, and developed quite a personality. She's learned what to chew, where to go to the bathroom, what pleases, and what upsets you—quite an accomplishment.

When I envision a well-behaved dog, I see a dog who listens without effort and obeys when asked; one you can take anywhere; a dog with spirit; a devoted friend who plays with the kids and curls up next to your bed at night; a confidante who never spills your secrets, and a playmate who's never too busy. It's the ultimate bond: a unity between two different species. It's a special relationship shared only between dog and human.

Happy Birthday to your puppy!

Some of you may be thinking, "I don't have a well-behaved dog yet! She *still* turns inside-out when company comes to the door. She *still* can't seem to hear me when I call her in from the yard. She *still* knocks things off the coffee table!" Don't worry. Like some people, certain dogs seem to linger in the adolescent stage. Some are just late bloomers. Keep working with your long line. It will come.

When I envision the owner of a well-behaved dog, I see someone who understands that a dog isn't a person and loves her for her differences. Someone who has taken time to patiently teach his or her puppy how she's expected to behave. Someone who remembers to give her extra water on a hot day, plays ball after a hard day at work, and makes sure she has a safe and comfortable place to sleep. In short, I see you.

So what's next? Are you finished?

I doubt you're finished. Training needs time to mature before it ends. You can choose to continue in specialty training or just keep up with the commands you've learned. Using them conversationally, you'll find they drop nicely into your day-to-day activities.

Practice "Sit" and "Sit-Stay" for greetings. Use "Wait" when going in and out of your home—lots of times!

Sit-Stay is great for greetings or before dinner or a ball toss.
Down is a goody to help your dog gain some self-control.
Down-Stays work nicely when visiting friends or your veterinarian or when you need some quiet time.
Heel is great when you need to call your dog to your side or for controlled walking.
Come. Need I say more?

Your other commands—*Wait, Okay, Stand, Leave It,* and so forth—have their place in everyday conversation too! Don't forget to use them. I know some weeks can be really hectic, and it's hard to find the time, but trust me—your dog notices!

If you want to continue in your training, however, you've got a lot of options! Many breeds' clubs conduct special breed events, like herding or retrieving trials, water rescue, sledding or carting, lure coursing and coursing Schutzhund. You can also try competitive obedience trials, which have different levels of training requirements. For information about obedience trials, write the American Kennel Club: 51 Madison Avenue, New York, New York 10010. For more information about breed-specific activities and the clubs that sponsor them, ask your breeder or vet or visit a local bookstore. Still other activities are less specific and open to both pure and mixed breeds. I've listed the three I've enjoyed with my dogs.

Agility

Agility, originally introduced in England in 1978, is the fastest growing sport in the dog fancy. Looking at a course for the first time, it looks like a gigantic jungle gym. Going through it with your dog is more fun than words can express. However, training requires patient conditioning, teamwork, and cooperation. The result of this effort is exhilarating! Dogs love the challenge of moving through a series of obstacles; owners get excited about teaching their dog to navigate under their direction; and spectators cheer the rapport that exists between trainer and dog. If you have the chance to watch a competition or a practice—take it. If you think it looks right for you, join! I've

All dogs can do agility, just look at this Pomeranian! (Jane Simmons-Moake)

done it with my dogs and loved it. For more information on what it is, write the American Kennel Club at the address listed in the previous paragraph, or ask your breeder or veterinarian whether he or she knows an agility group in the area.

Canine Good Citizenship

CGC is a fun, noncompetitive training and acceptance test given by obedience clubs and animal shelters throughout the country. The CGC program, introduced by the American Kennel Club in 1989 to offset breed-specific legislation, has blossomed. Thousands of dogs across the country have earned their CGC certificates from the American Kennel Club—purebreds and mixed breeds! For a dog to earn a CGC title, it must pass all 10 parts of the test, which examines the dog's sociability skills, the owner's handling and care, and the dog's reaction to an approaching stranger. Passing this examination is a great achievement. Again, ask your breeder or vet how to get involved.

Pet Therapy

Pet therapy is similar to many other forms of therapy. It helps patients, young and old, healthy and disabled, communicate feelings and reach out with the help of a pet. Dogs are the most frequently used "therapists," and it's a wonderfully fulfilling activity if you and your dog have the right temperament. The demand for pet therapists (dogs and their humans) in nursing homes, psychiatric wards, prisons, children's hospi-

Pet therapy helps patients express feelings and reach out with the help of a pet, like this Cocker Spaniel puppy.

tals, and other in-patient facilities has grown tremendously over the years. This type of work requires a special dog who is extremely friendly, gentle, and adaptable. If you're interested in this activity, telephone your local humane society and find out where classes are held to train and certify you and your dog for this very special calling.

In Closing

Whether or not your time and energy allow you to continue training doesn't really matter. True, a higher education enhances focus. Most people are content to have a dog who will come reliably and stay moderately contained when company arrives. It is the time you have spent training and conditioning your dog as a puppy that matters most.

Some say the process of training never ends. I disagree. One day, your dog will listen because she wants to. One day, you can retire your long lines and stop going to all those obedience classes. One day, you will be able to communicate your directions without effort or forethought. One day, she'll behave habitually.

It is the process of *learning* that doesn't end. You will always be different, and life will always change. She will get older, and her needs will shift. You may move, have a baby, or start a new work schedule. You must *learn* together how to cope. Training gives you a common language to communicate. Our higher ability to reason and understand gives us the responsibility to make the necessary adaptations. Borrowing from the poem in the beginning of the book, you must be your dog's leader, keeper, friend, and voice. Your efforts are always worth your reward.

I want to leave you with a list of key points to keep tucked in the back of your mind. Refer to them as often as necessary, and good luck. I hope I've helped.

10 Key Training Tips

1. *Be patient.* Your dog is not perfect. He sees the world though his own eyes.
2. *Be persistent.* Teaching him to obey is necessary for his safety and your sanity.
3. *Don't repeat yourself!* Dogs hear sounds, not words. Repeated commands sound different.
4. *Don't watch your dog when he baits you.* Eye contact reinforces behavior.
5. *Don't bend over to correct or direct behavior.* Low posture equals play or submission.
6. *Praise your dog!* Nothing reinforces good behavior better.
7. Use your commands conversationally. Speak in Doglish, not English.
8. *Use your hand signals.* They teach your dog to watch you for direction.
9. *Use "No" when necessary.* It develops your dog's conscience.
10. *Appreciate your dog's wonder.* He has his own spirit. Separate and unique.

Part 4

Your Puppy's Health

15

Preventive Health Maintenance

INTRODUCTION

This chapter deals with the basics of preventive health and daily maintenance of your puppy. From cleaning and grooming to feeding and basic nutrition. We will also briefly touch on topics like some home remedies, holistic alternatives, spaying and neutering, and pet health insurance.

This mixed bag of information is a collection of veterinary tidbits, along with generally accepted puppy-rearing practices. It's an accumulation of advice from breeders, dog handlers, groomers, animal health technicians, veterinarians, and dog enthusiasts. Most of all, it's advice I give my clients so they can take the best care of their pets.

VACCINES

A vaccine is a suspension of pieces of infectious organisms (bacteria or virus), administered to an animal to prevent that infectious disease. The theory behind a vaccine is quite complex; but simply, when we give a vaccine, we administer those parts of an infectious organism (bacteria or virus) that stimulate an immune response from the host (the animal getting the shot).

The host's body makes antibodies (proteins made by the immune system) to match the small antigens (proteins on the surface of the organisms) in the vaccine. The antibodies combine with their corresponding antigens whenever they touch them. By combining millions of antibodies with the antigens found on the surface of bacteria or viruses, these organisms are rendered inactive and are incapable of causing disease. In other words, by being coated with a layer of antibody proteins, a bacteria or virus is *inactivated*. This process is how a vaccine *prevents* disease. Most vaccines only work if given before exposure to the disease. Below is a list of canine diseases for which vaccines are available.

The first five viruses are usually combined into a 5-in-1 vaccine, abbreviated DHLP-P:

- Canine Distemper
- Leptospirosis
- Adenovirus Type 1 or 2
- Parainfluenza
- Canine Parvovirus
- *Bordetella bronchiseptica* (kennel cough)

- Borreliosis (Lyme disease)
- Canine Coronavirus
- Rabies

These vaccines are available separately or in combination. We generally use the DHLP-P distemper vaccine and "split-out" (give individually) the other vaccines.

How Vaccines Are Given

There are three different ways to administer vaccines to animals. They can be given by subcutaneous injection (under the skin), intra-muscular injection (in the muscle), or by intranasal route (nose drops). Each vaccine has an approved mode of administration, determined by the Food and Drug Administration (FDA).

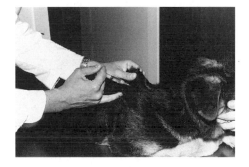

A *subcutaneous injection* is commonly given in loose skin of the scruff area of the neck. There is no

Giving a vaccine via subcutaneous injection.

postvaccine soreness (although there can be mild itching), and it is an easily accessible area. These reasons make it a very popular mode of administration.

It is generally thought that *intramuscular injections* enter the blood stream quicker than subcutaneous ones and can stimulate a stronger immune response. There can often be muscle soreness for a day or two post vaccination. Some vaccines are required to be given this way.

Intranasal administration is via nose drops. Only one vaccine (*Bordetella bronchiseptica*) is available now in this form for dogs. This vaccine starts a very strong and effective immune reaction locally.

When Should I Vaccinate?

The age we start vaccinating is dictated by how long the dam's immunity lasts. We have learned through testing that most maternal antibodies last anywhere from 2 to 20 weeks. In 30 percent of puppies, maternal antibodies are gone by 9 to 10 weeks; over 90 percent of the mother's immunity is gone after 16 weeks. Therefore, we have developed vaccine schedules to fit the average case. The basic principles of vaccination are listed below.

- Start the vaccination as young as two to four weeks of age if the puppy was orphaned and did not have any of the mother's first milk (colostrum); otherwise, start vaccinating the puppy at eight weeks.
- Vaccinate for those diseases that are endemic in your area.
- Monitor your pup for 20 minutes after vaccination for any signs of an allergic reaction.
- Booster the vaccine at the specified interval to keep the level of immunity protective.

Are There Any Drawbacks to Vaccines?

We occasionally see two types of reactions in puppies: allergic anaphylactic reactions, which are very serious and rare; and vaccine reactions (immune-mediated hypersensitivity), which are mild and more common.

Sometimes, the vaccine just doesn't take, leaving puppies susceptible to disease. There are many reasons why this might happen, including:

- Each animal is different and has a different immune system. Therefore, the response from it will vary from dog to dog.
- If the dam's immunity lasts longer than the normal 16 weeks, subsequent vaccines will not take.
- The vaccine has expired.
- The vaccine was administered improperly; that is, an intramuscular vaccine was given subcutaneously.
- Nothing is 100 percent. Vaccines generally approach 90 percent to 95 percent efficacy.

A Glimpse into Vaccine Diseases

Most of the vaccines available on the market today are for diseases that have plagued the canine kingdom for centuries. The most recent addition is the *Borrelia burgdorferi*, or Lyme vaccine (discussed thoroughly in Chapter 16). Assume all puppy diseases are not contagious to people unless otherwise stated.

1. Canine Distemper

This is a highly contagious viral disease. Dogs become infected with the virus through the upper respiratory tract (eyes, nose, and throat) by contact with contaminated feces, saliva, and sputum from infected dogs.

The first clinical signs are fever, conjunctivitis, sneezing, coughing, and labored breathing. There is often a thick pus discharge from the eyes and nose. Pneumonia is common. This can last for one to two weeks. At this point, the dog goes into a digestive tailspin. Vomiting and diarrhea start, causing weight loss and dehydration. Of the dogs who survive this stage, about 50 percent go on to develop neurological symptoms, which can include blindness, circling, falling over, tremors, and seizures. Dogs with neurological symptoms are in critical condition. There is no other treatment for the virus other than supportive care. Even if the puppy survives, it most likely will have permanent neurological damage that would necessitate euthanasia.

2. Canine Adenovirus Type-1 (Infectious Hepatitis)

This is another contagious virus of dogs that causes an inflammation of the liver, something we call *hepatitis*. The virus is spread through the bodily fluids of an infected dog.

The first symptom is a nonspecific fever. It progresses to loss of appetite, vomiting, abdominal pain, and an inflamed liver. Occasionally, jaundice (a yellowing of the body tissues) is seen and is classic for liver damage. Some dogs also develop a cloudiness, or hazing to the cornea (surface of the eye) called "Blue Eye." Those dogs that survive the initial disease can have chronic liver damage or permanent eye impairment.

3. Canine Adenovirus Type-2

This virus is another strain of the adenovirus described above, but it causes a respiratory disease. Many research scientists feel that this virus can occur alone or in combination with other organisms to cause kennel cough (scientifically known as *Infectious Tracheobronchitis*). Symptoms include sneezing, nasal discharge, coughing, wheezing, runny eyes, and labored breathing. The danger of secondary bacterial bronchial infections and pneumonia always exists.

4. Leptospirosis

This disease is caused by the *Leptospira* organism, which is a spirochete (a corkscrew-shaped bacteria). These organisms enter the body through the mucus membranes, such as the mouth, conjunctiva, and genitals, and invade the blood vessels of the liver, kidneys, and urinary bladder. Infected puppies have body aches, high fever (102–104°F) vomiting, loss of appetite, nose bleeds, abdominal pain, uveitis (inflammation of the inside eye), liver enlargement, blood in stool, and jaundice (a yellowing of the mucus membranes and skin). If the case is severe, the dog may die suddenly. More commonly, the cases are milder and chronic.

5. Canine Parainfluenza

Think of this as a flu virus of dogs. It's similar to the adenovirus type-2 described above, which causes infection of the upper respiratory tract and sometimes the bronchi and lungs. Sneezing, runny nose and eyes, and coughing are common signs. There is usually fever. In adults, the virus isn't that serious, but in puppies, it can cause high morbidity.

6. Canine Parvovirus

This is one of the newest viruses to hit the dog world. It was first discovered in 1978 in the United States. This new virus comes on like a ton of bricks. The symptoms are sudden, explosive, watery, foul, and bloody diarrhea that won't respond to any medical treatment. There are generally high fevers and acute abdominal pain. Vomiting is also persistent. This virus is highly contagious through fecal contamination and is thought to be a major factor in *fading puppy syndrome*, where newborns die within their first week of life for unknown reasons.

This virus is a complicated one because there is more than one strain of parvovirus. Check with your veterinarian to find the parvovirus vaccine that will be the best protection for your puppy.

7. Canine Coronavirus

This is another intestinal virus of dogs, but it is not as devastating as the parvovirus described above. The average case of coronavirus starts as vomiting and intractable diarrhea. There is usually fever. There is a much higher success rate in treating coronavirus cases; only very young and debilitated puppies don't survive.

8. Kennel Cough (Bordetella bronchiseptica)

This bacteria is thought to be the main component of the *Infectious Tracheobronchitis* complex of diseases known as kennel cough. *B. bronchiseptica*, adenovirus type-2, and canine parainfluenza in combination cause kennel cough. This disease is characterized by sudden bouts of a dry, hacking, persistent cough that sounds like a goose honking. The dog literally stays up at night coughing. This, in turn, keeps the owner up and prompts a call to the vet. This bacteria is extremely contagious and becomes airborne, which means it actually floats in the air on saliva, nasal, and sputum droplets, infecting dogs in the immediate area.

Kennel cough comes in two forms: uncomplicated and complicated. Uncomplicated kennel cough refers to an average case of the disease, where the dog coughs for one to two weeks and spontaneously gets better. Complicated is more severe, with symptoms lingering beyond two weeks. Very young or very old dogs are most prone as are dogs with upper respiratory problems, pushed-in faces, allergies, asthma, and congenital defects of the bronchial tubes.

9. Rabies

Just the name of this virus strikes fear in the hearts of most people: It is almost 100 percent fatal, and people are also susceptible. Rabies natural hosts are wildlife, such as foxes, skunk, raccoons, and especially bats.

Pets can become infected with rabies by being bitten by a rabid animal because the virus is shed from the infected animal's saliva. It can also be spread from saliva contamination of open wounds. Therefore, if your puppy comes home with an obvious wound and saliva or blood is on its fur, put on protective gloves before handling him. The classic symptoms are neurologic. The virus enters the body through the wound or bite and travels along nerves until it reaches the central nervous system, spinal cord, and brain. It then settles in the salivary glands.

Obvious signs are sudden behavioral changes, sudden aggression, paralysis of the jaw that leads to the classic "foaming at the mouth," circling, blindness, uncoordination, change of voice, and seizures. Due to the gravity of this disease and public health significance, if a dog is suspected of rabies, it is quarantined by the applicable health department. If it dies within the specified time frame (usually 10 to 15 days), an autopsy must be done to submit brain tissue to the proper state authorities for testing.

All persons in contact with the infected dog may need to go through a series of postexposure vaccines. State and county health departments oversee these procedures. Many veterinarians and animal health personnel get prophylactic preexposure vaccines. All puppies should be vaccinated for rabies starting at three to four months of age and boostered routinely. Many states have laws requiring rabies vaccines of all dogs.

10. Lyme Disease (discussed in Chapter 16)

FEEDING AND NUTRITION

The old saying "you are what you eat" is especially true in animals. If just one nutrient is out of proportion, or deficient, disease will result. Extensive research has been conducted about the daily requirements of the food groups, vitamins, and minerals for dogs; in fact, the average American dog eats a more balanced and complete diet than the average American. There is a standardized minimum level determined for each nutrient, stated by the National Academy of Sciences Nutrient Requirements (NRC) for dogs.

When a commercial dog food claims to be "complete and balanced," this means that it meets these daily requirements. This standard has been set by the AAFCO (Association of American Feed Control Officials).

What Is a Nutrient?

Nutrients are substances that are required to sustain life. There are six of them:

Water	Large quantities of water are needed daily to prevent dehydration and for normal bodily function.
Proteins	Proteins are the building blocks of muscle, connective tissue, enzymes, and hormones.
Carbohydrates	These are sources of energy, sugars, and fiber for normal digestion.
Fats	Fats are essential for absorption of fat-soluble vitamins. They provide a storage for energy in times of fasting, provide fatty acids for the coat, and make food more palatable.
Vitamins	Vitamins are needed in small quantities for bodily functions.
Minerals	Minerals are needed for strong bones, cellular function, and cell stability.

Let's look at each more closely. This will give you an idea of why these nutrients are so important in the diet.

1. Water

Water is the single most important nutrient. The reason is, life can continue for weeks without nutrients in the food groups, but without water, clinical dehydration occurs within days. Severe dehydration is terminal. There are two ways to naturally get water: by drinking and by consuming water in foods.

Most dogs self-regulate their water. This means they sense their body dehydrating and seek water. Therefore, water should always be available. Several factors can increase their water requirements and intake: heat, humidity, exercise, salty foods, and water loss from the body (fever, vomiting, and diarrhea). *Puppies need a lot of water, and restricting it can put your puppy at risk of dehydrating. The only time water can be safely withheld is at night.*

Clear eyes, good coats, healthy appetites, and general good health — like these Pekingese pups display — are signs of a good diet.

2. Proteins

Proteins are the building blocks of muscle and connective tissues. Dogs get their protein in their diet—usually from animal-based ingredients and certain bean products. Proteins are digested and broken down into *amino acids,* which are used in the production of muscle fibers, hormones, and enzymes. There are 22 different amino acids. Some of these can be manufactured by the dog's liver. Others must be taken in their diet. These indispensable amino acids are called *essential amino acids.*

We grade proteins as either low or high quality. High-quality proteins are ones that meet three requirements. The first is that the proteins have a high *biologic value,* which is the percentage that is absorbed and used by the body. Poor quality proteins are not retained by the body, and they are excreted in the urine. Another feature of a high-quality protein is that it contains many *essential amino acids. Digestibility* is the third factor to qualify a protein as high quality. This means that the protein is actually digested, and doesn't just pass in the feces.

High-quality proteins can be found in animal-source foods such as beef, lamb, and poultry. Meat by-products and vegetable sources (such as soybean) are not as good. The quality of the protein becomes more important when there is a deficiency of it in the diet. The minimum protein level in a puppy's diet should be around 25 percent. For the body to use the most protein from the food as it can, there has to be a certain amount of calories in the food. In other words, there may be lots of high-quality protein in the diet, but if there aren't enough high-energy calories, the body can't use the protein.

If there is more than the dog can use, the rest will be excreted in the urine. This means that the proteins have to be filtered through the kidneys. All this excess filtering is very stressful to the kidneys. *Therefore, when it comes to protein, more isn't necessarily better. Stick to a diet that has high-quality protein that is 25 percent on a dry basis (versus wet food).*

3. Carbohydrates

This group of nutrients contains *starches, sugars,* and *fiber*. Breads, pasta, cereal, rice, potatoes, vegetables, biscuits, cookies, and grains are all carbohydrates. Carbohydrates supply the majority of energy in a dog's diet. If too many carbohydrates are eaten, they don't get excreted out of the body like protein, they get stored as fat. Carbohydrates are needed for the body to use proteins, but too many carbs leads to obesity. *There must be a balance between sugars and fiber for proper digestion. Fiber should be between 3 percent to 4 percent of the diet on a dry basis (versus wet food).*

4. Fats

There has been a lot of publicity about fats lately, most of it bad. In people, diets high in fats have been linked to heart disease, obesity, and certain types of cancer. The saturated fats seem to be more the culprit. Saturated fats are found in animal fats, hydrogenated vegetable oils, and tropical oils such as palm, seed, and coconut oils. The unsaturated fats found in unprocessed vegetable oils seem to be the healthiest ones.

Having said that, let me now enumerate the good things fats and oils do. First, fats are needed in the diet to allow absorption of fat-soluble vitamins (namely, A, D, E, and K). Second, fats contain essential fatty acids needed for the synthesis of cell membranes, hormones, and a healthy coat and skin. Deficiencies of fatty acids lead to skin and coat problems. Third, fats make foods *palatable*, meaning tasty. Fourth, fats are easily digested and are stored as a quickly mobilized energy source—namely, fat. In other words, if a diet rich in fats and oils is eaten regularly, the excess fats will end up as fatty deposits. *Premium puppy foods generally are not less than 20 percent fat on a dry basis (versus wet food), due to the high demands for fats in this age group.*

5. Vitamins

Do you need to give vitamins to your puppy? The answer is a bit complicated. Let's start by saying that most of the commercial dog foods on the market are "complete and balanced"—they contain the daily requirements for all nutrients, including vitamins and minerals. Most experts agree that it is better to get vitamins from natural sources than from vitamin tablets. If, however, you have a puppy that is very athletic or works every day, he will have a higher requirement for these nutrients. Talk to your veterinarian about supplements in such cases.

6. *Minerals*

Minerals are fundamental building blocks of bone and teeth and are needed for cellular functions. Minerals are also salts, which are crucial to maintaining tissues and cells. Some are needed in fairly large amounts in the diet, including:

- calcium
- iron
- phosphorus
- potassium
- sodium
- zinc

Others, like copper and iodine, are only needed in trace amounts, also from the diet. Below is a chart that shows where some of these minerals come from.

Minerals

Mineral	Natural Source	Function
Calcium	green leafy vegetables	strong bones and teeth, cellular function
Copper	nuts and beans	needed for blood cells, nerves, and bone
Iodine	seafood, kelp	needed for normal thyroid function
Iron	meats	oxygen transport of red blood cells
Magnesium	dairy foods, fish, grain	needed for bone, muscle, heart function
Phosphorus	grains, nuts, dairy	bone, teeth, kidney function
Potassium	dairy, fish, meats, fruit	nerves, heart rhythm, kidney function
Selenium	nuts, grains	fat preservation, anti-oxidant
Sodium	most foods	body water balance, all nerve function
Zinc	seafood, meats, eggs	healthy skin and coat

Even though some of them are only required in minute amounts, without them, there would be illness.

Are All Dog Foods Alike?

The simple answer is no. Most commercially available foods are complete and balanced, but that's where the similarity ends.

The first way to classify dog foods is based on which age group they are formulated for: a puppy, adult, or senior (less active). Since this is a puppy book, we'll focus on the puppy foods.

The second way to classify dog foods is by their quality. Here are the basic categories: performance, premium, high quality, average, and economy foods. What these categories are based on is the percentage of protein, fat, and fiber in the food as well as on the quality of the main ingredients and whether preservatives or artificial ingredients are used. Generally speaking, the performance and premium foods have higher levels of protein and fat, with reduced fiber for a smaller stool. They are also more natural foods, with few if any artificial ingredients or preservatives. Too much protein can be stressful to the kidneys, but that's after years of consuming a high-protein food. This is not a concern in puppies. Puppies have higher requirements for protein, fat, vitamins, and minerals than do adult dogs, except perhaps for lactating bitches or dogs used for intense work or sport.

"Guaranteed Analysis" and Ingredients

How can you tell which foods are considered premium or high quality? Read the labels! On each package or can of dog food, there is a label with a guaranteed analysis listing. This is a rough measure of how much protein, fat, and water (moisture) are in the food on a dry matter basis (discounting the water). The reason they are rough estimates is they are listed as "not more than. . ." maximums for water and fiber, and "not less than. . ." minimums for protein and fat values. Use this table to give you an idea of what to expect from a premium food.

Guidelines for Guaranteed Analysis in Premium Foods

Nutrient	Minimum %	Maximum %	Main Ingredient Source
protein	25	N/A	chicken, lamb, beef, egg
fat	15	N/A	chicken fat, beef tallow, lamb fat, vegetable oil
fiber	N/A	4	ground corn, rice, barley, corn gluten, bran, beet pulp
water	N/A	10	N/A (not applicable)

The other important thing to read on the food label is the list of ingredients. This is a list of all the ingredients in descending order. In other words, the first ingredient is what there is the most of, and the last one is in the least amount. This information is important to know because if the main protein source is listed third, for example, then you'd be concerned there is a low-protein content in the food.

What, How Much, and When to Feed Your Puppy

Let's start with *what* to feed your puppy. Most veterinarians will recommend a dry food. These foods are generally more nutritious and better balanced by virtue of being mostly food and not water like the canned foods (canned foods are close to 75 percent water). Also, as mentioned earlier in this chapter, dry foods are better than canned foods for maintaining healthy teeth and gums. Canned foods are also more likely to put tartar on the teeth. I recommend keeping the canned food less than 25 percent of the daily intake by weight if the owners insist on feeding it. Think of it as a treat and not a main staple of the diet. As far as the semimoist foods are concerned, we regard them as the "junk" foods, laden with sugars, artificial colors, and preservatives. These should be avoided.

Do you have to feed your puppy a premium diet? Well, no you don't. But the better the food, the healthier your puppy will be inside and out: stronger bones and connective tissue, bright eyes, healthy teeth and gums, resilient skin, lustrous coat, high energy, good muscle tone, and an even temperament. Do you have to buy the most expensive food on the market? No, get one that meets the requirements listed in the above table. This should be easy to find in a puppy formula. We don't recommend buying bargain food that is mostly corn meal or cereal. As far as where to buy your food, high-quality puppy foods are available at both pet supply stores and grocery store. All you have to do is read the label! *Always feed your puppy a diet formulated for puppies. Adult maintenance foods don't usually have the level of nutrients needed for a growing puppy with a high metabolism.*

How much to feed is the next issue. Most bags and cans of dog food have a chart on the back label that gives feeding instructions, but we have found these guidelines often overexaggerate how much a puppy will eat at one sitting.

Daily Amounts for Dry and Canned Foods

Weight in Pounds	Cups† per Day of Dry Food	Cans* per Day of Canned
1–10	1–1½	½–1
11–30	2–2½	2
31–45	4	2½
46–60	5–6	3–3½
61–75	6–7	4–4½
76–90	7–8	4½–5
over 100	8–9	5–½

†Based on 8-ounce cups   *Based on 15-ounce cans

Please use this chart as a guideline only. Watching weight gains and consulting with your vet are the best ways to determine if you're over- or underfeeding your puppy.

The last consideration of feeding is *when* to feed. A feeding schedule is *very* important for housebreaking. Never free-feed your puppy, meaning the food is in the bowl all the time. If you do, we can almost assure you your efforts for housebreaking will be wasted. *The reward of a regular feeding schedule is easier housebreaking.*

Follow the feeding schedule in this chart for an easy program.

Feeding Schedule

Age	Feedings per Day	Snacks Allowed
6 weeks to 3 months	4	yes, often
3 months to 6 months	3	yes, often
6 months to 1 year	2	yes, but occasional
after 1 year	2	try to limit between-meal snacks

Most people find that dividing the total daily quantity of food into two equal portions keeps their dog from ever becoming too hungry. Some dogs become nauseated or weak if they go 24 hours without eating. This can lead to obsessive behavior and dry heaving. We find that dogs thrive better with two feedings a day, even as adults.

Are Table Scraps Okay?

Some of the reasons we don't advise feeding your puppy table scraps are:

- They put more tartar on the teeth.
- They are usually more fattening.
- They may be more difficult to digest.
- They may cause vomiting and diarrhea.
- They spoil the puppy who won't eat his dog food.
- They rarely contain the nutrition your puppy needs and gets from dog food.

However, the vast majority of new puppy owners do feed table scraps. Why? Perhaps that special way he looks at you when you're eating his favorite dish. If you insist on feeding scraps, follow these guidelines:

Do's	Dont's
• Stick to pieces of chicken, beef, lamb, or turkey, but never bones—other meats can be difficult to digest.	• Never treat your puppy like a garbage disposal.
• Vegetables are okay if they're cooked.	• Stay away from pork, veal, venison, duck, or other gamy meats, as they are too fatty.
• Rice, potato, and plain pasta are okay carbohydrates.	• Stay away from raw vegetables, except carrots.
• Wholesome foods like cottage cheese, baby food, bread, cheese, and yogurt are okay in small quantities.	• Never feed processed foods like potato chips, crackers, pretzels, canned nuts, or other salty foods.
• Dogs may eat small pieces of fruits, including canned fruit.	• Dogs should never be given candy, especially chocolate, because it is toxic to them.
• Table food should only be a treat once in a while, if at all.	• Never feed leftover Chinese food, pizza, Mexican, or other spicy foods unless you're willing to clean up the mess when it backfires.

CARING FOR THE BODY

Your Puppy's Teeth

Teeth are as important to your puppy as they are to you. Maybe more so; after all, we don't use our teeth to hold, carry, and play with our toys. A dog's dentition is definitely worth protecting and saving! We humans try to hold onto our teeth as long as possible by brushing every day, flossing, and going to the dentist for regular professional cleaning. Imagine if you did *nothing*. Eventually your teeth would just rot out.

Because dogs don't do anything to their teeth, many begin loosing them in midlife. Just look at a seven-year-old dog's teeth. Unless he's unusual, there will be lots of tartar, discoloration, odor, and black areas of decay (a cavity or caries), not to mention cracked and missing teeth.

Let's be fair about this. Animals in general have a higher resistance to tooth decay, for several reasons. First, their saliva is more resistant to bacterial growth than ours. Second, dogs generally chew on harder things than we do. This mechanical scraping helps keep tartar from accumulating. Third, the enamel coating of a dog's teeth is generally thicker than ours. *Despite these positive forces, without basic dental care dogs will end up with tooth decay, tooth rot, cavities, root abscesses, cracked teeth, periodontal disease and ultimately, tooth loss.*

What are the steps you can take to prevent such a tragedy? Read on and start now while your puppy is young to help ensure many years of a beautiful, healthy smile:

1. See how clean, white, and glossy your puppy's teeth are? The gums are healthy with no evidence of disease. That's the way they should look for the life of your dog.
2. Dry is better. Feed your puppy a high-quality dry kibble food. Only use canned food or table scraps as a treat once in a while. The kibble will help keep his teeth clean.

See how clean, white, and glossy your puppy's teeth are? That's how they should look for the life of your dog.

3. Brush your puppy's teeth at least once or twice a week. Use one of your old toothbrushes and baking soda. Add just enough water to two tablespoons of baking soda to make it pasty. Spread the paste onto the head of the toothbrush or directly on the outer surfaces of the teeth. You'll have to lift up the lips to do this. (If you want to be fancy about this, there are commercially available doggie toothpaste and toothbrushes.) *If*

your puppy is introduced to this procedure early, it won't be a struggle later in life. The key is to start at the gum line and brush downward in a circular motion. Concentrate on the outer surfaces because this is where most of the tartar and plaque accumulate. Brush vigorously for two minutes. If your puppy gets tired sooner, take a short rest, then continue. No rinsing is needed. You can get away with only brushing once or twice a week because, unlike in humans, plaque takes several days to mineralize into tartar. Obviously, the more you brush, the healthier the teeth and gums will be.

4. *Regular professional cleaning* by your veterinarian is necessary. It involves a combination of hand scaling and ultrasonic cleaning that literally blasts tartar off. Each tooth is scaled separately, then all are polished with a tooth polish. The reason is that during the scaling, microscopic lines are made in the enamel. If these aren't smoothed out by polishing, then they will provide a place for tartar to accumulate.

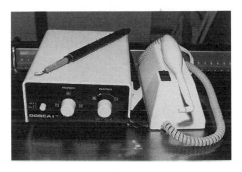

Modern veterinary dental equipment for professional cleaning.

Following at least two or three of the above steps will greatly increase your puppy's chances of keeping the beautiful set of teeth he was born with for his whole life.

Your Puppy's Ears

Dog ears come in all different shapes and sizes. Look at the cropped, erect ears of a Doberman Pinscher compared with the long, floppy ears of a Basset Hound. Each ear is different and has its own personality. A puppy can have a left ear that's always having problems, while the right one is fine. Even dogs within a breed can be different. The point is, each dog and each ear is different, and you shouldn't generalize. However, one of my jobs here is to make recommendations that pertain to the average case.

To begin, let's walk through the basic anatomy of an ear. On the outside is the earflap, or *pinna*. This is a flap of cartilage sandwiched between two layers of skin. All ears are assembled the same regardless of the size, shape, or breed. At the junction of the pinna and the skull, the ear turns into a conical tunnel called the *outer ear canal*. There are two parts to the outer ear canal: the vertical and horizontal canals. Think of the ear canal as an inverted *L*. At the bottom of the horizontal canal lies the *tympanic membrane*, or eardrum. This membrane separates the outer ear from the middle ear.

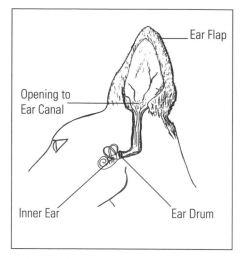

A diagram of the inner structures of the canine ear.

Care of the Ear Flap

The three most common ailments of the earflap are cropped ears, fly bites, and frostbite.

In puppies where the breed dictates cropping, the veterinary surgeon will "crop" (cut) the ear in a standard pattern for that breed at about 12 weeks of age. Antibiotics may be dispensed following surgery to prevent infection. The skin margins often bleed and ooze serum for several days after surgery. If the breed calls for erect ears, the cropped ear is kept in an upright, erect posture with use of a cotton support rod taped into the outer ear canal. Then a piece of tape is used between the ears to form a bridge, which keeps the ears vertical.

The black fly, may fly, deer fly, and horsefly all love the inside of tender young earflaps. In many parts of the country, these biting flies come out in the spring. The bites leave large welts that itch and bleed. These can be treated with topical antibiotics and cortisone ointments.

Frostbite most commonly sets in on the tip of the earflap because there is reduced blood flow and less hair there. Frostbite literally means the freezing and killing of tissue. At first, the skin turns white and loses feeling. Once the dog is brought inside, the skin starts to thaw. At this point it becomes very red and painful. This is due to a tremendous inflammatory response to the damaged skin. After a few days, the dead skin starts to turn black and dry up.

If frostbite is diagnosed, the veterinarian slowly thaws out the skin with warm water bottles. The skin that is still viable will survive. The skin that died is surgically removed after a waiting period of two to four weeks.

Care of the Outer Ear Canal

By far the most common problem we see in the ear canal is infection. Most people refer to these as "ear infections." We will be more accurate and call them "infections of the outer ear canal" or, scientifically put, *otitis externa*. There are three basic types of outer ear infections:

1. ear mites
2. bacterial infections
3. yeast infections

The environment of the ear canal is very important in encouraging the growth of bacteria or yeast. If the ear canal is dry and clean and air gets in readily, bacteria and yeast cannot grow. Bacteria and yeast grow best in an environment that is dark, damp, and warm with reduced air flow. It usually takes a veterinarian to be able to differentiate between the bacterial and yeast etiologies. Their clinical presentation can look very similar. In fact, we often need to do a culture of the ear canal to see what's growing.

The following list of steps prevents ear disease.

1. Pluck That Hair.

Plucking hair from the ear with a pointy-nosed hemostat. You can use your fingers at home

One of the most common causes of outer ear problems is excess hair in the outer ear canal. All dogs have some hair in their ear canal, but certain breeds have more than their share. What the hair does is keep the ear wax from working its way out of the ear canal. In effect, it traps it like a wick. Wax accumulation coupled with warmth, dampness, darkness, and no air circulation leads to ear infections. Most groomers pluck out the ear hair as part of a grooming, which means for many breeds it gets done every four to six weeks. At home, you can pluck out hairs with your fingertips slowly, a few hairs at a time. As you can imagine, your puppy may not take to this too kindly, but just remember, not all things that are good for you are fun. Groomers and veterinarians often use tweezers or a pointy-nosed hemostat to pluck with instead of fingers. If done properly, there will be minimal discomfort to your puppy. Have your groomer or vet show you how.

2. Clean Those Ears Regularly.

You can do this at home. To be of any real benefit, you should clean your puppy's ears weekly. Use a commercially prepared dog ear cleaner. It should have a ceruminolytic agent to break up the wax. Some have menthol and eucalyptus extracts to soothe the irritated ear canal. A few have antiseptic agents to discourage bacterial and yeast growth. If your puppy has wet ears, use an ear cleaner that has an astringent (drying agent). There are dozens of ear cleaners on the market; ask your vet which one is best for your puppy.

Regardless of which cleaner you use, the technique is the same. Follow the guidelines below.

1. Tear off a piece of cotton about two inches long. I like to use cotton on a roll.
2. Soak the cotton in your chosen ear cleaner.
3. Using your finger, gently swab the inside of the ear canal with the wet cotton.
4. Use circular motions to wipe out the ear canal.
5. If there is a large accumulation of dirt or wax, pour a small amount of cleaner into the ear canal, massage it in with your hand, then swab it out with dry cotton.
6. *Never use cotton-tipped swabs* because these can damage the eardrum if improperly angled.
7. Continue until no more dirt comes out with the swabbing. It may take a dozen or more swabbings to clean a dirty ear.
8. Do the same for the other ear.

3. Keep Those Ears Dry.

If your puppy swims a lot or must be bathed often, there is an increased risk of developing ear problems. Place cotton in the outer ear canals before swimming or bathing to keep water out. If that's impossible, rinse out the ear canals with an astringent after swimming or bathing to dry the ear and remove any residual water.

How to Medicate Ears

In most situations, a thorough cleaning of the ear is necessary before
applying any medication. After all,
placing medication on top of wax or
infectious debris doesn't do a great
deal of good.

Most ear medications are ointments. These are a bit greasy, but
they make good vehicles to deliver
the active ingredients to the site.
Applying ointment into an ear canal
is a simple procedure once you know
how. Follow these instructions:

Applying ear medication.

1. Make sure the ointment you're using hasn't expired. The expiration
   date is on the crimp (end) of the tube.
2. Make sure the ears are clean. If they're not, read the section above
   on cleaning the ear.
3. Hold up the earflap so the opening to the external ear canal is
   visible.
4. Most ear ointments have a tip or nozzle. While holding the tube
   upside down and vertical, insert the tip into the canal opening only
   as far as you can see. This may mean ½ inch in a Miniature Schnauzer to 1½ inches in a Labrador Retriever.
5. Squirt enough ointment into the ear canal to fill it. This can be
   anywhere from 5 drops in a Yorkshire Terrier to 25 drops in a Saint
   Bernard.
6. Thoroughly massage the ointment into the ear canal so that it
   works its way to the bottom. Remember, the ear canal is in the
   shape of an inverted *L*.

Your Puppy's Eyes

The eye is a complicated anatomical structure. Other than traumatic injury, the
majority of eye afflictions are inflammations and infections of the tissues
surrounding the eye. When we say the *eye*, we really mean the three main

components of the eye: the *globe,* which is the eyeball itself; the *eyelids* (upper, lower, and nictitans); and the *conjunctiva.*

The globe of the eye is the eyeball itself; the surface of the eye is called the *cornea.* The upper and lower eyelids are skin with eyelashes projecting from the outer margins. The *nictitans,* or third eyelid, is a protective veil the dog can raise to cover the cornea. The third eyelid has a slip of cartilage in it to keep its shape and rigidity and a gland of the nictitans, which acts as a lymph node to fight infection and secrete lubrication. The conjunctiva is the mucus membrane that surrounds the eyeball. This is the pink tissue that gets very red and swollen in a case of *pink eye* and *conjunctivitis.*

Care of the Eyelids, Conjunctiva, and Eyeball

Congenital eye defects such as entropion (which is an inward rolling of the lower eyelid), ectropion (which is an outward rolling of the lower eyelid), cherry eye, as well as other diseases of the eye, are described in Chapter 18, "Puppy Pediatrics." In this section, we will cover the steps you can take to keep the eyes healthy.

- Keep hair short around the eyes so it doesn't get into the eyes and irritate them.
- If your puppy is one that has a lot of crusty discharge, wipe it away often. Use warm water on a washcloth or tissue. Wipe in a downward motion so you don't run the risk of poking the eye. You may need to do this daily in some breeds like the Poodle, Lhasa Apso, Shih Tzu, and Pekingese.
- Keep your puppy from lunging face-first into bushes and plants because they can get poked in the eye by the branches.
- Avoid playing any rough games that could involve trauma to the eye such as throwing sticks or pointed objects for him to catch. Only use smooth, rounded, or soft playthings, like tennis balls, Frisbees, or soft handballs.
- Reduce the possible irritants in your home and yard that may cause eye irritation. Some of the things that are very irritating to puppy's eyes are dust, paint or adhesive fumes, sawdust or plaster dust, indoor plants, mold spores, city soot, aerosol spray propellants, carpet cleaners, certain fabric fibers, outdoor pollens and grass cuttings, dried soil, and car exhaust.

- Have your puppy checked routinely for internal parasites because some of them can cause eye damage.
- Avoid physical contact with other dogs or cats that have mange, ringworm, or any other skin ailment of unknown cause.
- Never hit your dog in the face or head for fear of causing eye trauma (you shouldn't be doing that kind of thing anyway).
- At the first sign of redness, hair loss around the eyes, swelling of the conjunctiva or eyelids, eye itching, or any watery or thick discharge of the eyes, consult your veterinarian!

Applying Eye Medication

There are two basic types of ophthalmic medications that are commonly applied to the eyes: drops and ointment. Below are directions for applying each of these.

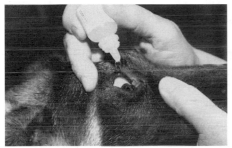

Applying eye drops.

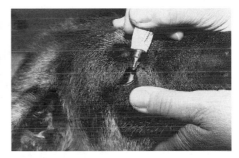

Applying eye ointment.

1. *Drops.* To apply an eye drop to the eye, raise your puppy's nose upward about 30 degrees. Gently pull back the upper lid so that the white of the eye is showing. Drop one drop onto the white of the eye. Hold the nose up for 10 seconds.
2. *Ointment.* To apply ointment to the eye, raise your puppy's nose upward about 30 degrees. Gently pull down the lower lid so that a pocket forms between the lower lid and the conjunctiva. Squeeze ¼ inch of the ointment into the pocket. Let go of the lower lid and allow the dog to blink. Blinking will melt the ointment and spread a thin layer evenly over the eye.

Your Puppy's Nails

The nails of a dog are very similar to our nails. There is a point of dead thickened skin and an inner core of fleshy tissue that contains the blood and nerve supply. The inner core is called the *quick*. The quick is what produces the nail, and it is from there that the nail grows out. Anyone who has cut a dog's nail too short knows that it hurts the dog, and it probably bled a lot.

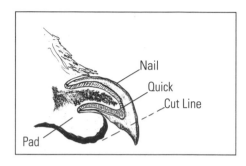

Cross sections showing the nail growing out of the toe and the nail itself. Dotted line shows where to cut.

The nail grows out of the nail bed, which is the center of the toe. The nail is firmly attached in the nail bed. The pad is the bottom of the toe. It has a black, horny, rough layer of dead skin. Beneath that is a pad of fleshy, fatty tissue that is full of blood vessels.

In the outdoors, nails are very important for normal walking. Dogs use their nails for traction and tactile feeling. Unfortunately, many dogs nowadays live indoors and walk on hard floors and roads. The nails are still important to these urban dogs, but if they get too long, they can cause a loss of traction. Therefore, dogs on hard flooring should have their nails trimmed often.

There are several things that can go wrong with nails. We will describe each one in detail.

1. Bacterial and Fungal Infections of the Nail Bed

Small scratches allow opportunistic bacteria and fungi to enter the skin and nail bed. Bacterial infection causes inflammation and pain of the skin around the base of the nail. A pus discharge is often present. A fungal infection is similar, except the skin is crusty, and there may be intense itching. Treatment involves soaking the paw in warm water with an antiseptic or antifungal agent for 5 to 10 minutes three times a day; applying topical antibiotic or fungal creams or powders; administering oral antibiotics or antifungal drugs to combat a deep infection; and as a last resort, if the above steps fail, surgical removal of the nail.

2. Brittle and Cracked Nails

Many dog nails become dry and brittle, especially the longer they are. Superficial cracks and splits are of little consequence. The superficial layer may peel. If the nail crack is deeper, it can go into the quick of the nail bed. This is very painful and can lead to infection. Try to keep the nails short to prevent this.

3. Ingrown Nails

Ingrown nails are particularly common in toy breed dogs, where the owner doesn't trim the nails often enough. Since canine nails grow in a curved fashion, there is the potential that the point of the nail can curl around and pierce the pad. If left untreated, the nail continues to grow into the pad. Infection ensues shortly thereafter. Treatment is simple: The offending nail needs to be cut short and pulled out from the pad by your veterinarian. Since this condition is so painful, a local or topical anesthetic is needed to numb the area. The paw is then soaked in warm antiseptic solutions or Epsom salts three times daily for a week. Oral antibiotics are usually prescribed as well.

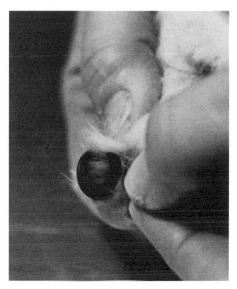

An ingrown toenail.

4. Broken Nails

This is perhaps the worst of the nail ailments. When we say broken, we mean broken off at the base. You can imagine how painful that must be. This occurs when an overgrown nail gets caught and enough pressure is applied to break it off at the base. If the nail breaks off cleanly, the fleshy stump of the quick will be exposed. This is extremely sensitive and will bleed. At this point, the paw must be soaked in a warm antiseptic solution or Epsom salts three times daily for a week. The vet will often put a bandage on the paw to cover the quick. If the quick continues to bleed, it may need to be chemically cauterized to stop the bleeding. If the nail doesn't completely break off and is left dangling by a thread, the veterinarian needs to trim off the nail. Since this condition is so painful, a general anesthetic may be needed. Once desensitized, the nail can be trimmed off. The exposed quick is treated the same as described above.

Why Shorter Is Better

Reading through the descriptions of all the things that can go wrong with nails, you will notice that the majority of them are due to being overgrown. Nails that are too long are prone to injury, splitting, cracking, breaking off at the base, and infection. If you are reluctant to cut your puppy's nails yourself, have your veterinarian or groomer do it as soon as a curved tip grows out. If your dog's nails are clear, you can visualize the quick. *Stay away from it!* If the nails are black, you won't be able to see the quick, which makes it much more difficult. *Dogs have very good memories. If you cut their nails too short and make them bleed, they may never let you or anyone else try again.* New puppy owners should learn how to cut their puppy's nails. Here's how:

- The front nails grow longer and wear slower than the hind nails. Therefore, concentrate on the fronts. The average dog needs his nails trimmed every two months.
- Declaws are the small nails halfway between the toes and the wrist (on the front legs), and the toes and the hock (on the hind legs). They are not used for walking and usually don't wear down at all. This means they tend to grow long and curl. Don't forget to trim them.
- Dogs that walk on roads, concrete, sidewalks, and gravel tend to wear down their nails much faster than dogs that only walk on lawns, dirt, carpeting, or hardwood flooring. In fact, dogs that regularly wear down their nails may not need them trimmed.
- Get your puppy used to it early. Start trimming his nails at 8 to 10 weeks of age. Handle the paws every day to get him used to people

Use guillotine-style clippers to trim your puppy's nails. They're easier to use and make it harder to cut too short.

touching his paws. Dogs naturally don't like it, but they can learn to accept it. Be gentle, and hold each toe in your fingers. Count to 10 (that's about how long it'll take you to cut the nail). It may take a week of practice before you actually attempt to cut one.

- If your puppy gets aggressive—like growling and trying to bite while attempting to cut his nails—stop and consult a professional.
- Use the guillotine-style trimmers; they are easier to maneuver and make it harder to cut the nail short.
- Hold the paw with your left hand if you're right handed, and vice versa.
- Cut the nail parallel to the floor, and only cut off the tip of the nail. The line at which you cut starts where the tip begins to curve.
- Cut each nail slowly and carefully. Don't rush this. You may only get a few nails done at one time.
- If the nail is left sharp from the cutting, you can take a nail file and round off the end.
- What do you do if, by accident, you cut a nail short? Buy a product that stops the bleeding or plunge the bleeding end of the nail into a bar of soap. This will work just as well.

Your Puppy's Coat

There are several types of coats. We all think of dog fur as hair. It is, but it's very different from our own. In most breeds, the "coat" is really made of two layers: the overcoat and the undercoat.

The *overcoat* is the longer and coarser hairs that make up the outer, protective layer. It protects against sun, water, thorns and brush, animal bites, and heat. The oils that the dog's skin secretes keep this layer waterproofed. Some breeds, such as the Maltese, only have an overcoat.

The *undercoat* is the layer made of finer and shorter hairs. Some people refer to this coat as the *downy* layer. In fact, the undercoat is an insulating layer. Some breeds have more of this layer than others.

Dogs' coats come in different *lengths* (ultrashort, short, medium, and long); *thicknesses* (fine and coarse); *textures* (smooth, rough, flat, wirehaired, curly, wavy, silky, woolly, etc.); and *colors* (white, black, golden, chocolate, brindle, red, tricolor, and many more).

Shedding

All dogs shed to some degree. There are light shedders, normal shedders, and heavy shedders. Shedding is the turning over of the coat based on photoperiod (hours of light in a day) and seasons. A thick coat will grow in for the winter, and the shedding will be less. In the spring, the shedding season starts, and the dog will lose much of the undercoat that grew in during the winter. Breeders call this sudden onset of shedding "blowing coat." Other than seasons, there can be other reasons why dogs suddenly drop a lot of hair:

- Short-term, excessive nervousness or excitement (from being at the vet's office or groomer)
- Longer term stress (from being at a boarding kennel)
- Malnutrition, vitamin (such as vitamin E) and mineral deficiencies (such as zinc)
- Hormonal changes in females: spaying, heat cycles, pregnancy, false pregnancy
- Allergies and allergic dermatitis
- Parasites: mites and mange, fleas, lice
- Genetic causes: patterned baldness, congenital alopecia
- Diseases: dermatitis, pyoderma, hot spots, ringworm, autoimmune diseases, hypothyroidism, and Cushing's disease

Basic Home-Grooming Techniques

Some breeds require regular professional grooming. These include the Akita, Alaskan Malamute, Bichon Frisé, Cairn Terrier, Chow Chow, Cocker Spaniel, Lhasa Apso, Maltese, Schnauzer, Pekingese, Pomeranian, Poodle (all varieties), Shetland Sheepdog, Shih Tzu, Siberian Husky, Springer Spaniel, West Highland White Terrier, and Yorkshire Terrier.

Tools of the Trade

Before you can get started with basic grooming at home, you need to know what tools are available and which one you use for what job. Some of these are for short coats, others are for long and dense. Apply the following guidelines.

A *wire slicker brush* is the most common brush people buy for their dog. It has angled wires to brush the coat and is designed to get through medium to short coats. It doesn't detangle mats. If used on a dense coat, it tends to skim over the surface of the coat.

Slicker and universal brushes (top) and a variety of combs.

A *universal wire brush* is very similar to the slicker brush, but is tougher and can work through some mats. This is a popular tool for brushing out dogs.

There are several different *combs* on the market. They come in all different tooth widths, from fine and medium to coarse—or a combination. Combs are best at getting out mats or teasing snarls. Combs with ultrafine teeth are called *flea combs*. They are used to trap and comb out adult fleas from the coats of dogs and cats.

Handheld *rakes* are great for pulling out dead undercoat from a densely coated dog. Make sure you get the ones with rounded teeth; otherwise, you could scrape the puppy's skin. These must be used gently.

Shedding blades look like a bowed saw blade with saw teeth. They are used to pull out the dead overcoat. You must be very careful with them; too much pressure will cause scrapes and abrasions to the skin.

A *mat comb* should only be used by an experienced professional. It has wide razor-sharp teeth for cutting into mats.

Scissors are used to cut hair. They must be kept sharp and clean to cut well. There are different types of scissors for different grooming needs.

Clippers are electric shavers that have interchangeable blades. They are used by professionals and experienced amateurs who have learned their capabilities. Clippers can cut through the toughest of mats and can shave as close as a razor.

Dog *shampoos* are similar to people shampoos, but there are some differences. One of the biggest is the pH. A dog shampoo is pH balanced for canine hair. A good shampoo will be easy to work with, lather well, smell nice, and rinse thoroughly with no residue. There are many different types of shampoos, from insecticide to medicated. They can contain ingredients to clean, detangle, medicate, reduce itching and flaking, deodorize, and whiten.

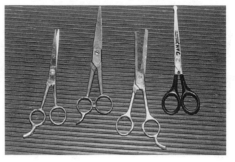

From left to right, shedding blade, rake, and mat comb; an assortment of scissors.

Getting Started

Before getting into the meat of the matter, clean the ears with an ear cleaner and cotton as described earlier in this chapter, and place cotton in your puppy's ears to keep water out during the bath.

Step 1: Brushing and Combing.

Before the water touches your dog, you have to brush out the coat *thoroughly*. Matted hair turns into cement when it gets wet. The rule is you should spend more time brushing and combing out the coat than you do bathing. Do specific areas one at a time; that is, do each leg individually, then work on the tail. Cover the entire body in a logical fashion so you don't miss any areas. Use your brush first, then go over it again with the comb. Then end with another brushing. This will really get all the snags and tangles out. Don't miss those hard-to-get areas like under the tail, behind the ears, and between the hind legs. When you're finished brushing the coat, it should have a luster, soft feel, and most of the dead hair should come out. Brushing also spreads the natural oils of the coat.

Step 2: The Bath.

Once the brush-out is done, it's time for the bath. Indoors, the bathtub works best; weather permitting, some people use the garden hose outside. Completely wet the coat, starting at the head, and work your way to the tail. Use tepid water. Then apply the shampoo, again starting at the head. Work up a good lather. Use your fingers to thoroughly work the lather into the coat. Rinsing is next. Use plenty of warm water. Rinse until you can't feel any soapy residue. When finished, ring the water out of the coat with your fingers. At this point, the dog usually shakes the excess water all over you, and you both get a bath!

Step 3: Drying.

After squeezing the water out of the coat, use a thick, cotton towel to towel dry the coat. You may need two or three towels for a large long-coated breed. If you have a hair dryer, you can use it on the low setting, never closer than 12 inches from the skin. In warm weather, you can skip the blow drying.

Step 4: Final Brushout.

The last step in the process is to brush the coat out again. Wow, what a difference!

How Often?

If your puppy likes to get dirty, you can bathe him as often as once every two to three weeks. Be careful not to overbathe, however, because this can dry out the coat. Most people with breeds that require professional grooming have it done every six to eight weeks. Ask your groomer how often your puppy should be done.

Spaying and Neutering

Many people use the term *fix* to describe making their dog unbreedable. The actual terminology is *spay* for a female and *neuter* for a male. The typical time for neutering or spaying is when the puppy is six months old. This age is chosen for the following reasons:

1. *For a bitch*: Since most bitches don't start coming into heat until six to eight months of age, you are preventing them from going into their first heat cycle. This has definite benefits in preventing certain types of cancer; it also eliminates the risk of unwanted pregnancy.
2. *For a male dog*: Most male dogs don't yet reach puberty by six months of age. Neutering them at this age prevents the male *behaviors* from developing. Most of the male physical characteristics are developed by this time, so neutering doesn't stunt their growth.

Both procedures are surgical, require general anesthesia, have a recuperation period of a couple of weeks, and must be performed by a veterinary surgeon.

The *spay* procedure on a female dog is a surgical ovariohysterectomy. What this means is both ovaries and the body of the uterus are surgically removed. When a male dog is neutered, the two testicles are surgically removed, leaving an empty scrotum. The advantages and disadvantages of spaying and neutering are summarized below:

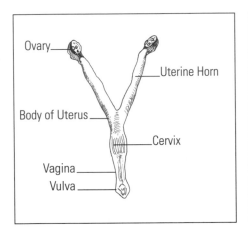

Female reproductive tract.   Male reproductive tract.

Advantages of Spaying

- No more messy heat cycles.
- No chance of breeding or pregnancy.
- You avoid the behavioral changes (restlessness, aggression, roaming, and whining) during heat cycles.
- The lack of estrogen hormone prevents breast cancer later in life. Bitches spayed before their second heat cycle have a 95 percent reduction in mammary carcinoma, as compared with intact bitches.
- There is no chance of ovarian, uterine, or cervical cancer.
- You're doing your part to prevent the surplus of unwanted puppies.

Advantages of Neutering

- Once the testicles are removed, the hormone testosterone disappears and with it the male behavior many people find objectionable such as lifting the hind leg to urinate and "mark" his territory, male aggression, male dominance and territorial behavior, roaming to find a mate, and mounting objects and people.
- Testicular cancer is prevented.
- All prostatic diseases, such as cancer, prostatic enlargement, and prostatitis (infection of the prostate) are prevented.
- Most people find a neutered male a better house pet, especially if they have young children.
- You're doing your part in preventing the surplus of unwanted puppies.

Disadvantages of Spaying and Neutering

- Weight gain is common because the base metabolism is lower.
- You cannot ever breed or show a spayed or neutered animal.
- Some people notice a reduction in activity after the operation.
- The risks of the anesthesia and surgery in general are low, but ask your vet if there are any special considerations regarding your puppy.

Cryptorchids, a Special Consideration

Cryptorchidism is when only one testicle makes it down into the scrotum, leaving the other one in the abdomen or in the *inguinal ring*, the opening where the testicle makes its descent. This is a genetic problem. Most puppies that haven't "dropped" both testicles by the time they're four to five months old, won't. This leaves a problem when it comes time to neuter the dog. You cannot just remove the one testicle that has descended into the scrotum. If the surgeon leaves the internal testicle, there will still be sufficient testosterone levels to maintain all the male behavior, and the dog could still breed a bitch in heat. Being that this is an inherited problem, these dogs should be neutered so that they cannot propagate this defect by breeding. The other reason you should have your cryptorchid dog neutered is because studies have shown that the internal testicle is much more likely to become cancerous later in life than the external one in the scrotum. The constant higher temperatures inside the abdomen increase the risk of cancer.

HOME REMEDIES AND HOLISTIC ALTERNATIVES

Some of you may find this section interesting. Not many of us are aware of the whole world of *holistic* medicine. It is as ancient as mankind. A holistic approach to health incorporates a balance between mind and body as well as a respect for nature and natural processes and the belief that animals as well as people fit into the scheme of nature. Both medical and spiritual forces are used to heal. Holistic medicine encompasses homeopathic medicine, naturopathic medicine, acupuncture, chiropractic medicine, acupressure, nutrition, and herbology. Think of the holistic approach as a healthy, natural way of life. This section will give you a brief history of holistic medicine and how it can apply to your new puppy, plus more specific examples of remedies and treatments that are purely natural.

A Brief History of Homeopathic Medicine

The definition of homeopathy, according to Dr. George Vithoulkas, a world-renowned homeopathic physician, is "that branch of medicine whose methodology is based on the Principles of Similars ('likes are cured by likes'). The homeopathic physician does not treat the symptoms, but considers the symptoms the outward signs of the body's attempt to cure itself."

There are three basic approaches to homeopathic medicine: nutrition, detoxification, and exercise. The German physician Samuel Hahnemann is considered the father of modern homeopathy. He was an acclaimed healer in 18th-century Europe, who documented natural substances that caused disease-like symptoms, ultimately leading to a cure. He compiled these substances and their dosages in several volumes called the *Materia Medica*. These books were in full use throughout Europe by the 19th century. Many of the natural substances that had been used for centuries by the ancient Romans and Greeks are extracts of botanical and herbals, diluted and dissolved in water or alcohol. The concentrations may be as low as one part per million. The book ends with a *Repertory*, which is an alphabetical list of medical ailments with the homeopathic cures following it.

What can be said about homeopathic medicine today? There are vast differences in our current knowledge versus over a century ago. Even with this high level of medical comprehension, there is a whole new resurgence of homeopathy, indicating it is not just a leftover from a time long gone, but an active, progressive, credible alternative to traditional western medicine. Homeopathy offers natural cures for such ailments as:

- anemia
- arthritis
- bronchitis
- colitis
- constipation
- digestive disorders
- ear infections
- kidney and urinary bladder infection
- muscle cramps and weakness
- nosebleeds
- pneumonia
- skin diseases
- tonsillitis and sore throats
- toothaches
- vaginitis
- viral diseases
- vomiting and nausea

The majority of veterinarians are trained in traditional medicine, just as physicians are. If a veterinarian professes to practice homeopathy, he or she learned it after graduating veterinary college. To find a homeopathic veterinarian in your area, write the American Holistic Veterinary Association, 2214 Old Emmerton Road, Bel Air, Maryland 21015.

Examples of Homeopathic Treatments

It is beyond the scope of this book to expound on the science of homeopathic medicine. However, we can give you a few examples of natural treatments for some ailments. Traditional medicine also offers treatments for these, but consider the alternatives.

1. *Anemia:* Anemia is a low red blood cell count. Many times, this is a deficiency of iron in the diet. Foods rich in iron would include green leafy vegetables, meat, and liver. Instead of using medication to stimulate the bone marrow to produce more blood cells, give the body what it needs, and let it naturally produce them.

2. *Arthritis.* Arthritis is an inflammation of a joint. It can occur in an old dog or in a young dog with a congenital problem. The idea is to reduce the inflammation of the joint and by so doing reduce the pain. In a young puppy, reduce the amount of food given; this keeps the weight down and slows the rate of growth, which can alleviate some bone growth deformities. There are plants that have been shown to reduce joint inflammation, such as garlic, alfalfa, *Rhus Toxicodendron,* and *Ledum.*

3. *Vomiting.* Puppies are very prone to nausea and vomiting because they eat almost anything they can put in their mouths. Holistically speaking, there are a few remedies that tend to settle an upset stomach. First, withhold all food and water for 12 hours. To keep the puppy's mouth from drying out, leave out a bowl of ice cubes. Second, there are foods that are bland on the stomach and easy to digest. Some of them are white rice, boiled chicken, cottage cheese, yogurt, baby food strained meats, and crackers. These can be supplemented for dog food for two to three days while the stomach is returning to normal. Third, there are some natural herbs that have soothing effects on an upset stomach. They are ginger, peppermint, and ginseng. These are usually made into teas and drank. Reintroduce his puppy food gradually.

PET HEALTH INSURANCE

With the rising costs of high-tech veterinary services, the costs of pet health care are getting too much for many people to afford. People like the modern services that veterinarians can offer, like ultrasounds, CAT scans, bone scans, board certified specialists, intensive care units, and large referral centers, to name a few. But these high-tech procedures come with high price tags.

In human medicine, most of these procedures are covered by major medical health plans. Pets are not covered under any human health plan; in fact, only a few underwriters in the country insure pet ailments. Their plans cover major medical expenses and typically do not cover preventive, or wellness visits or vaccines—but they can help defray expenses nonetheless. Pick the plan that is best for your new puppy. All plans have a deductible, many have maximums per illness. Then there are the annual premiums—the amount of money you pay to the insurance company per pet. No plan pays 100 percent of the health costs. A plan may cover only 70 percent (which means there is a 30 percent copayment), and there are hidden catches such as preexisting conditions that may be excluded from coverage or birth defects, cosmetic surgery, any and all fertility-breeding and whelping costs, grooming, and vaccinations.

Here are a few guidelines to use when shopping for an insurance plan (taken from the American Veterinary Medical Association's [AVMA] policy statements and *Guidelines on Pet Health Insurance and Other Third Party Animal Health Plans*):

1. Pet owners should have the freedom to select a veterinarian of their choice.
2. Referrals should be allowed.
3. The policy should be accepted by the state insurance commissioner.
4. The policy should be licensed in the state in which it is sold.

Here are a few questions you should ask when shopping for a policy:

- How long has the company been insuring pet health care?
- Is the insurance carrier licensed for pet health?
- What is the annual deductible on the policy?
- What is the copayment (the portion the insured has to pay)?
- Will it cover any preexisting conditions?
- What is excluded from the policy—vaccines, wormings, well visits, heartworm tests, etc.?
- Are there certain diseases that aren't covered by the policy?
- What are the limits per illness, and are there annual caps?
- What is the premium payment? Is it paid all up front or monthly?
- What age can the puppy be covered?
- Can the policy be terminated by the carrier and for what reasons?
- Is there an upper age limit?
- Does the puppy need to go through an exam to sign up?

If your puppy is accident prone or sickly, it may be a very good idea to have him insured for accidents and illness. You may gladly pay the yearly premium instead of a stack of veterinary bills.

16

Fleas, Ticks, Worms, and Other Bugs

INTRODUCTION

This chapter is devoted to all the common "bugs" of puppies. We use the term loosely. We are really referring to the *parasites* of dogs. A parasite is an organism that lives on or in another living thing; in this case, your puppy. Some parasites live peacefully with their host, others do not, causing disease. Parasites are generally either bugs, worms, or protozoan microscopic organisms.

The good news is that most of these parasites are more of a nuisance than a real health concern. Don't be surprised if you start to find yourself itching while you read about some of these bugs. There are many days where our staff at the clinic all imagine we have bugs crawling on us after a long day of seeing fleas, ticks, or mange. I have actually gone home after a particularly "buggy" day and used a flea shampoo on myself!

FLEAS *(Ctenocephalides)*

All of us know how annoying these bugs are. They have been a nuisance to man for as long as there has been written history. The Egyptians were plagued with them and wrote about how to exterminate them in 1555 B.C. It was common throughout much of the world through the 19th century for people in all socio economic classes to be infested with fleas. These fleas are different from the ones that infest animals. All fleas can be seen with the naked eye. They're about the size of sesame seeds. They are brownish-red and run very fast. When off the dog, they can jump six feet in one hop. They stay on the surface of the skin and run through the fur. Your puppy picked them up by going outside in a grassy area or from another dog or cat who had them. Fleas have four stages in their 30-day life cycle: the egg, larvae, pupae, and adult, described below.

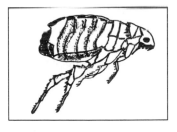

Diagram of an adult flea.

The *egg* is white, oval, and glossy. Most are laid on the pet and then fall off in the house, especially where the dog sleeps. A single female can lay about a dozen eggs per day. The eggs hatch in one to two weeks under the right temperature and humidity conditions (warm and humid).

The *larvae* emerge from the egg. These look like small worms. They stay in the rug or bedding or crawl under furniture, where it's dark, molting several times over weeks to months. The last stage of the larva spins a cocoon and is now called a pupa.

Pupae undergo changes in the cocoon that turn them into adult fleas. This process is quite variable and can take weeks to months. A mere vibration of the floor can stimulate the adult to hatch out of the cocoon, hungry for a host.

The *adults* are what most of us see on the dog. They bite and suck blood. They are like heat-seeking missiles, targeting any warm body. Their feces are black specks, called "flea dirt." If an owner doesn't actually see the adults on the dog, they usually see the black specks. Adult fleas can live for over a month under the right conditions.

Flea Allergy Dermatitis

Flea saliva is very irritating to most dogs, and often starts an allergic reaction. The dog develops red swellings and intense itching at the bite site. This causes the common biting and scratching owners report. Some dogs have such a violent reaction that they develop a secondary bacterial infection, lose their hair, and even resort to self-mutilation. We call this *Flea Allergy Dermatitis* (FAD).

As you can see from this life cycle, fleas reproduce very quickly. In fact, several adults can multiply to a couple thousand in one month! Your pets, house, and sometimes family members all become infected with these blood-sucking bugs. Fleas are commonly found on a dog's lower back near the base of the tail, between the legs, underside of the abdomen, and inner thighs. Occasionally, they will crawl to other areas, but they don't stay long. The common site for flea bites on people is the ankle.

These bugs not only cause itching and allergic dermatitis but also can carry disease. The dog flea can carry the tapeworm, *Dipylidium caninum*. Therefore, any puppy infested with fleas should be either tested or treated for tapeworms.

Treatment for fleas is twofold: the dog *and* its environment need to be treated. The reason is that treating only one will not break the life cycle, leading to an uninterrupted breeding cycle. *People who only treat the dog or the house will never get rid of their flea problem.*

Treating the Dog

There are so many ways to treat your puppy and so many types of flea products that it gets confusing. Here is a list of guidelines to follow:

1. Always follow the label directions on all flea products. Don't assume one product is like another.
2. Be careful to use products that are FDA approved for use in puppies.
3. Use the product only as often as the label says.
4. Be careful and follow all the hazard warning label instructions.
5. Treat all the animals in the house on the same day.
6. If you like to see a "quick kill" of the adult fleas, shampoos and dips work best. (It's so rewarding to see the little bugs wash down the drain!)
7. If your puppy isn't cooperative for a bath, use sprays. These don't require you to soak the animal with anything. Usually a gentle misting over the entire animal except the face is all that's needed. Rub the spray into the dog's coat. This gets it down to the skin where the fleas live.
8. Powders, collars, and mousses are all adjuncts to the above-mentioned techniques.
9. Permethrin oil pouches have proved very effective. They are easy to apply, longlasting, kill both fleas and ticks, and can be used with other products. Unfortunately, they are not for use on puppies under six months of age and can leave the coat a little greasy.
10. We recommend the use of insect growth regulators whenever possible to break the reproductive cycle of the adult fleas. There is a new once-a-month flea pill that uses an insect growth regulator that sterilizes the female flea.

To help you find and understand the flea-fighter that's best for your puppy, let's review their common ingredients. This information is relevant regardless of the brand.

1. *High-potency active ingredients:* Carbamates (carbaryl), organophosphates (chlorpyrifos, cythioate, diazanon, dichlorvos, fenvalerate, fenthion, methylcarbamate, butoxypropylene, piperonyl butoxide, malathion), and rotenone.
   - Very effective, with few fleas being resistant.
   - Kills adults only (except for chlorpyrifos, which can kill larvae).
   - These should not be used in puppies under 16 weeks old and used with caution in older puppies.

- Potentially toxic side effects include excess salivation, dilated pupils, muscle twitching, vomiting, and diarrhea. These should be treated promptly by a veterinarian.

2. *Moderate potency active ingredients:* Pyrethrin, microencapsulated pyrethrin, allethrin, synergized pyrethroids, and permethrin.
   - Kills adults only.
   - Some preparations can be used in puppies as young as eight weeks.
   - Mild and few side effects, which often resolve when product is washed off pet.
   - Very effective and generally safer than organophosphates, carbamates or rotenone.
   - Some insect resistance.
   - May need frequent applications due to instability under bright light (less so for the microencapsulated and pyrethroids forms).

3. *Mildest potency active ingredients:* Orange peel derivatives (D-limonene, Linalool).
   - Kills adults only.
   - Can be used on puppies as young as six weeks of age.
   - Mild and few side effects.
   - Modest efficacy, prolonged contact with the flea is needed to kill.

4. *Insect growth regulators:* Methoprene, Fenoxycarb.
   - Prevents the normal progression of the flea's life cycle. In effect, prevents the egg or larva from becoming an adult.
   - Safe for puppies as young as eight weeks old.
   - Safe and effective alternative or adjunct to insecticides.
   - Used very effectively with an adulticide for controlling recurrent flea infestations.
   - Unusual to see any insect resistance.

5. *Home remedies:* Brewer's yeast, garlic cloves, menthol, eucalyptus, citronella, herbal extracts.
   - More of a repellent than an insecticide.
   - Many people swear by these, although there is little scientific evidence they work.

- No toxicity—most are either food additives or botanicals.
- Can be used on young puppies six weeks old.

6. *Once-a-month flea pill* that sterilizes the female flea when she bites.

Flea-fighting products come in a variety of forms: shampoos, sprays, powders, collars, dips, pouches of oil and mousse foam. Each is briefly described below.

1. *Shampoo.* These are just like shampoos you'd use on yourself. The dog is wet then lathered with the shampoo. It is important to leave the shampoo on the dog for 10 minutes to assure it works. Always start lathering on the head and work your way to the tail. Be careful to keep the shampoo away from the eyes. A thorough rinsing is needed to wash out any soap residue. Remember, once the shampoo is rinsed out, there is no residual activity. This means the dog has no protection left on it.

2. *Sprays.* These are liquids that contain insecticides that are sprayed directly on the dog. They may have a water or alcohol base. Most of them dry quickly and have a strong chemical odor. Directions must be followed closely. Sprays usually last several days; they must be reapplied regularly.

3. *Powders.* These are body powders that have an insecticide. They are messy, and many dogs are allergic to them, sneezing for days after application. Powders need to be reapplied regularly.

4. *Collars.* These are neck collars that release an insecticide over time. Collars work best in small breeds, where there isn't much distance between the collar and the base of the tail, where fleas like to live. These have a definite life span, usually several months. People often forget how old the collar is and let it expire. Collars seem to work best when used with other flea products.

5. *Dips.* These are strong concentrates that are mixed with water and sponged on the dog but not rinsed out. Another name for these dips is "drench." When dry, a fine residual powder is left on the fur and usually lasts from two to four weeks. If you use a dip, you should not use any other insecticide products with it for fear of overdosing your dog and causing a toxicity. Be advised, very young, old, or sick dogs should not have dips.

6. *Oil pouches.* These are small pouches of permethrin oil that get applied to the skin of a dog's back. The fine oil spreads evenly over

the dog's body and stays on the skin for up to one month if it's not washed out.

7. *Mousse.* This is a foam spray that has an insecticide as an active ingredient. It is particularly useful when you cannot wet the animal's coat. This is like a dry shampoo. It's useful on the face, where other products may be awkward to apply near the eyes.

There are other products available, from electronic collars to oral insecticidal tablets where the insecticide gets into the dog's bloodstream and kills the flea when it bites. Our concern with the tablets is that there is a continual serum blood level of an organophosphate in a young, developing puppy. We do not recommend these products under normal circumstances, although we concede their merit under certain conditions, such as year-round flea problems in southern states.

Treating the House

As described earlier, there are many products available to kill fleas. The products designed for the house are not to be used on the dog because they contain active ingredients in too high a concentration to be safely used on pets. *Please refer to the earlier description of the products for further information on active ingredients.*

Home products are available in sprays, powders and foggers. The better products contain active ingredients to kill the adults as well as insect growth regulators. People can treat their own house or have the place professionally done by an exterminator.

The different forms of insecticide products for the premise are described below:

1. *Powders.* These are dusting powders that contain a variety of active ingredients to kill adult fleas. The product needs to be dusted over most of the floor, including under furniture. Carpets are targeted more than hardwood or tiled floors. These tend to be messy, and most owners vacuum up the powder because of the mess. People with allergies should be especially careful while using these products. Always follow the manufacturer's directions.

2. *Sprays.* These come as either pump, or "trigger," sprays or pressurized aerosols. They contain a variety of active ingredients to kill adult as well as preadult fleas. Long residuals are common. These are much less messy than powders, but there are fumes and a strong odor from most of them. People with allergies should be especially careful while using these products. Always follow the manufacturer's directions.

3. *Foggers*. These are cans of pressured insecticide that are set off in rooms that need treatment. They spew a fog of insecticide that fumigates every nook and cranny of a room. These are highly effective and usually contain adulticide as well as insect growth regulators. The drawbacks are that the house has to be vacated during the process and aired before you return. Also, most foggers' instructions require all counters where food is handled to be covered, due to the fine residue of insecticide that falls out. Birds, aquariums, and some plants also need to be removed from the house. As you can see, this is a more involved process than other products need. People with allergies should be especially careful while using foggers. Always follow the manufacturer's directions.

When doing your house:
1. Always follow the label directions on all flea products. Don't assume one product is like another.
2. Be careful to use products that are FDA approved for use in homes. Most labels will list the appropriate surfaces the product is safe to use on (drapes, upholstery, wood floors, rugs, etc.).
3. Use the product only as often as the label says.
4. Be careful and follow all the hazard warning label instructions.
5. Treat all rooms the dog goes in.
6. Start by vacuuming all the floors and carpets in the house. Make sure you vacuum under furniture and baseboards. Throw out the vacuum bag afterward so you're not harboring fleas in your vacuum.
7. Launder all pet bedding. This area is a favorite place for fleas to live and eggs to hatch. If laundering is not possible, throw it out.
8. Remove all small items from the room, like plants, baskets, towel racks, pillows, and so forth. The fewer items, the better the product can infiltrate.
9. Use products that contain both an adulticide and an insect growth regulator. We want to kill both the adults and the eggs! Otherwise, you'll need to do everything again in three or four weeks.
10. Exterminate when pets, people, and kids are out of the house. The pets should be treated for fleas at the same time, either outside or at your veterinarian's office or groomer.
11. Leave enough time for the process. It doesn't pay to rush the procedure. Remember, if you forget a step or don't cover the entire area, you'll only have to repeat the process again.

12. Because veterinarians are professionals in flea control, consult with one. They are happy to help you with your flea problem, and many have their own system for flea control, including the necessary products.

What Went Wrong?

The most common reasons for failure in treating a flea problem are:

1. Treatment of the pets was not done *at the same time* as the house.
2. Treatment of *all furry pets* in the house, especially cats, must be done *at the same time*.
3. Ineffective products were used, perhaps due to resistance of the flea to the active ingredient.
4. Not enough product was used to effectively kill the fleas. *Follow directions!*
5. Furniture was not moved when applying a product for the house. You must get under all furniture.
6. When treating the dog, get into every crevice of the animal (except the eyes)—between toes, behind ears, under tail, and between legs. These are some of the fleas' favorite hiding places.
7. A product was used that didn't contain an insect growth regulator, so only adults were killed. All those eggs in the rug and floor crevices are still going to hatch.
8. The product was outdated. Check for expiration dates.
9. You forgot to throw away the vacuum bag after vacuuming for fleas. In effect, you made a flea hotel in your vacuum.

TICKS

Ticks are small, wingless insects that normally live outdoors. They vary in size from a poppy seed to a large grape, depending on the stage, species, and state of engorgement (how much blood they've consumed), and they come in two varieties, hard and soft. The ticks that parasitize dogs are hard. This means that there is a shield (called a *scutum*) to protect the body. There are four stages in the tick life cycle:

Diagram of an adult tick.

Eggs are laid by females in a single batch of thousands. Egg laying is done in the environment, not on the host. The eggs hatch into larvae in several weeks. The larvae then look for a host to feed on, usually the first warm-blooded animal who walks by.

The *larvae* hatch from the eggs and find a warm-blooded host, either a wild or domestic animal. It feeds once for several days, then drops off into the environment and molts into a nymph stage tick. In tick-borne diseases, the larva doesn't carry the disease.

The *nymph* stage also needs to feed on a warm-blooded host. After a few days of molting, the new nymph is ready to hitch a ride and grab a meal. After feeding for about a week, it drops off again to molt. This process can take months, but once it's done, an adult is the product. In tick-borne diseases, the nymph can carry the disease.

As you can see, the *adult* tick is the result of a very lengthy process that involves months, three moltings, and lots of cooperation from three different hosts! Adult ticks can live for nearly two years. They carry tick-borne diseases like Rocky Mountain spotted fever and Lyme disease.

Ticks are often found in certain locales or in pockets. One neighborhood may be crawling with them, while the adjacent area may be devoid. Why? These insects thrive in certain environmental conditions, namely, damp and shady areas. Sunny pastures or dry land may not be able to sustain their life cycle. Wooded, grassy, and thickly settled land with shrubs are perfect areas to find ticks.

Ticks are natural climbers. This means that once on a dog, they climb upwards until they reach the head and neck (unless they get lost on the way, which sometimes happens). This explains why most ticks are found on the head, especially the ears.

Once the tick settles into a comfortable spot, it "bites" the dog. This involves inserting its barbed, long nose into the dog's skin to feed. The barbs make the apparatus much like a fishhook, which makes removing these tenacious little bugs very difficult.

Removing a Tick

All dog owners are faced with removing a tick from their dog from time to time unless the dog never leaves an urban surrounding. The technique we use in the clinic is to "stun" the tick with rubbing alcohol (unless it's near the eyes, in which case we use mineral oil). This process involves soaking a cotton swab with rubbing alcohol and placing it on the tick for 30 to 60 seconds. This application disrupts the tick and often causes it to start backing out of the dog—but remember those barbs. These ticks don't just let go. They need to be pulled out, which takes some force. Grasp the head of the tick as close as possible to the skin. You may need to use tweezers for this procedure. Give a quick twist and

Removing a tick with tweezers.

pull to remove the tick. What often happens is the barbed probe breaks off and is left in the skin. We call this "leaving the head in." Not to worry. The small black spot is like a splinter and usually works itself out on it's own. Remember, because of the barbs, you can't just pull the tick out like a splinter. You'd actually have to cut it out to remove it.

Most vets and dog owners don't go through all that for a tick. And despite popular belief, the head does *not* grow into a new tick. The remaining bump left from the tick bite should be cleaned with a topical antiseptic. An antibiotic ointment should be applied twice daily for a week to prevent infection. Try not to overhandle the tick so it doesn't break in your hand.

Tick Prevention

The best way to prevent tick bites is to keep your puppy inside. This is impractical for most of us outdoor-loving people. But you can keep them out of heavily wooded areas and tall, grassy fields. Here are some other tips:

- Avoid wooded areas and fields you think wild animals inhabit.
- Apply a tick and insect repellent to your puppy before taking him outdoors.
- Wear light-colored clothing so it's easier to see ticks. Wear white socks and tuck your pants into them. Remember, ticks grab onto you and your puppy's legs as you walk by.
- Inspect yourself and your puppy after each outside walk.

Tick Products

Most of the information about flea products pertains to ticks as well. But not all. You must read labels. If a product is approved by the FDA for ticks, it will say so on the label. Most products have a minimum age requirement. Generally speaking, the stronger the active ingredient, the older the puppy has to be for it—up to six months old in some cases.

Diseases That Ticks Carry

Ticks can be vectors (carriers) of disease. Not all diseases are in all areas of the country. Below is a list of the three common tick-borne diseases in the United States, with a brief description.

Rocky Mountain Spotted Fever (RMSF)

This is a rickettsial disease caused by the *Rickettsia rickettsii* organism. The vector is the *Dermacentor* tick. Only certain areas of the United States have this disease, most notably the southeast, though it has been reported as far north as Long Island, New York.

When a dog is bitten by a tick that carries the RMSF, the symptoms ensue within two weeks. The organism causes a disturbance in blood clotting, leading to internal and subcutaneous (under the skin) bleeding. A rash develops, along with fever, vomiting and diarrhea, bloody urine and feces, nose bleeds and respiratory difficulty. Neurological signs such as seizures have been reported. A diagnosis is made by observing the clinical signs, finding a low platelet count on a complete blood count and seeing a high positive result on the RMSF titer blood test. Treatment generally consists of several weeks of antibiotics, usually of the tetracycline family.

Canine Ehrlichiosis

This is another tick-borne disease. Like Rocky Mountain spotted fever, the organism in ehrlichiosis is a rickettsial organism, namely *Ehrlichia canis*. The vector is a *Rhipicephalus* tick. Affected dogs develop a severe anemia, edema of the extremities, and bleeding disorders. The white blood cells of these dogs are invaded by the organism and are rendered defective. There is a profound deficiency of *thrombocytes* (platelet cells responsible for blood clotting), which leads to excessive bleeding. The invading organism is often seen by the veterinarian on a blood smear. Treatment is the same as for RMSF above.

Lyme Disease (Borreliosis)

Lyme disease was first reported in Lyme, Connecticut, in 1977. This disease originally was thought to affect only people. We have since learned it can affect most mammals. It is caused by the spirochete, *Borrelia burgdorferi*, a corkscrew-shaped bacteria.

The natural host of the spirochete is the deer tick. This tick lives outdoors in grassy and wooded areas. The adults normally attach and feed from wild animals, especially the white-tailed deer. The nymphs are about the size of a poppy seed and peak between May and July. Latest reports show that about 25 percent of nymph deer ticks and about 50 percent of the adults carry the Lyme

The deer tick in its various stages: from left to right, larva, nymph, adult female, adult male.

disease. It generally takes 24 to 48 hours of feeding on the host for the tick to transmit the disease. By early autumn, the nymphs molt again into adults. Adults generally live for two years.

Exposure to the ticks is through brushing up against grass, shrubs, tree branches, and other vegetation that harbor the insects. They literally wait for a warm-blooded creature to walk by, and they climb onto the animal or person, toward the head, then "bite" or attach themselves to the skin. Staying out of woods and grassy pastures dramatically cuts down on exposure. Since it takes 24 to 48 hours to pass the Lyme disease to you from an infected tick, pulling them out shortly after attachment prevents Lyme disease. Use of insect repellents such as tick sprays, collars, dips and powders will also discourage the tick from attaching itself to you or your pet.

Symptoms of Lyme disease in animals are very similar to those in people, and include:

- fever
- loss of appetite
- swollen, aching joints
- general body aching
- lameness

Loss of appetite is due to the fever. The spirochete gets into the joints, where it stimulates an inflammatory reaction. There can be permanent damage to the joint surfaces, leading to chronic arthritis. It can take weeks to months for an exposure to incubate into disease and symptoms. The classic "bull's-eye" rash, often seen in people, is not reliable in animals, and most tick bites (regardless whether or not there is Lyme disease) leave a raised lump for days at the site of attachment. Therefore, the most reliable indicator of disease is either clinical symptoms or a continually rising Lyme titer blood test.

If left untreated, Lyme disease can progress to life-threatening cardiac, neurologic or renal (kidney) failure.

Diagnosing Lyme Disease

Diagnosis is made by putting together the patient history ("Our puppy is always in the woods") and clinical presentation. We also take a Lyme titer, which is a quantitative measure of the animal's immunity, or antibody level, to a particular disease. One titer result is not always enough to make a diagnosis; I like to run two or even three to follow a trend in the numbers.

There is some discussion about the accuracy of these tests. There is a low percentage of "false negatives," which means that the titer may come back negative despite the presence of Lyme in the animal's system. This is usually because there is a window of about four to six weeks after exposure when the titer is on its way up but is not into a positive range yet. Taking another test four weeks later will often reveal that the titer has risen into the positive range. Another confusing factor is that many dogs who are seropositive (meaning they have a positive titer test) are not sick and show no symptoms (and may never). Finally, there can be cross-reactivity of antibodies with other bacteria. This means that the titer blood test is not 100 percent specific to the *B. burgdorferi*. These are called "false positives."

One recent advance is a titer test called the Western Blot test, which can differentiate between antibodies from an actual infection of Lyme disease and antibodies from the Lyme vaccine. This becomes very useful when testing a dog that received the *Borrella* vaccine.

There are Lyme vaccines available on the market. They boast between 80-93 percent efficacy. They are killed vaccines and cannot give your puppy Lyme disease. Since they are relatively new, there is still some question as to their protection and safety. The vaccines appear safe, but common sense says that the vaccine should be used in Lyme-endemic areas, where there is a real threat of contracting the disease. Our protocol is to test each puppy's titer before vaccination. If the puppy is positive, we treat it first, recheck the titer in one month, then vaccinate if negative. The reason we don't vaccinate seropositive dogs is that many of the symptoms of Lyme disease come from the body's own immune response to the spirochete. This is in the form of inflammation of the joints and tissues of the kidney, where the spirochete invades.

When a vaccine is administered, it boosts immunity to the disease by stimulating the dog's immune system in making antibodies to the organism. The antibodies, Lyme spirochete, and other immune process complements can combine to cause inflammation in the tissues. We call this an immune complex reaction. Although these antibodies are different from the antibodies seen in a natural infection, there may be some cross-reactivity. It has been postulated that in a small group of dogs with a positive titer but no symptoms, the vaccine may cause Lyme-like symptoms through an immune complex reaction and an autoimmune arthritis. To date, there is only partial research data on this, and much further work needs to be done.

WORMS

Unlike external parasites, internal ones can cause severe disease and even death if left untreated. Imagine dozens of spaghetti-sized worms that are clogging up your heart valves, as is the case in canine heartworm disease. That's how dangerous some of these internal parasites can be. Puppies are particularly susceptible to internal parasitism. In fact, many of the intestinal worms of puppies are transferred from the mother.

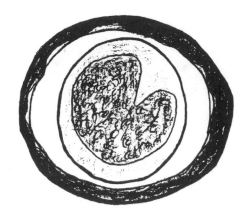

Roundworms (*Ascariasis*)

Roundworms live inside the host and measure from 4 to 20 cm in length. The larvae go through four different molting phases to reach the adult. Each larva has a specific place it lives in the body. Most of the larvae are migratory, which means they don't stay in one place very long. Adult worms settle in the small intestine, where they feed on ingested food, robbing the host of nutrition. The

A diagram of the roundworm egg (top) and photo of an adult roundworm.

roundworms that infect dogs are of the genus *Toxocara* or *Toxascaris*. Let's look at the complicated life cycle of the dog roundworm:

Adults lay eggs in the intestines; newly hatched larvae burrow through the intestinal wall and enter the blood stream that goes to the liver; the larvae wander through the liver, then enter the blood stream that flows through the heart and pulmonary arteries to enter the lungs; larvae then migrate through the bronchi and are coughed up the trachea; once coughed up, they are swallowed and complete their development in the stomach and small intestines where it starts all over again.

Just imagine the havoc and damage done from several dozen of these migrating larvae! In pregnant bitches, some of the larvae make their way to the placenta, where they affect the developing fetuses and invade the mammary tissue so that they are ingested by the suckling pups. In this way, these worms can infect a litter of puppies either in utero (in the uterus) or by shedding larvae in the milk of the bitch.

Adult dogs can harbor these larvae in their tissues for years. The larvae are difficult to exterminate because they are mostly resistant to the drugs used to worm dogs. Therefore, litter after litter, a bitch can whelp puppies with roundworms even though the bitch was wormed several times with standard worming drugs.

The symptoms of a roundworm infestation in a puppy are:

- abdominal bloating
- excess gas production
- foul-smelling, loose diarrhea
- bloody stools
- thin, emaciated puppies
- a chronic cough
- poor, dry coat
- insatiable appetite
- passing adult worms in vomit or feces
- chronic poor doer
- inflammation of the inside eye

Control of Roundworms

The most common roundworm wormers are Piperazine and Pyrantel pamoate. These drugs are given orally and *only kill the mature adult worms*, so two wormings are needed three weeks apart (that's how long it takes larvae to become adults) to rid a puppy of a complete cycle.

Prevention of roundworms involves cleaning up after the puppies often to reduce fecal contamination of the premise. Remember there are worm eggs shed in the feces, which after several days become infective to all dogs. Worming of all the puppies, starting as young as two to three weeks and again three weeks later, will lower the chance of your puppy's having worms. Ask your breeder whether your puppy was wormed in this fashion.

Some breeders only have a chance to worm their litter once before selling the puppies. In this case, your vet will have to complete the worming. Have your veterinarian run fecal exams at each visit until the puppy is 16 weeks old because not all worms show up on the first or even second fecal exam.

Hookworms

The hookworm that infects dogs is called *Ancylostoma caninum*. It got its name from the three hooklike teeth it uses to anchor itself to the gut lining. These worms don't just rob their host of food and nutrition like the roundworms, they suck blood—a lot of it. Puppies with a heavy infestation can die from anemia (loss of red blood cells). These worms are very small (measuring only millimeters in length), very prolific, and congregate in large numbers. Their life cycle is described below.

Adult hookworms in the small intestine lay eggs in the gut; these pass out into the environment through the feces; the feces can infect puppies orally, or larvae hatch from the eggs and burrow through the skin of a puppy. If the egg was ingested, the larvae develop in the intestines; if the larva entered through the skin, it migrates into the

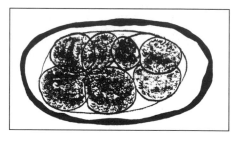

A diagram of the hookworm egg.

bloodstream and ends up in the lungs. There it goes into the trachea, gets coughed up, swallowed, and the larva then matures and infects the intestines.

There are four common ways a puppy can become infected with hookworms.

1. From eating feces infected with hookworm eggs.
2. A dam bitch can infect her fetuses in utero if she's infected herself.
3. The dam sheds hookworm larvae in her milk. The puppies become infected by nursing.
4. Third-stage larvae can actually burrow through the tender skin of young puppies, infecting them through this dermal route.

As with roundworms, adult dogs can harbor hookworm larvae in their tissues for years. They can be equally difficult to eliminate.

Symptoms of a hookworm infestation are similar to those for roundworms but also include anemia with pale mucus membranes and insatiable appetite.

Clean up after the puppies often to reduce fecal contamination of the premise. Remember, worm eggs are shed in the feces, which after several days becomes infective to all dogs. Also, the hookworm larvae can burrow into tender puppy skin if the puppy is allowed to walk through infected feces or contaminated soil. Worming of all the puppies by the breeder, starting as young as two to three weeks and again three weeks later, will lower the chance of your puppy's having worms. Ask your breeder if your puppy was wormed in this way. Hookworm larvae have been known to burrow through human skin as well!

Whipworms

Whipworms are small worms shaped like a whip or riding crop that live in the large intestines and colon of dogs. They are approximately five centimeters long and very thin. The scientific name for whipworms is *Trichuris vulpis*. These worms attach themselves to the inner lining of the

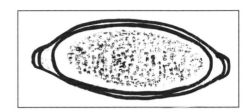

A diagram of a whipworm egg.

colon, where they feed. Their life cycle is very simple and direct compared with roundworm or hookworms.

Adult whipworms lay eggs while attached in the colon. Larvae develop within the eggs and hatch in two weeks. These larvae attach to the inner lining and take another week to develop into adults. Within two to three months, they start laying eggs.

The only way a puppy can become infected is to eat whipworm eggs in contaminated feces. You may think this is unlikely, but remember puppies will eat anything. There is no infection during pregnancy or through the milk, as we see in roundworms and hookworms.

The symptoms for whipworms all stem from the colitis (inflammation of the colon) caused by the feeding adult worms. The most common ones are:

- abdominal bloating and cramping
- excess gas production
- foul-smelling, loose diarrhea
- bloody or mucus-coated stools
- thin, emaciated puppies
- poor, dry coat
- insatiable appetite
- chronic poor doer

Control of Whipworms

Whipworms are treated by administering anthelmintic drugs (wormers). The most popular drug used now is Fenbendazole, which comes as a powder. The powder is mixed in the food of the puppy and given for three consecutive days. Due to the two- to three-month life cycle of the whipworm, a new crop of larvae hatch during that interval. Since there is some question about whether the larvae are killed along with the adults, many veterinarians repeat the worming in that interval.

Tapeworms

These are perhaps the most notorious of all internal worms, probably because they are the most visible. These are flat, white, ribbon-like worms that live in the small intestines of many animals, including dogs. Adult tapeworms are segmented and can measure several feet long because there are hundreds of segments attached in a row. There are two different tapeworms that infect dogs: *Dipylidium caninum and Taenia.* The head of the adult tapeworm is a club-

A diagram of a tapeworm egg.

shaped anchor with hooks, which attaches to the inner lining of the small intestine.

The tapeworm life cycle always involves an intermediate host (another creature). In the case of *Dipylidium caninum*, it is the common dog and cat flea; in *Taenia,* rodents and rabbits. The life cycle is described below.

The head of the adult tapeworm makes segments. Each segment is an independent functioning unit that contains packets of eggs. Each segment breaks off one by one and wiggles its way out the anus or comes out in the stool. The segments break and release eggs, which fleas, rodents and rabbits may feed on. Once inside the intermediate host, the eggs hatch, and a larval tapeworm invades the tissues of the insect or animal. The dog becomes infected by eating a contaminated rodent or rabbit (in the case of *Taenia*) or swallowing a contaminated flea, often while grooming itself (in the case of *Dipylidium caninum*). The larvae invade the small intestines of the dog where they develop into adults.

The symptoms of tapeworm infection are:

• weight loss in spite of a voracious appetite
• rectal itching

- observing the small, white, grainlike segments in stool or around rectum
- occasional mild abdominal and digestive upsets

Control of Tapeworms

The key to controlling tapeworms is to eliminate the intermediate host from the picture. In the case of *Taenia* tapeworms, the dog must be kept from eating small wild animals; in the case of *Dipylidium caninum*, you must rid the dog of its flea infestation. This is guaranteed to work, but you may need to continue treatment for one month after ridding the dog of fleas. Treating dogs with tapeworms requires only one dose of a specially formulated drug.

Heartworm Disease

Heartworm is a cardiovascular parasite: Instead of living in the intestines like the worms described so far, this one lives in the chambers of the heart and in the blood vessels of the lungs. The parasite that causes heartworm is *Dirofilaria immitis*. This worm is spread through the bite of mosquitoes.

The life cycle of heartworm involves an intermediate host, namely, the mosquito. As with all worms, there are adult and larval forms, each one following its own path. The life cycle is described below.

The common mosquito bites a dog who has heartworm disease. The mosquito feeds on blood from the dog and becomes infected with the young larvae circulating in the bloodstream, called *microfilariae*. These microfilariae enter the mosquito's digestive tract, molt twice and migrate to the salivary glands as a third-stage larva. When the mosquito bites another dog, it injects this third-stage larva into the subcutaneous tissues; from there, the larvae molt into fourth-stage larvae and stay in the tissues for about four to five months. The final molt produces the fifth-stage larvae, which migrate into the right side of the heart and pulmonary arteries where after another month, they mature into adults. The adults begin producing microfilariae in two to three months.

It takes about six months from the time a dog is infected with the third-stage larvae until adults appear. Only once the adults are present can they reproduce and make microfilariae. The adult worms can grow up to several inches in length and look very much like spaghetti. As you can see from the life cycle, outdoor dogs, especially those that spend time near wetlands where mosquitoes breed, are more likely to contract heartworm disease than indoor dogs.

Most of the symptoms of heart-worm disease stem from adults clogging the heart and lungs. Please note that symptoms don't usually begin for several months to three years after infection because it takes this long for the adults to occupy the heart and start causing congestive heart failure and obstructive pulmonary disease.

Common symptoms are:

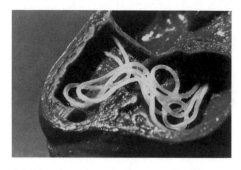

Adult heartworms can grow several inches in length and look like spaghetti (as in this model).

- a chronic, persistent cough
- general body weakness
- weight loss
- exercise intolerance
- fluid accumulation in the liver and abdomen
- dilated pulmonary blood vessels
- venous dilation and congestion
- kidney disease

Control of Heartworm Disease

This disease is much easier to prevent than it is to treat. We recommend that all puppies get put on a heartworm prevention medication as young as eight weeks of age. *All adult dogs must be tested negative for heartworm prior to being given any type of heartworm prevention.*

There are two types of heartworm prevention medications: ones that need to be given daily, and ones that are given monthly.

Daily medications only kill the third-stage infective larvae, which are injected into the dog by the mosquito. Since the third-stage larvae can molt into fourth-stage larvae within one day, the medication must be given daily to work. The main ingredient, Diethylcarbamazine, is effective and safe for use in puppies. One word of caution: If a dog with heartworm disease and circulating microfilariae is given diethylcarbamazine, many of the microfilariae will die, causing a sudden antigen overload. This can precipitate a fatal shock.

Monthly medications kill the third- through fifth-stage larvae, killing them before they can mature into adults, thus preventing heartworm disease. There are two different active ingredients, ivermectin and milbemycin oxime. Milbemycin oxime has been shown to also kill other internal parasites, such as adult roundworms, hookworms, and whipworms.

Many people like the daily medication because it's cheaper and has been used for many years, while others prefer the monthly medication because of its convenience and broad-spectrum features. Regardless of the type of prevention used, there are a few guidelines to remember:

- It is preferable to keep your puppy on heartworm prevention year round, especially if you live in a warm climate where mosquitoes are out continually.
- If your puppy is on heartworm prevention year round, he should still have an annual heartworm test.
- If you live in a climate that has winters that eliminate the mosquitoes, you can stop the prevention two months after the first hard frost and restart one month before the first mosquito appears. Remember, you must test for heartworm before restarting.
- If you skip more than a week of daily heartworm prevention or more than 30 days of the monthly heartworm prevention, your puppy should be tested before restarting.
- Because all heartworm preventives are dosed according to the weight of your puppy, if you have a breed that is growing quickly and changing its weight every week, it may be wise to start the puppy on a chewable daily prevention that is easy to dose until his weight stabilizes, then switch to a monthly one. This switch must be done within 30 days of stopping the daily prevention.

In the unfortunate event of your puppy contracting heartworm disease, an early diagnosis is crucial for a favorable outcome. For this reason an annual heartworm test is recommended (if you don't use a preventive on your puppy, it is crucial to have him tested twice a year). Once the diagnosis is made, your veterinarian will discuss treatment options. Treatment is slow and dangerous. Prevention is a much safer option.

Worms that Pose a Public Health Hazard

Roundworms. Roundworms can infect people, especially children. The mode of transmission is fecal-oral, which means the person or child has to put infected dog feces or fecal-contaminated soil into their mouth. A horrifying thought, but young children do these things, and adults sometimes forget to wash their hands after cleaning up after the puppy.

Once the larvae hatch in a person's stomach and small intestine, they migrate to strange places like the liver, kidney, brain, and eye. Just from their presence, damage to these sites is common. All families with young children who have a puppy with roundworms should consult their physicians.

Hookworms. Like roundworms, hookworms pose a threat to people, especially children. Hookworm larvae can burrow through tender foot skin, so if children run barefoot through a hookworm-contaminated yard, they risk the larvae invading their skin.

Hookworm larvae migrate through the skin, causing red, raised, serpentine eruptions that are intensely itchy—you can actually see the worms under the skin! Fortunately, the skin is as far as they get. If either your dog or your cat is infected with hookworms and you have young children, make sure they wear shoes outside!

Whipworms. Neither people nor cats get whipworms.

Tapeworms. The tapeworms that infest dogs pose few health hazards for people. A couple of cases have been reported in children who ate fleas off their pets; luckily, there was no disease or pathology caused by this. However, there is a tapeworm that can seriously affect people. It's the *Echinococcus* tapeworm, and its larvae can cause large, tumor-like cysts in people's liver, lungs and brain. This tapeworm's intermediate host is sheep; therefore, people who have sheep should be very careful not to let their dogs eat any raw lamb meat nor should they consume it themselves.

MITES, LICE, AND MANGE

Ear Mites

Mites are microscopic bugs that feed on the outer layers of the skin (epidermis). They live for two months and have a three-week life cycle. They inhabit the surface of the ear canal and do not burrow in the skin. Before treating for them, the mites should be identified because this disease mimics other types of ear infections.

Symptoms are intense itching of the ears, shaking of the head, constant scratching of the ears, a dark brown waxy discharge that looks like "coffee grounds," and crusting and flaking of the upper ear canal. Occasionally, the incessant scratching may cause bleeding of the outer ear.

Treatment consists of a thorough cleaning of the ear canals with a wash that loosens wax. Since most of the waxy debris is deep in the ear canal, cleaning usually means flushing it out. This should be done by a veterinarian. If it is done too vigorously, you run the risk of rupturing the eardrum. Once the ears are clean, an ear mite preparation is put into the ear

It is generally thought that mites don't inhabit the house or infect people. However, under certain conditions these mites can live in the house and cause an allergy in people similar to that of house mites. Therefore, ear mites should be considered a minor human health hazard.

Lice (Pediculosis)

Lice are small insects measuring only two millimeters in length that live on the hair shafts. They literally cling to the hair with their claws. They spend their entire life cycle on the host, feeding on the flaking outer layer of skin (epidermis) or by sucking blood. Lice lay their eggs on hair, firmly cementing them to the hair shaft. The eggs look like small white dots.

Symptoms of lice are intense itching and scratching with hair loss. If there is a heavy infestation of the blood-sucking type, there can be an anemia from the blood loss. These signs can be mistaken for other skin diseases. Your veterinarian can differentiate these similar but different diseases.

Treatment is fairly easy. Most of the products made to kill fleas and ticks also kill lice. Pyrethrin is well suited for this. If there are mats of hair, they should be shaved before shampoos or dips. All grooming tools should be washed in a pyrethrin-based solution to kill any that linger. All other dogs that have touched the patient should be tested for lice. Any dog suffering from anemia should be treated with iron supplements.

These lice are very host specific and do not cross species. This means that human lice stay on people, and dog lice stay on dogs. Dog lice are not contagious to people and visa versa.

Mange Mites (Cheyletiella or "Walking Dandruff," Demodectic and Sarcoptic)

Mange mites are similar to the ear mites described earlier. The difference is that mange mites don't live in the ears. Each of the three distinct manges described are very different in some aspects but similar in others. All three are caused by mange mites and live in or on the skin. All three are common in young puppies and cause intense itching and skin disease. All three are diagnosed the same way (by a veterinarian performing a skin scraping and identifying the mite under a microscope). They differ in the prognosis, severity, treatment and human health hazards.

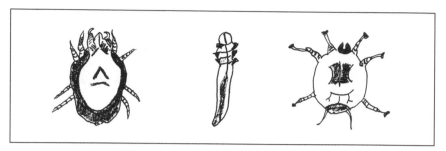

The mange mites, from left to right, chyletiella, demodex, and sarcoptes.

Cheyletiella, or "Walking Dandruff"

This mange is caused by *Cheyletiella* mites, which live on the surface of the skin. They crawl and creep along the back spine, leaving a bad case of dandruff in their wake. Cheyletiella are large compared with other mites, but you still can't see them with the naked eye. They are not as host-specific as lice and can be shared between dogs, cats, rabbits, and occasionally people. These bugs don't suck blood, but they do live off the fluids of the skin. They spend their entire life on the dog; they do not inhabit the house.

The most noticeable symptom is an intensely itchy case of dandruff along the dog's back—so severe that regular shampooing will not control it. Simply put, this is an itchy dandruff that won't quit.

Once diagnosis of *Cheyletiella* is made, treatment is started immediately. These bugs are easy to kill using pyrethrin-based flea and tick preparations. A thorough shampooing and a complete cleaning or fumigation of the dog's bedding and sleeping quarters are essential. Do these every week for two to three weeks. Powders and sprays work well too but are messy.

This mite can infect people, causing very itchy red bites that drain fluid and leave a yellow-crusted lesion. The infections are usually self-limiting and may resolve in three to four weeks. People who suspect this in themselves should consult a dermatologist for treatment options.

Demodectic Mange

This mange is caused by the *Demodex* mite, a cigar-shaped mite that lives in the hair follicles. These mites are normally present on all dogs and many other animals. However, when they overpopulate, they cause a severe dermatitis. These mites are transferred by the dam to the puppies shortly after birth via nursing. In a normal puppy, these mites will be kept to low numbers by a normal-functioning immune system. Puppies that are stressed, burdened with parasites, underweight, sick with other illness, or immunosuppressed will be more likely to get this mange. It is not contagious to people and is barely contagious to other normal adult dogs. Luckily, these bugs cannot live off the host, so they don't infect the house. There are two forms of demodectic mange: localized and generalized.

Localized Demodex

This means the mange is confined to a small area, usually around the face, head and legs. It results in patches of itchy, bald, red, raised skin. The lesions often start at three months of age.

Treatment usually involves daily application of a rotenone ointment to the lesion. Interestingly, if no treatment is done, most cases resolve on their own because the puppy's immune system matures, usually by six months. Prognosis is fair to good.

Generalized Demodex

Generalized Demodex is much more widespread on the body, covering large patches of the head and neck, chest, flank, and abdomen. It may start as localized but quickly spread. There is such a severe inflammatory response that the dog may run a fever and have enlarged lymph nodes. There is often a secondary bacterial infection. The overpopulation of mites grows out of the hair follicle and into the surrounding dermis (deeper layer of the skin). This in turn causes abscesses, at which point the disease is lifethreatening and carries a poor prognosis.

Generalized demodex is much more difficult to treat. Because as much as 50 percent of the body may be involved, we use dips to cover the entire dog. This must be done by a veterinarian, not a groomer, because this dip is a strong chemical. The dog is dipped every other week, for three to four treatments. Due to the secondary bacterial infection, the use of antibiotics formulated for skin usage may be needed. Some veterinarians are tempted to use strong anti-inflammatory drugs such as cortisone to relieve the itch and pain. This should be avoided at all cost because cortisone will lower the dog's already faltering immune system and make matters worse. Short-coated breeds appear to have a predisposition for generalized demodex.

Sarcoptic Mange

Sarcoptic mange, also known as *scabies*, look like little crabs under the microscope. They live by burrowing in the upper layers of the skin, where they lay

their eggs and make tunnels. The life
cycle is three weeks. The areas of the
body most often affected are the legs,
tail, underside of abdomen, and head.

Symptoms are an inexhaustible,
intense itch that spreads. The skin
becomes inflamed, red and crusty and
the hair falls out. From the incessant
itch, the dog invariably scratches
constantly, which leads to open sores
and secondary bacterial infection. To
watch this process, one would think

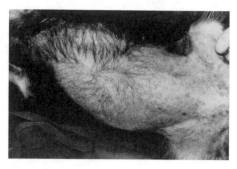

This dog has sarcoptic mange on its abdomen.

the dog is literally being consumed by something. A veterinarian who has seen
this often enough will come to recognize a certain odor from the skin. In our
clinic, we say the dog smells "mangy." But the illusive nature of this mite makes
it particularly difficult to diagnose. One report states that mites are only found
in 50 percent of the cases. If a veterinarian even suspects this disease, treatment
should be started even without actually finding the mites on a skin scraping.

Treatment used to be dips of a lime-sulfur shampoo that smells like rotten
eggs and stinks up an entire clinic for a day or two. Treatment of choice now is
two injections two weeks apart of the Ivermectin anthelmintic. Although this
drug is not yet approved by the FDA for this purpose, it is widely used in small-
animal medicine as well as in laboratory animals. It is effective for most mange.
Luckily, these bugs cannot live off the host, so they don't infect the house. Anyone who touches the patient is at risk of getting it. Generally, these mites don't
like human hosts (we don't have enough hair for them), and most human
cases spontaneously resolve without treatment within four weeks of the dog's
being treated.

The Mange Mites

Mite Name	Symptoms	Diagnosis	Treatment	Human Hazard
Cheyletiella	Excess flaking	Skin scraping	Pyrethrin dips	YES
Demodectic	Itching, bald spots	Skin scraping	Goodwinol or Mitaban dips	NO
Sarcoptic	Intense itch, yellow crusts	Skin scraping,	lime-sulfur dip Ivermectin inj.	YES

OTHER BUGS: COCCIDIA AND GIARDIA

Coccidia

These are a form of Protozoan, one celled microscopic organisms, most of which are free-living, meaning that they are not parasitic. Coccidia, however, are parasitic. They are also specie specific. The genus of coccidia that infects dogs is *Isospora.*

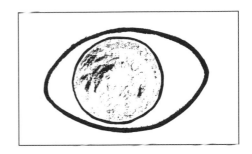

A coccidia egg.

The life cycle of coccidia is relatively complex, but dogs get it via oral contamination with feces from infected animals.

Coccidia invade and destroy intestinal epithelial cells, causing an inflammation of the intestinal lining called enteritis. Puppies most susceptible to coccidia are those under stress (shipping, overcrowding, pet shops, etc.). Symptoms are loose, watery or bloody stools, vomiting, malnutrition, abdominal bloating, weight loss, and straining to defecate.

Control of Coccidia

Not all animals with coccidia are symptomatic; they are called carriers. If the dam bitch is a carrier, all the puppies in her litter will be exposed. Control of this disease involves identifying all carrier animals in a kennel or household, cleaning up all infected feces and treating all infected dogs. Treatment is very easy and effective with the right antibiotics.

Giardia

Giardia canis is another protozoan that infects dogs. These one-celled organisms are free-living in outdoor water sources, such as ponds, streams and brooks. What's different about these protozoa is they have a whiplike tail (flagella) to propel them. When these *giardia* are free-living outdoors, they cause no harm, but when a dog becomes infected by ingesting outdoor water or feces of animals that contain the infective cyst, they cause intestinal disease.

The various and sometimes nebulous symptoms of *giardia* infections are chronic and persistent diarrhea; loose and mucus-coated stools; abdominal bloating weight loss; and chronic listlessness.

Control of Giardia

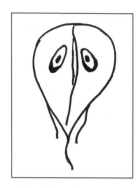

A giardia protozoa.

The best way to control *giardia* is to limit exposure to outside water sources. This is clearly difficult if your dog swims. Bring clean drinking water on your outings so your puppy has the choice of drinking that when he gets thirsty. The other way to avoid contracting this disease is to keep your puppy from eating wild animal droppings.

The treatment of *giardia* in dogs is with antiprotozoal drugs. This parasite is very difficult to diagnose, so most vets treat for it if there is a presumptive diagnosis of *giardia*, with chronic mucous diarrhea.

17

Household Dangers and First Aid

INTRODUCTION

Most of us have all kinds of hidden dangers lurking in our homes. Everyday items can pose a threat to a curious puppy, who may be teething and chewing on everything in sight. Simple things like lamp cords, cleaners, antifreeze for your car, indoor plants, insects, children's toys, and small items left within reach can be chewed or swallowed. You should puppy proof your home before your puppy comes home to reduce the chances of his getting into hazardous materials.

This chapter covers proofing against poisonous plants, toxins, chemicals, lamp-cord electrocution, and ingestion of foreign objects; plus it covers first-aid needs for heat stroke, choking, bleeding emergencies, burns, bug bites, and shock.

PUPPY PROOFING

Household Plants

Indoor plants add a natural atmosphere to our homes and liven up any living space. Unfortunately, some of them are toxic to pets if ingested. The effects can range from mild stomach upset to neurological problems or death. The following charts show you the plants' common names, followed by the symptoms associated with their toxicity. There are also some first-aid tips on removing the plant from your dog's stomach once he's eaten it.

Poisonous Household Plants

Plant Common Name	Symptoms
Cactus	needle injury, scratched eyes, needle in tongue
Dumb Cane (Dieffenbachia)	numbing of mouth, blistering in mouth, excess salivation, swollen tongue
Marijuana	hallucinogenic
Mistletoe*	vomiting and diarrhea, slowed pulse
Philodendron	mouth burns and blistering, throat irritation, excess salivation, swollen tongue
Poinsettia Sap	vomiting and diarrhea
Tobacco	vomiting, nausea, excess salivation, increased heart rate

*Denotes a potentially lethal plant toxicity

Poisonous Outdoor and Garden Plants

Plant Common Name	Symptoms
Acorns*	kidney failure
Apple Seed*	vomiting, trouble breathing, coma
Azalea Bush	excess salivation, vomiting, excess swallowing
Bird of Paradise Flower	vomiting, diarrhea, abdominal pain and cramps
Castor Bean*	abdominal pain, shock, low blood pressure
Cherry Tree Seeds	vomiting, trouble breathing, coma
Daffodil Flower Bulb	nausea, vomiting
English Holly	vomiting, diarrhea, abdominal pain and cramps
English Ivy Berries*	vomiting, diarrhea, abdominal pain and cramps
Honeysuckle	vomiting, diarrhea, abdominal pain and cramps

Plant Common Name	Symptoms
Horse Chestnut, nut	vomiting, diarrhea, abdominal pain and cramps
Iris Flower Bulb	vomiting, diarrhea, abdominal pain and cramps
Lily of the Valley	vomiting, diarrhea, heart arrhythmia
Morning Glory Flower	hallucinogenic
Nutmeg	hallucinogenic
Oleander*	vomiting, diarrhea, heart arrhythmia
Potato Skins with green buds	dry mouth, vomiting, diarrhea
Rhododendron Shrub	excess salivation, vomiting, excess swallowing
Rhubarb	vomiting, diarrhea, depression
Skunk Cabbage	burning of mouth and tongue, excess salivation, swollen throat
Tulip Flower Bulb	vomiting, diarrhea, abdominal pain and cramps
Wild Mushroom*	central nervous system disturbances, coma and death
Wisteria Flower	nausea, vomiting
Yew Shrub Berries*	vomiting, diarrhea, wide pupils, heart arrhythmia, convulsions

*Denotes a potentially lethal plant toxicity

First Aid for Plant Poisoning

Although there are many types of plant poisoning, there are a few basic first-aid techniques that pertain to most. These measures in no way replace prompt veterinary care; rather, they are the steps you should take immediately upon noticing the plant being eaten.

Step 1: Identify the plant. It's a good idea to know ahead of time what plants you have in your home and yard. Don't wait for an emergency to have to identify the plant.

Step 2: Try to figure out how recently your puppy ingested the plant. Get a rough idea—was it minutes or hours ago? Try to visualize how much of it was consumed—was it one leaf or half the plant?

Step 3: Call your veterinarian or local poison control center for advice. They will ask you what plant it was, how long ago, and how much of it was eaten. If you cannot reach anyone, go to step 4.

Step 4: The single most important way to treat plant poisonings is to remove the source of the toxin. This usually means getting the plant out of the dog's digestive tract. There are several ways to do this:

If the plant was consumed within two hours:

1. Induce vomiting by giving several teaspoons (for small and medium dogs) or several tablespoons (for large and giant dogs) of hydrogen peroxide orally. Repeat as needed to stimulate vomiting.
2. Another way to get a dog to vomit is by giving 1 teaspoon (for small and medium dogs) or 1 tablespoon (for large and giant dogs) of the emetic, Ipecac Syrup. It's available in all pharmacies and is a valuable agent to stimulate vomiting. Allow the puppy to drink 1 cup of water because this will hasten the vomiting. Repeat as needed to stimulate vomiting.

If the plant was consumed more than two hours ago:

1. Inducing vomiting will be of little help because the plant probably has left the stomach and is heading down the small intestines. The aim here is to move the plant material as quickly through the digestive tract as possible.
2. Use a laxative to quickly expel the plant material from the intestines. Mineral oil is a safe and effective one. Give 1 teaspoon to small dogs (under 25 lbs.), 1 tablespoon to a medium-sized dog (26–50 lbs.), and 2 tablespoons to a large or giant dog (50–100 lbs.). This won't work immediately, but you will see the offending plant material pass through in the stool, usually within 24 hours.
3. Magnesium sulfate, or Epsom salts, is another laxative you may have in the home. The dosage is ½ gram per pound mixed in water. The puppy has to drink this for it to work. This cathartic will work quicker than mineral oil and will produce very watery diarrhea.

*Step 5: **Call your veterinarian!*** Depending on the type of plant and the severity of the poisoning, he or she will be able to do several other things to help your puppy.

Poisonous Household Substances

This section outlines the common household, kitchen, and yard substances that are toxic to puppies. Some are not going to surprise you, but others will. A general rule of thumb is, if the product label has a warning on it, then it probably is hazardous in some way. It may be a skin and eye irritant, or it may be toxic if ingested.

This chart gives the common name of the substance, its symptoms, and basic first-aid steps to take while someone calls the veterinarian or poison control center.

Common Household Toxic Substances

Substance	Symptoms	Basic First Aid
Acetone	vomiting, diarrhea, depression, weak pulse, shock	induce vomiting,[†] give baking soda in water orally
Ammonia	vomiting blood, abdominal pain, skin blisters and burns	wash skin with water and vinegar, give diluted water and vinegar orally or 3 egg whites
Antifreeze	vomiting, coma, kidney failure, death	induce vomiting[†], administer 1 oz. of vodka orally followed by water, can be repeated
Aspirin	vomiting, excess bleeding, acid odor to breath	induce vomiting[†], give baking soda mixed in water orally to counteract acid overdose
Bleach	burns of skin and mouth, vomiting	induce vomiting[†], give 3 egg whites

Substance	Symptoms	Basic First Aid
Carbon Monoxide	dullness, depression, dilated pupils after being in a garage with a car	mouth-to-muzzle resuscitation, get to fresh air immediately
Charcoal Lighter	vomiting, breathing distress, shock, coma or seizures	induce vomiting[†], give laxatives[‡]
Chocolate	vomiting, diarrhea, depression, heart arrhythmia, muscle twitching, seizures, coma from high levels of Caffeine and Theobromine	induce vomiting[†], give laxatives[‡], lethal doses of 1/3 oz. per lb. for dark chocolate, and 1oz. per pound for milk chocolate
Deodorants	vomiting	induce vomiting[†]
Detergents and Soap	vomiting	induce vomiting[†], give 3 egg whites or milk orally, watch breathing
Furniture Polish	vomiting, breathing distress, shock, coma or seizures	induce vomiting[†], give laxatives[‡]
Gasoline	skin irritation, weakness, dementia, dilated pupils, vomiting, twitching	induce vomiting[†], give vegetable oil orally to block absorption, get into fresh air
Kerosene and Fuel Oil	vomiting, breathing distress, shock, coma or seizures	induce vomiting[†], give laxatives[‡], give vegetable oil orally to block absorption
Lead	vomiting, diarrhea, anemia, neurologic symptoms, blindness, seizures, coma	induce vomiting[†], give laxatives[‡], remove source of lead—paint chips, car battery, leaded gasoline, plumbing solder, grease, pellets, fishing anchors, golf balls, shotgun shot

Substance	Symptoms	Basic First Aid
Lime	skin irritant, burns	wash skin with copious soap and water
Lye	vomiting blood, abdominal pain, skin blisters and burns	wash skin with water and vinegar, give dilute water and vinegar orally or 3 egg whites
Organo-phosphate Insecticides	excess drooling, weakness, seizures, vomiting, dilated pupils	wash off insecticide, administer atropine sulfate as the antidote
Paint Thinner	vomiting, breathing distress, shock, coma or seizures	induce vomiting†, give laxatives‡
Phenol Cleaners	nausea, vomiting, shock liver or kidney failure	wash off skin, induce vomiting†, give 3 egg whites or milk orally
Rat Poison	excess bleeding, anemia, cyanosis	induce vomiting†, requires vitamin K injections
Rubbing Alcohol	weakness, incoordination, blindness, coma, dilated pupils, vomiting and diarrhea	induce vomiting†, give baking soda in water to neutralize acidosis
Strychnine	dilated pupils, respiratory distress, rigid muscles, seizures and spasms with loud noises or stimulus, brown urine	induce vomiting†, keep dog in a dark, quiet room until taken to your veterinarian
Turpentine	vomiting, diarrhea, bloody urine, neurologic disorientation, coma, breathing distress	induce vomiting†, give vegetable oil by mouth to block absorption, give laxatives‡
Tylenol	depression, fast heart rate, brown urine, anemia	induce vomiting†, give 500 mg vitamin C per 25 lbs., followed by baking soda in water

† See method in the previous section on plants.
‡ Administer according to instructions in section on plants.

Lamp Cord Shock

Many puppies chew on lamp cords and break through the protective plastic coating, at which times a sudden shock of electricity goes through the wet mucous membranes of their mouth. I've seen mild cases with no permanent damage and serious shocks that are potentially lethal.

For a small puppy, even a mild shock can be more than that. For the instant the shock occurs, the electric current flows through the mouth's mucous membranes, often leaving burns. The puppy may seem dazed for several minutes immediately following the shock and often runs around the room crying, trying to run away from it.

Treatment is twofold. First, try to reduce the pain and swelling in the mouth by applying ice cubes to the burn. Second, if the burns are bad, antibiotic oral gel can be applied to them to prevent infection. Luckily, a dog's mouth is naturally clean and heals quickly, so little follow-up attention is required. Contact your vet to see if there is something else to be done.

When a young, small-breed puppy is severely shocked by an electric cord, the dog shows symptoms of unconsciousness, blackened mouth and gums, breathing distress, circulatory shock, and possible seizure. These puppies need *immediate* professional help. The only thing you can do at home is start CPR and mouth-to-muzzle resuscitation, as described later in this chapter.

Ingesting of Foreign Objects

As part of puppy proofing your home, remove all objects that could fit in the palm of your hand from floors, chairs, counters, closets, and wastebaskets in bathrooms and kitchens. You can't believe the things a dog will eat. Below is just a partial list of things I have seen dogs eat:

children's toys	paper clips
Christmas ornaments	rings
coins	rocks
cooking knives	rubber bands
crayons	tampons
earrings	shoelaces
electric cord plugs	socks
fishhooks	sponges
marbles	toilet paper
pantyhose	

Symptoms are basically the same regardless of what the object is. The puppy starts vomiting, gagging, dry heaving, and coughing. This may persists for hours or intermittently for days. The puppy stops eating and drinking, or if it tries, the food or water comes right up. After a day or so of this, most owners become concerned. At this point, the puppy may be obstructed, meaning the object has blocked the natural flow of materials through the intestine. Intestinal obstructions are life threatening.

Upon presentation at the veterinary office, the puppy is weak, hunched over, feeling pain in the abdomen, and has pale mucus membranes. The dog may be salivating from the nausea.

Once a diagnosis is made and the object is identified, the next step is to try to get the material to pass out of the body. In some cases, the veterinarian will need to remove the object surgically. If the patient isn't too debilitated, dehydrated, or uncomfortable, a mineral oil treatment can be attempted. If the object isn't too large, it will start to pass in 12 to 24 hours. The key is knowing when to stop waiting and when to consider surgery.

Once the object is out of the body, the dog seems to respond almost immediately. If surgery was performed, there is a recuperative period of several days when only liquids are fed. If the mineral oil passed the object, the dog can resume normal eating.

CONDITIONS REQUIRING FIRST AID

Heat Stroke

Heat stroke is also known as *hyperthermia*. This condition occurs when body temperature exceeds 105°F. Breeds most prone to this are those with small nasal passages like the Pekingese, Bulldog, Lhasa Apso, Boston Terrier, and Pug. The only place on a dog's body where it can sweat is its pads of the feet. Dogs rely on panting for heat exchange to cool the body. Therefore, anything that restricts the air flow through the nasal passages of a dog will increase its chances of overheating.

Symptoms of impending heat stroke are intense panting, weakness, racing heart rate, fainting, excess salivation, and coma. If the dog remains hyperthermic for more than 10 minutes, there is the chance that irreparable brain damage will occur. There isn't much time to waste in these cases: Survival depends on removing the dog from the dangerous environment and cooling off the body *gradually*. Bathe in cool (not ice-cold) water, and get the puppy to a veterinarian quickly. *Never leave your dog in a closed car on a warm day (anything over 65°F).*

Choking

Puppies are particularly susceptible to choking because they are always chewing on something. If they take a deep breath to bark or pant or when startled, the object can become lodged at the back of the throat. Immediately, the puppy will start to cough, gasp, or heave.

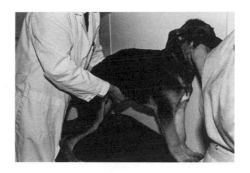

Performing the Heimlich maneuver on a puppy.

There are four techniques you can use to treat choking. The *first* is to try to pull out the object with your fingers, though this may be difficult. The *second* method is a variation of the *Heimlich maneuver*. Grasp your fists together and forcibly push them into the dog's abdomen, just behind the sternum. Your thrusting motion pushes on the diaphragm, which in turn forces air out the windpipe. This often dislodges the object. Do this vigorously and repeat several times.

The *third* method involves performing a tracheotomy, or making a hole in the windpipe. This is typically done by a veterinarian. If it is impossible for you to get to a vet within a few minutes and the puppy is fading or unconscious, you may have to perform this yourself. *This is a life-saving measure only.*

While the puppy is unconscious, locate the rings of the trachea. With a sharp paring knife, poke a hole in between two rings, about two inches from the larynx. You will feel a rush of air being sucked in the hole as you penetrate. Keep the hole open with a drinking straw—a temporary fix until you can get professional help.

Once the airway has been reestablished, you may need to perform basic CPR and mouth-to-muzzle resuscitation, described later in the chapter. This is a frightening thing to deal with, but keep your wits about you, and things may be all right.

Bleeding (other than from toenails)

Superficial cuts and scrapes are of no concern and usually heal with little to no treatment. This section concerns more serious bleeding—profuse bleeding that should be stopped; otherwise, anemia and other life-threatening changes can occur.

Regardless of the type of hemorrhage, it must be stopped at once. Use these techniques:

- Try to raise the affected body part above the level of the heart.
- Apply pressure sufficient to stop or at least to slow down the bleeding.
- Try to wrap the area with bandaging in the form of cloth strips, towels, shredded T-shirts, Ace bandages, or anything else you may have. Apply them tight so they won't fall off, but not so tight to stop all circulation.
- Apply ice packs to the area. Cold temperatures slow down blood flow.
- In cases of spurting blood that a bandage cannot stop (the blood keeps soaking through the bandage), a *tourniquet* needs to be applied. A tourniquet is a strap that gets applied above the wound, shutting off the blood supply to that area. Since most of these deep lacerations are on the paw, the tourniquet placement is on the leg, above the wrist (for a front leg), or hock (if it's a hind leg). A tourniquet can be made from string, strips of cloth, a belt, a rubber band, or anything else that can be tied around a limb. It has to be tight enough to stop the circulation. *A tourniquet can only stay on for 10 to 15 minutes before permanent damage to the limb occurs. If it takes longer than that to get to a veterinarian, you have to release the tourniquet every 10 minutes for 3 to 5 minutes to allow blood flow.* During that time, you will have to use your hands and a cloth to apply pressure directly to the cut to keep the bleeding under control.
- If the bleeding is from a scrape and a large area of skin is bleeding, use a soft cloth to apply gentle pressure on top of the wound. Wrap cloth or bandaging material around the area to keep a constant, low pressure on the wound.
- If a nosebleed occurs, use a tissue to apply pressure inside the nostril. Always keep the nose elevated. Use ice packs on the side of the muzzle. If you have nasal decongestant spray in the house, you can give one spray in the bleeding nostril. The decongestant constricts the capillaries and slows down the bleeding. Always have nosebleeds checked by your veterinarian because they can be a symptom of another ailment.

Burns

Burns can be caused by three different sources—thermal, chemical, and electrical—resulting in three types of skin burns:

First-degree burns are superficial burns involving the top layer of skin. The area becomes red and very painful, and the top layer of skin is usually lost.

Second-degree burns are deeper. They are very painful and bleed or ooze. Blistering is common. These burns take longer to heal.

Third-degree burns are the most severe and involve the full thickness of the skin. The skin appears to melt away, exposing the deeper tissues underneath. The area becomes red, swollen, and blackened, and bleeding may be minimal because blood vessels are also destroyed.

To treat burns, first remove the source of the burn. If it's chemical, flush the area with copious amounts of water; apply ice packs. If it's superficial, apply topical antibiotic ointment twice daily. If it's deeper, seek veterinary care immediately. Cover with a light bandage to keep clean.

Common Burn Sources

Thermal :
- car mufflers and tailpipes
- flames (candles, fireplaces)
- heating pads
- scalding water
- stoves

Chemical :
- acetone
- ammonia
- bathroom cleaners
- battery acid
- bleach
- gasoline
- liquid drain cleaners
- paint thinner
- road salt

Electrical :
- car batteries
- electrical cords
- hobby batteries
- wall outlets

Bee Stings and Other Bites

Most insect bites are an annoyance and cause itching and swelling at the bite site. A few are more serious, however. Dogs can be as allergic to bee stings as people. The bites and stings of the following insects have been known to cause severe reactions in puppies: fire ant, brown spider, black widow spider, wasp, honey bee, bumble bee, hornet, and yellow jacket.

At the very least, the bug bite usually causes a local reaction of swelling, pain, ulceration, and redness of the skin, which can last for days. The dog scratches at it and can make an infected mess of it. Treating with topical corti-sone and antibiotic ointments can prevent this. Many vets recommend giving an antihistamine if the swelling persists for a day. If the bite is venomous, there are systemic reactions as well. These might include fever, joint pain, muscle aching, vomiting and diarrhea, and a generalized allergic reaction called *anaphylaxis,* in which the animal quickly goes into shock.

Anaphylaxis

This is a sudden, intense allergic reaction that can be mortal within minutes from respiratory failure. Once an allergic substance enters the body, histamine is released from certain cells in the immune system. If a small amount of hista-mine is released, there will only be a local reaction—hives, redness, swelling, and itching. If, however, a massive amount of histamine is released, the entire body goes into a *histamine shock*, where blood pressure drops and the lungs fill up with fluid within minutes. The animal quickly goes into shock, respiratory, and cardiac failure and dies.

The only way to stop this violent reaction is to administer the antidote to his-tamine, *adrenaline.* People can get bee-sting kits from their physicians that inject a preset dose of epinephrine to counteract the histamine. If you have a dog with a known hypersensitivity to bee stings, you may want your veterinarian to prescribe a treatment in case of emergency. Timing in such cases is everything.

Snake Bites

There are many different snakes in this country, and the majority of them are nonvenomous: They bite, but they don't carry any poison. The bites can become infected, however.

The poisonous snakes in North America are of the pit viper family. These snakes have a hole (pit) between their eye and nostril, and they have elliptical pupils instead of round ones like the harmless snakes. They also have large fangs. The pit vipers found in North America are:

- Cobra
- Copperhead
- Coral Snake
- Cottonmouth
- Diamondback Snake
- Rattlesnake
- Water Moccasin

The symptoms of a snake bite are explosive swelling around the two fang holes, bruising, and disfigurement of the face if the bite was there. Neurological symptoms with seizures, coma, and death can ensue within two to four hours. The timing of the treatment is critical. The last dog I treated for snake bite was a 90-pound black Labrador named Jake who was bitten on the upper lip by a cottonmouth. Jake's face was so swollen that his eyes were shut, and he was having trouble breathing. Neurological symptoms hadn't started yet because the owner was able to bring him to me within 30 minutes. The two fang holes were bleeding. Jake survived the bite but not without weeks of recovery. I had to treat him aggressively with IV fluids, opening and flushing the bite holes, and injections of antivenin with the antidote I got from the local human hospital.

First Aid for Snake Bites

These are steps you can take to increase the chances of your puppy's survival if he's bitten by a snake.

1. Do not stress the dog or make him move unnecessarily. This only spreads the venom faster. Keep him lying flat.
2. Use a string, belt, strip of cloth, or anything else you may have that can act like a tourniquet and tie it above the bite if it is on a limb. This slows down circulation and impedes the spread of the venom. Loosen the tourniquet every 10 to 15 minutes to avoid completely obstructing blood flow.
3. Flush out bite holes with water or hydrogen peroxide.
4. Get your puppy to a veterinary facility as fast as you can. Some venom only takes a couple of hours to kill. The veterinarian will immediately start intravenous fluids, treatment for shock, and antivenin injections to neutralize the venom.

Shock

Shock is a term that is used to describe the state that occurs when there is dangerously low blood pressure or blood circulation to crucial areas of the body (brain, muscle, or major organ systems). Shock can be due to sudden blood loss or sudden drop in blood pressure or in response to fright and trauma.

Shock is a life-threatening condition that can lead to irreparable damage to nerve tissue, brain, kidney, cardiac muscle, and major organ systems. The body makes an attempt to increase the blood flow to these crucial areas while shutting off blood flow to not-so-critical ones like the intestines. Life cannot be sustained for very long without all these organs functioning, which is why it is so important to try to reverse these changes as quickly as possible.

Symptoms of shock are the same regardless of the type or cause. Below are the most noticeable ones:

- low blood pressure
- increased heart rate to try to compensate for low blood pressure
- quick breathing as an attempt to increase the oxygenation of the blood
- unconsciousness or disorientation
- fixed dilated pupils
- collapse, fainting, or coma

A veterinarian will treat shock very aggressively with intravenous fluids and drugs to increase the blood pressure and blood perfusion of the organs. Some common methods and drugs used to treat shock are outlined in the following table. Some of these you can do, others must be done by a vet.

Shock Therapy

Treatment or Procedure	Effect on System
IV fluids*	increase blood volume to better perfusion of organ systems
Open airway	this ensures that there is no obstruction to breathing
Stop all bleeding	hemorrhage control measures for arterial and venous hemorrhage
Keep in lying down position with head downward	this keeps the blood flow directed to the head and brain where it is most crucial
Keep warm with heating pads and blankets	during shock, body temperature usually falls causing hypothermia (to temperatures below 99°F)
Blood transfusions	this corrects blood loss
Check for heart rate and quality of pulse	heart rate usually increases during shock (150–250 beats per minute), and the pulses get weak and "thready"

Treatment or Procedure	Effect on System
Check mucus membrane color and capillary refill time	the mucus membranes of the mouth become white in shock, and when you press on gums, it takes more than 2 seconds for the color to come back
Monitor for urine output, if none, increase IV fluids and give diuretic drugs*	when the blood perfusion to the kidneys is low, urine production will stop. This is reversed by increasing the amount of fluids given intravenously, and with diuretic drugs that increase urine production.
Injections of cortisone*	this drug stabilizes blood vessels, increases oxygenation of the blood, and increases blood flow

*Denotes treatment must be performed by a veterinarian.

CPR: MOUTH-TO-MUZZLE RESUSCITATION

There are times when a dog goes into cardiac arrest and needs to be resuscitated. Cardiac arrest occurs when the heart stops beating or beats in an abnormal way, causing a sudden drop in blood pressure. Events that may bring on acute cardiac arrest include: acute viral and bacterial diseases; electric shock; getting struck by lightening; poisonings; shock; and trauma.

There are three main objectives to CPR. They are the ABCs of CPR:

A is for *airway*. You must establish a patent airway.
B is for *breathing*. You must breath for the animal.
C is for *cardiac* function. You must help pump the blood from the heart.

The key to successful CPR is timing. Beginning immediately and performing it right are the keys to success. Never be afraid to start CPR. If the animal responds quickly, you can stop. All you've wasted was some time and effort.

The first thing you must do when a dog goes down and is unconscious and in shock is to keep an open breathing *airway*. Make sure that nothing is caught in the throat and that the dog isn't swallowing its tongue. Position the head so that it is normally outstretched and not bent. Pull out the tongue so it is not in the back of the throat. Remove any foam or froth that might be in the back of the throat with a paper towel.

Since the dog isn't *breathing*, you must breathe for it. This is done by a procedure we call "mouth-to-muzzle" resuscitation. You do this one of two ways:

Demonstrating mouth-to-muzzle resuscitation.

1. If the puppy has a short muzzle, like a Pekingese, put your mouth over the entire face of the dog so that its nose and mouth are in your mouth. Blow air into the dog by exhaling. Don't do this with all your force. Do it enough to make the chest inflate slightly, then release the pressure by taking your mouth away. Do this every 25 to 30 seconds.
2. If the breed has a long muzzle and snout, you can cup your hands together to form a tunnel. Keep the mouth of the dog closed and wrap your cupped hands around the nose of the dog. Blow air by exhaling into your hand tunnel until you see the chest inflate slightly. Then release the pressure by taking your hands away from the nose. Do this every 25 to 30 seconds.

Since a dog in this condition is in acute *heart failure*, its heart isn't beating or pumping blood efficiently if at all. You must help pump the blood for the dog. Do this by laying the dog on its side and clasping your hands together, one on top of the other. You will need to kneel beside the dog, bend over its chest, and place your left hand over the heart area of the chest. Then, place your right hand on top of your left one, perpendicular to it. Lean over and with your weight push down in short bursts of pressure over the heart. This is the pumping action. Push on the chest, count to five, then do it again. Keep repeating this for 5 to 10 minutes or until you can get to a veterinary facility.

It is preferable for two people to perform CPR at the same time. One person does the heart pumping, the other the breathing. If you are alone, you must alternate between breathing and pumping as best you can.

During the CPR process, you should be checking for signs that the dog is responding. If you see any of these, celebrate! You may have just saved your puppy's life. These signs would be the following:

- Breathing starts on its own.
- A pink color returns to the mucus membranes of the mouth.
- A strong heartbeat is felt through the chest wall over the area of the heart.
- Consciousness returns.
- Pupils return to normal size.

18

Puppy Pediatrics, a Glossary

This chapter is designed to be a reference guide—and only a guide—for the most common medical disorders of young dogs. The disorders are listed alphabetically. Let your veterinarian diagnose a problem, then use this chapter to look up the disease and educate yourself about it. It does not include conditions specific to Chapters 15, 16, and 17.

A
Absence of Teeth
Addison's Disease
Allergic Dermatitis (atopy)
Anal Gland Problems
Anemia (AIHA)
Aortic Stenosis

B
Bloat and Stomach Dilation-Volvulus
Bronchitis or Pneumonia
Brucellosis

C
Calluses
Collapsing Trachea
Conjunctivitis (bacterial)
Constipation
Coprophagy (eating feces)
Corneal Ulcer
Cranial Cruciate Sprain and Rupture

Cuts and Scrapes
Cystitis

D
Deafness
Diabetes Mellitus (juvenile)
Diarrhea and Colitis
Dry Eye

E
Earflap Trauma
Ectropion
Elbow Dysplasia
Enamel Defects
Entropion
Epilepsy

F
Facial Paralysis or Palsy
Flatulence
Fractures

H

Head Trauma
Heat Cycles (irregular)
Hip Dysplasia
Hot Spots and Pyoderma
Hypoglycemia
Hypothyroidism

I

Impetigo and "Staph" Infections

J

Joint Swelling

L

Lactose Intolerance
Legg-Calvé-Perthes Disease
Lick Granulomas

M

Megaesophagus
Muscle Strains, Pulls, and Cramps
Muscular Dystrophy

O

Orchitis (Infectious)
Osteochondritis Dissecans (OCD)
Otitis Externa (bacterial)
Otitis Externa (yeast)
Overshot or Undershot Jaw

P

Panosteitis
Patent Ductus Arteriosis (PDA)

Portosystemic Shunts
Progressive Retinal Atrophy (PRD or PRA)
Prostatitis
Pulmonic Stenosis

R

Retained Deciduous Teeth
Ringworm

S

Scrotal Dermatitis
Sinusitis
Strangles (puppy)

T

Teething
Tendonitis
Tetanus
Tonsillitis
Trick Knees

U

Umbilical and Inguinal Hernia
Undescended Testicles

V

Vaginitis (puppy)
Vomiting and Inappetence (gastritis)
Von Willebrand's Disease (VWD)

W

Wobblers

Absence of Teeth. This inherited condition can range from having only a few teeth missing such as the incisors or a premolar to entire rows of teeth. By eight weeks of age, all the puppy teeth should have cut their way through the gum line. These dogs should not be bred because this trait is hereditary. There is no treatment for *anodontia*, and there is no sex predilection.

Addison's Disease. This is a condition where there are low levels of the body's natural cortisone (glucocorticoids). Glucocorticoids are needed for maintaining metabolism of the body's cells. Without enough, the animal will go into a state of breakdown and, ultimately, shock. The puppies are weak, have a slow heart rate and digestive problems. They don't develop normally, are runts, and have poor coats. Treatment of this disease consists of supplementing the puppy with glucocorticoids. This can be done orally or via injection.

Allergic Dermatitis (atopy). Dogs have allergies and allergic reactions just as people do. If the dog 1) eats, 2) breathes in, or 3) touches something it's allergic to (called an *allergen*), there will be a chain of events that leads to an allergic reaction. What exactly is an allergy? It's a bodily reaction against a substance to which the individual has a sensitivity. In other words, if your dog is allergic to dust and he goes into the back of your closet that hasn't been dusted in years, the dust will get into your dog's eyes, nose, and respiratory system. Once there, the body reacts to it by causing inflammation, swelling, and pain locally. There are also secretions along with the inflammation. In the eye, the secretions are in the form of excessive tearing; in the nose, it will be a clear, watery discharge; and in the sinuses and lungs, it will be thicker mucus.

What kinds of things can cause an allergic reaction in the skin of dogs? Things like dust, feathers, bug bites, cleaners, cosmetics, pollen, paint fumes, carpet fibers, mold, other animals, and smoke. All of us have some of these things in our houses. If your puppy is developing a chronic allergy that's causing skin rash, itching, hives, and hair loss, you may want to try to find out what your dog is allergic to. Your veterinarian can test your puppy to find the offending allergens.

The first thing you should do if you suspect an allergy is eliminate those things your dog is allergic to. If that is impossible, you can treat the allergy itself. Skin allergies are treated with cortisone and topical medications to reduce the itch and inflammation. The cortisone blocks the allergic reaction in the deeper layers of the skin. If the reactions are severe, oral or injections of cortisone can be given. If a food allergy is suspected, a bland hypoallergenic diet of lamb and rice is usually fed. Very few dogs are allergic to lamb or rice.

If your veterinarian thinks your puppy is a candidate, an individualized serum can be made for all the things he's allergic to. The puppy gets small amounts of this serum injected regularly. This is the only way to desensitize your dog to the things he's allergic to and to cure the allergy.

Anal Gland Problems. Anal glands, or sacs as some books call them, are skunk-like glands all dogs have. There is one on either side of the rectum at 5 and 7 o'clock. The glands are used to mark their territory. The problem is the glands tend to get diseased, either impacted or infected. Impacted glands are overfilled, distended, itchy, and painful. Dogs try to express the glands themselves and itch at their rectum or "scoot" their bottoms on the floor. Treatment is to have your veterinarian manually express the glands empty. If a gland stays impacted too long, it becomes infected. At first, the gland drips a bloody, yellow, pus discharge. If the infection continues, the gland will abscess (meaning break open to the outside) and drain the bloody fluid just described. The best prevention for anal gland abscesses is to have your veterinarian express the gland empty as soon as the dog starts showing symptoms of having rectal itching. In severe or chronic cases, the diseased glands can be surgically removed.

Anemia (Autoimmune Hemolytic [AIHA]). This is an odd condition where the puppy's immune system actually seeks out and destroys its own red blood cells, resulting in anemia. Anemia is defined as a reduction of red blood cells in the blood below normal levels. The puppy suffers from poor oxygenation of its tissues. Symptoms include pale mucus membranes of the mouth, lack of energy (lethargy), amber discoloration of the urine, and a severely reduced red blood cell count. Treatment is aggressive with use of fairly high doses of corticosteroids, iron supplements, blood transfusions as needed, and possibly a splenectomy (surgical removal of the spleen) because this organ plays a role in the destruction of the red blood cells.

Aortic Stenosis. This congenital defect is the third most common heart defect seen in puppies. Stenosis means narrowing. In these cases the aortic valves (the valves are the doors that open and allow blood to flow through) are narrowed to the point of almost constricting the outflow of blood from the aorta. The aorta is the main artery that carries blood away from the heart and supplies oxygenated blood to the entire body. You can imagine the trouble caused by cutting this flow down by as much as half! Early symptoms are breathing trouble, loss of energy, coughing, and pale mucous membranes of the mouth. In other words, symptoms of *congestive heart failure*. The first thing the veterinarian hears is a loud murmur on the left side of the chest, which radiates up the throat. The heart rate is too fast and the pulse is weak. Treatment is surgical correction of the stenosis. A substantial percentage of puppies with aortic stenosis die suddenly of cardiac arrhythmia.

Bloat and Stomach Dilatation-Volvulus. *Bloat* is a condition where the stomach becomes overinflated with gas. Besides being extremely uncomfortable, this condition can be fatal. It all depends on how distended the stomach becomes. The second part of this disease is the *dilatation-volvulus*. This occurs when the stomach distends with gas and actually twists on itself, shutting off the inflow and outflow pipes. This makes matters critical; death can occur within a few hours. The causes of bloating and dilatation-volvulus are breed predilection (which means some breeds bloat despite your efforts to prevent it); overeating at one time; drinking a large quantity of water following eating; heavy exercise within an hour after eating; or feeding a poor quality kibble, which expands when wet inside the stomach. Since simple bloat is not lifethreatening, most veterinarians treat these cases with antacids and antigas medications, then observe for any signs of progression to dilatation-volvulus. Treatment of complicated bloat with dilatation-volvulus involves major surgery to untwist the stomach. These cases are always emergencies, and the patient is in critical condition.

Bronchitis and Pneumonia. *Bronchitis* is defined as the inflammation of the bronchi, or air passages, of the lungs. *Pneumonia* is the inflammation of the actual lung tissues involved in gaseous transport (oxygen and carbon dioxide). If there are both bronchitis and pneumonia present, it's called *bronchopneumonia*. This combination of the two is very common. The causes of bronchopneumonia in the dog are viral, bacterial, and allergic. Regardless of the cause, the symptoms are virtually the same: coughing, fever, loss of bark, and breathing difficulties and wheezing. Treatment with long-term antibiotics and expectorants (which help bring up the lung congestion) usually helps.

Brucellosis. This is a contagious venereal disease of breeding dogs and bitches. It will be described below under *orchitis* because males are more prone to the disease.

Calluses. Like lick granulomas, these afflictions are thickenings of the skin that develop over bony points. The common sites are the elbow and hock. These are common in large and giant breed dogs. The constant pressure of the dog's laying on these bony joint protuberances causes the skin to become dry, thickened, white, hairless, and flaky. Calluses are unsightly but are of little health consequence. Generally, they require no treatment other than padding the floor where the dog sleeps to relieve the pressure on the callus.

Collapsing Trachea. Think of the trachea (or windpipe) as similar to a vacuum cleaner hose made up of rings so that it's flexible. These rings keep the hose open and round. If there are missing or broken rings, then there is weakness at that spot, and it can collapse or flatten slightly under pressure. The defect can occur anywhere along the trachea, either in the

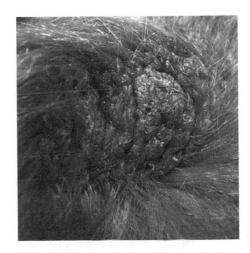

Calluses most often form on elbows and hocks.

throat or inside the chest. When an affected puppy is breathing heavily due to exercise or excitement, he sets off a coughing spasm that sounds like a "goosehonking" and lasts until the puppy calms down and catches its breath. There is limited medical treatment available. Such a puppy should be kept from doing strenuous type exercise, kept thin so that fat doesn't put additional pressure on the throat, and given cough suppressants. Always use a harness instead of a collar when on a leash.

Conjunctivitis (bacterial). The bacteria most often cultured from eye infections is *Staphylococcus*. It lives on the skin and is considered opportunistic, meaning that it is just waiting for an abrasion to allow its entrance into the skin. This can happen just from the puppy scratching or rubbing its eyes. If the infection involves the tissues around the eye, it's called *conjunctivitis*. The eyes become swollen and red, pus may exude from open sores, there may be whiteheads, it may itch, and the conjunctiva may be red and swollen closed. Fortunately, the eyeball itself is usually unharmed. Treatment of bacterial and conjunctivitis involves frequent washing of the eyelid, warm compresses to enhance healing, triple antibiotic ophthalmic ointments in the eye, and oral antibiotics.

Constipation. Constipation is the opposite of diarrhea. This is a condition where the stool becomes very hard and dry. Puppies can have trouble passing these hard stools. Specific treatment of the constipation will depend on the cause, but it includes laxatives, high-fiber foods, and enemas. Occasional uncomplicated constipation is nothing to worry about. Chronic cases should prompt a trip to the vet.

Coprophagy (stool eating). Puppies often eat their own stools or those of other dogs, birds, and cats, for a variety of reasons. It is a good idea to try to stop this bad habit because it can lead to vomiting, diarrhea, and internal parasites, besides being a poor health practice. People have tried to train their dogs not to eat stools; others attempt to make the stool very distasteful with Tabasco or other flavors. Increasing the fiber content of the diet also seems to help. Don't fret too much over this problem. Most dogs outgrow this bad habit by the time they're six months old. If they continue to do it after that, get some strong professional advise.

Corneal Ulcers. The cornea is the multilayered transparent covering of the eyeball. If there is any disruption to the integrity of these layers, an ulcer will develop. Think of a corneal ulcer as an erosion, or pothole, in the cornea. The most common cause is trauma to the eye. A scratch from a cat's claw or low branch can do it. Another common cause is an infection of the eye, also known as conjunctivitis. Symptoms are excess tearing; red and swollen eyes; squinting; and discolored areas of the cornea. Treatment of corneal ulcers depends on how deep they are. Superficial scratches are treated with antibiotic ointment; deep ulcers may require eye drops to reduce the pain and muscle spasms associated with deep ulcers. The eye may need to be sutured shut so that the conjunctiva, or third eyelid, acts like a natural bandage. Never use any medications that contain cortisone in cases of corneal ulcers; they inhibit healing and can make corneal ulcers worse.

Cranial Cruciate Sprain and Rupture. The *cruciate ligament* is one of the main ligament that holds the knee (also called a *stifle* in animals) joint together. Large and top-heavy breeds are more prone to this injury due to their size and the force put on their joints and ligaments. During intensive exercise or play, the ligament can be damaged. Twisting motion is the most common way this ligament is torn. With the feet planted firmly on the ground and the upper body twisting (say to catch a tennis ball), the cruciate ligament is at risk of injury. If the ligament is stretched, or partially torn, we call this a *sprain*. There will be immediate pain in the joint. They do limp quite a bit on it, but rarely will the dog be three-legged lame (holding that hind leg up). In fact, lameness is graded from one to five, with one being barely noticeable and five meaning the animal won't use the leg at all. Cruciate sprains are about a three to four. If the dog completely ruptured the ligament, pain will be almost unbearable, and the lameness will be a five. Treatment varies depending on whether the rupture was partial or complete. Partial tears and ruptures generally heal without surgery. The surgery to repair a complete cruciate rupture involves reconstruction of the ligament. Physical therapy and rehabilitation are excellent ways to get the stifle joint back into shape. Slowly building up the muscles around the joint will strengthen it. Whirlpool or just plain swimming are great to rehabilitate a joint. The key is a gradual return to function.

Cuts and Scrapes. Superficial cuts have the following signs: There is only a faint white line on the skin, no gaping wound; instead of bleeding, there is only an ooze of a straw-colored fluid; there may be hair loss without injury to the skin; and there is minimal redness and puffiness around the cut. Treat superficial cuts and scrapes with basic first aid at home. Wash the area twice daily with hydrogen peroxide, pat dry with a tissue or gauze, and follow with an antibiotic skin ointment. Apply only a thin film because any excess will prompt the dog to lick it off, which defeats the purpose. If you can cover the wound with a light dressing or bandage, do so. Some areas are impossible to cover, so you'll have to leave these bare. Warning signs that the wound requires further professional attention are bleeding through the bandage; a pus discharge that starts two to three days later, indicating infection; a foul, infectious odor that comes from the wound or bandage; and a wound that is in a place that could leave an unwanted scar. These warning signs tell you that your home first aid attempts are inadequate for the wound. A veterinarian may choose oral systemic antibiotics, wound flushing and debridement (removing of dead tissue), or sutures to close a deep laceration.

Cystitis. Cystitis means inflammation of the urinary bladder. There are two common reasons for this: (1) something is irritating the bladder lining such as bladder stones, or (2) an infection of the bladder. This section will describe infectious cystitis, meaning bladder infections caused by either bacteria or yeast. Bacteria can gain entry into the urinary bladder from outside contamination, especially from poor hygiene. Yeast will grow anywhere there is sugar to feed on. In a normal urinary bladder, there is a balance between bacterial growth and yeast growth, so neither gets over populated nor can cause disease. If the bacteria is removed such as in a dog on long-term antibiotics for an illness, the yeast flourishes in the absence of bacteria and overpopulate. This overpopulation causes yeast cystitis. Symptoms, regardless of whether it is bacterial or yeast, include straining to urinate or crying out during urination; increased urgency and frequency of urinations; or blood and pus in urine. There are four components to treating cystitis in dogs: (1) antibiotics to kill the bacteria; (2) urine acidifiers to lower the pH of the urine, which inhibits bacterial and yeast growth; (3) changing the diet to one that acidifies the urine and has a low magnesium content; and (4) removing or dissolving any bladder stones that may be present in the urinary bladder.

Deafness. Deafness is a congenital condition predominantly of Dalmatians. The puppy does not respond to sounds or voices. The actual mechanism of deafness is from a faulty inner ear, which is critical for transmitting sound from the environment to the nerve that picks up the sound and converts it into hearing in the brain. These puppies make great pets, but obviously some allowances will have to be made for their hearing impairment.

Diabetes Mellitus (juvenile). This is the most common hormonal disorder of puppies. In these dogs, there is a high level of blood glucose (sugar) present at all times, not just after feedings. Diabetes mellitus is characterized by consistently high levels of glucose in the blood and urine combined with a lack of insulin that regulates blood sugar levels. Symptoms include increased thirst and, therefore, increased urine output; cataract development of the eyes; loss of energy and weight (even though there is an abundance of glucose in the blood, without insulin the body can't use it, and these dogs are actually starving); poor circulation, and often, concurrent heart disease. This is a very serious disease. Factors that increase the chances of diabetes are obesity and poor breeding. Treatment is to give insulin injections daily, under close supervision of a veterinarian. With proper insulin management, most diabetics lead a normal life.

Diarrhea and Colitis. Diarrhea is defined as a loose stool. Colitis is severe diarrhea with straining and often bloody stools. The most common cause of diarrhea is "dietary indiscretion," or when a dog eats something he shouldn't, like dead animals, other animal's feces, garbage, bars of soap, paper, spoiled food, plants, etc. Below is a chart of other causes of diarrhea.

Common Causes and Types of Diarrhea

	Causative Agents	Consistency of Diarrhea
Viral	Canine Coronavirus Canine Parvovirus Canine Distemper Virus	watery and bloody stools watery and bloody stools watery and bloody stool
Bacterial	Salmonellosis Campylobacter Shigellosis	bloody and dark stools bloody and dark stools bloody and dark stools
Protozoal	Giardiasis Coccidiosis	mucous coating on loose stools mucous coating and bloody stools

	Causative Agents	Consistency of Diarrhea
Parasitic	Roundworms	loose and foul-smelling stools
	Hookworms	loose and foul-smelling stools
	Whipworms	watery and bloody stools
	Tapeworms	slightly soft stools, rectal itching
Immune-Mediated	Lymphocytic-Plasmacytic Enteritis	loose, greasy, yellow stools
	Food Allergy Enteritis	loose, greasy, yellow stools

Regardless of the specific cause of the diarrhea, there are some universal treatments that help slow down the passage of stool through the intestines and colon. Basic treatment of occasional diarrhea includes feeding small meals of a bland diet (chicken and rice or boiled chopped meat and rice) three to four times daily (other bland foods can be given, such as cottage cheese, bread, plain yogurt, potato or noodles); antidiarrhea medications; oral fluids and electrolyte replacement solutions to compensate for water and salt loss; and intestinal antibiotics in an attempt to promote digestive bacterial growth and inhibit the "bad" bacteria.

Dry Eye (Keratoconjunctivitis Sicca or KCS). KCS is the most common eye affliction of dogs. It should be suspected any time there is a chronically red eye with an ocular discharge. It's a condition where the puppy doesn't produce enough tears to keep the eye moist. If there is a deficiency of tears, the cornea will dry out. The

Dry eye is a condition where the eye doesn't make enough tears to keep it moist; instead, it produces pus.

body makes a desperate attempt to moisten the cornea by secreting a thick, yellow pus discharge. This in no way substitutes for tears, but it's the only thing it can do. Causes of KCS are varied, and include breed predilections (breeds with prominent eyes such as Pekingese, Bulldog, Cocker Spaniel); dogs who have had their cherry eye (gland of the third eyelid) surgically removed; eye trauma; and generalized dehydration. Treatment is easy with artificial tear medications available over the counter. Without the tear replacements, the eye will dry out and go blind.

Earflap Trauma. Breeds with long, drooping earflaps are most susceptible to trauma. Some common causes of earflap trauma are dog fights, getting an ear caught in a door, people stepping on one (a Basset Hound's number 1 cause), and fly bites. The trauma can range from a superficial scrape or wound to a full thickness laceration or puncture. Here are a few things to keep in mind if an earflap trauma happens to your puppy: Earflap wounds bleed a lot, so follow the first-aid tips in Chapter 17, "Household Dangers and First Aid," to stop bleeding. If the puncture is full thickness through the earflap, it will require suturing; many ear wounds leave permanent ear notches and disfigurement; and ears become infected easily, so precautions should be taken to avoid them.

Ectropion. This is a condition where the lower lid droops and everts outward. The look is of saggy, sad eyes. We see this most often in hounds, Saint Bernards and Cocker Spaniels. This feature is natural for these breeds and considered normal. Excessive drooping of the lower lid can lead to chronic conjunctivitis and excessive tearing. Therefore, in extreme cases, it needs surgical correction.

Elbow Dysplasia. This condition is a developmental flaw of the elbow joint of giant breed dogs. During development of the elbow joint, a fragment of the ulnar bone never fuses, leaving a chiplike piece of bone floating around in the elbow. Symptoms start as young as six months and are painful on flexion and extension of the elbow, especially with outward rotation of the paw, and dogs are lame on that limb. The elbow may become warm and swollen. Exercise worsens the pain. If left untreated, degenerative changes will occur in the elbow, ultimately leading to permanent arthritis. The arthritis can be managed with anti-inflammatory medication such as buffered aspirin or phenylbutazone. Surgical correction is needed in severe cases.

Enamel Defects. The enamel is the hard white coating of teeth. It is the hardest material in the body. The enamel is essential in maintaining tooth health. If, during the development of the tooth from its tooth bud certain factors are present, faulty enamel can result. Instead of enamel that is white, smooth, and impermeable, the defective enamel is thin, brown, and soft. This ultimately leads to tooth loss. Practically speaking, there is no treatment for this condition. But with advances in veterinary dentistry such as bonding, minor enamel defects can be corrected. There is no breed or sex predilection to this condition.

Entropion. In entropion, either eyelid rolls inward so the eyelashes actually rub against the cornea (surface of the eye), causing corneal abrasions. The lower lid is the most common. The symptoms are corneal irritation (which includes excess tearing), squinting, redness of the schlera (the white of the eye), and a thick discharge. The treatment is surgical correction. A slip of skin of the lid in question is removed, causing the lid to roll outward.

Epilepsy. Epilepsy is defined as a condition where there are regular malfunctions of the brain that lead to sudden bursts of involuntary electrical activity. We call

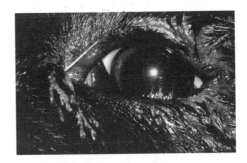

In this case of entropion, the lower eyelid is rolled in and the lashes rub against the cornea. (Dr. M. Neaderland)

these bursts seizures or convulsions. Most cases of epilepsy in puppies are *idiopathic*, which means we don't know the cause. Seizures come in two varieties. The first is called *petite mal*, which means "little seizure." These dogs may have only one part of their body involved, and they only last moments. The other type of seizure is called *grand mal*, and the entire body is involved for up to 10 minutes. These puppies shake, fall over, and kick and paddle. They also may void, thrash, and stiffen. Treatment is not needed if the seizures are more than a month apart or if the seizures are less than a minute in duration. If the seizures are closer together, then most vets use an antiepileptic drug.

Facial Paralysis or Palsy. Facial paralysis occurs when there is trauma to the facial nerve on one side of the face. This can happen because of a kick or blow to the side of the head. Without proper function of this nerve, the facial muscles sag and atrophy, and the eyelids droop. The lips on that side also droops. Most of these traumatic facial palsies are temporary and resolve spontaneously on their own.

This dog suffers from facial paralysis on the left side.

Flatulence (excess gas). All dog owners have, occasionally noted their puppies pass wind. If it only happens once in a while, well . . . that's natural. If it is frequent, it may be a symptom of a different problem. Excess gas is often a precursor to diarrhea. Some common causes of diarrhea associated with gas production include: viruses; bacteria; internal parasites; food allergies; and dietary indiscretion. Treatments for excess gas involve dietary changes to more digestible foods.

Fractures. A fracture simply means a broken bone. There are different types of fractures, but for all bones to heal, the two ends must be brought together so they are touching each other. This procedure is called *reduction* of the fracture. Sometimes this can be done just by manipulating the leg. Other times it must be done surgically under anesthesia if the muscles are contracting, keeping the two ends of the bone separated. To heal, the bone ends must be kept together and absolutely still. This is achieved with casts, splints, or internal hardware (wires, screws, plates, etc.). It is beyond the scope of this book to explain the different situations pertaining to fracture repair. Your veterinarian will have to decide which option to take for your puppy's particular fracture.

Head Trauma. Head trauma occurs most often when a dog is hit by a car. It can also occur from falling down stairs, being hit by a thrown stick or ball (usually a baseball), running into a tree while chasing a cat, being in a dog fight, and falling off a ledge and hitting the head. In people it's called a concussion. The clinical signs of severe head trauma are unconsciousness, shock, rapid or slowed breathing, small or dilated pupils that do not respond to bright light, and flickering eyelids. Treatment depends on the severity.

Heat Cycles (irregular). The scientific word for a heat cycle is *estrus*. This condition occurs when the bitch's ovaries start to produce the hormone *estrogen*, which is responsible for the physical changes her body goes through in preparation for breeding. The normal female dog's heat cycle is about every six or seven months. Each heat cycle may last from one to three weeks. Some bitches do not have normal heat cycles. If the interval between heat cycles (called the *interestrous period*) is shorter or longer than six to eight months, we consider that abnormal. The most common abnormal heats are due to *ovarian cysts* (cysts of the ovarian tissue that produce the estrogen hormone); *silent heats* (shorter than normal cycles with little external evidence); *split heats* (the bitch starts coming into heat, stops, then restarts several weeks later); and *hypothyroidism* (discussed under that heading in this chapter).

Hip Dysplasia. Hip dysplasia is the most common orthopedic deformity seen in large and giant sporting and working breeds. Dysplasia means "an abnormal development." This defect has an inherited origin. There seems to be many factors involved in the development of dysplasia. They include rate of growth; muscle weight compared to bone conformation; nutritional deficiencies or overuse; stress; excessive exercise too early in the developmental process; and other environmental factors. The deformity can be in either one or both hips. There are two components to this defect. First, there is a laxity or looseness of the joint so that the head of the femur doesn't sit inside the acetabulum properly. In dysplastic dogs, less than 50 percent of the femoral head sits in the acetabulum. Second, as the disease progresses, there is a deformity of both the acetabulum and head of femur. The result is instability of the hip joint, which translates into pain. These dogs have pain on manipulation, especially extension of the hip. They also experience pain when climbing up stairs, jumping, or doing anything that puts additional weight on the hindquarters. Most vets are qualified to diagnose hip dysplasia from x rays, but breeders usually request confirmation by a panel of veterinary radiologists of the *Orthopedic Foundation for Animals*. The x ray is sent to this foundation for an official report and rating. We call this getting an "OFA

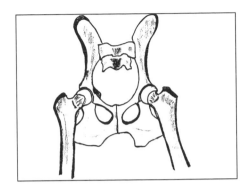

Normal hips and pelvis.

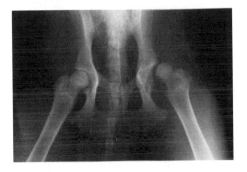

X ray of a dysplastic hip Note the displaced femur head in the hip socket.

rating." OFA will not rate a dog under two years of age. Although symptoms may start by six months, they can progress until the dog is two years old. Hips are rated excellent, good, fair, borderline, or dysplastic (mild to severe). Breeders are strongly urged not to breed dogs with a dysplastic report. Treatments available range from mild medical attention to radical surgical correction. Mild cases can be treated with weight reduction, limited exercise, and anti-inflammatory medications such as aspirin and phenylbutazone. Crippling cases are treated with any one of six surgical procedures.

Hot Spots and Pyoderma. "Hot spots" and pyoderma are skin infections involving the deeper layers of the skin. They often start as an itch or irritation such as an insect bite. A local hive or wheal develops, and the dog itches and scratches. As the dog continues to itch, more and more of the skin layers become involved, until the infection is deep within the dermis. Instead of there being whiteheads and pimples like impetigo, there is a large red, ulcerated area that bleeds and is very painful. There may even be a bull's-eye in the center where it started. They can be anywhere from nickel size to six inches in diameter. A firm diagnosis is important to rule out fungal infection, fleas, mange, and autoimmune diseases. Treatment usually includes prescribing antibiotics or topical anti-inflammatory drugs. It's important to keep the dog from scratching or licking at it, or it won't heal. If it can't be bandaged, then an Elizabethan neck collar will keep him from getting to it. The essentials to treating a hot spot are threefold: (1) antibiotics for the infection, (2) anti-inflammatory and anti-itch drugs to calm the itch and reduce the pain and swelling, and (3) a bandage, or covering, to keep the puppy from making it worse.

Hypoglycemia. Hypoglycemia means low blood sugar. The hormones glucagon and insulin control blood sugar levels. Insulin lowers blood sugar levels, glucagon raises them and is needed to mobilize sugars stored in the fat and liver when there isn't enough coming from food sources. This mobilization brings the blood glucose (the sugar of blood) up to normal levels. If a puppy goes too long without eating or is lactose intolerant and cannot digest its mother's milk, the blood glucose levels drop. These puppies are weak, underdeveloped, motionless unless coaxed, and mentally dull and disoriented. They can even have seizures. Some die within several weeks of whelping. Treatment of mild hypoglycemia is with oral glucose or other sugar supplements. The owners will also have to ensure that the puppy gets regular feedings. Severe cases of disorientation, collapse, or seizures require veterinary treatment.

Hypothyroidism. This literally translates to "below normal thyroid." These puppies have reduced circulating thyroid hormone. The symptoms of congenital hypothyroidism are underdevelopment, weakness, low energy, and dwarfed puppies. Teeth may be missing, the coat is thin and dry, and the puppy is a "poor doer." Treatment is daily thyroid hormone supplements, either natural thyroid from health food stores or synthetic hormone in tablet form. Either way, the T_4 (a blood test that measures thyroid level) should be rechecked monthly until the dose is tailored to the patient. Most puppies start to thrive and flourish with the supplement. By the way, the reverse condition, *hyperthyroidism*, rarely occurs in dogs.

Impetigo and "Staph" Infection. Perhaps the most common skin disease of young puppies under six months of age is impetigo. This is a *Staphylococcus intermedius* infection of the skin. This bacteria is notorious in skin infections in almost all species of animals and children. It lives on the skin and is considered opportunistic, meaning that it is just waiting for an abrasion to allow its entrance into the skin. The infection can involve the hair follicles, or bald areas, and causes small whiteheads. Infection can happen just from the puppy scratching at its skin or the dam mother licking the puppy. The most common site is between the hind legs, groin area, armpits, and inner thighs, where the skin gets soiled with urine and feces. Most of these infections are superficial, meaning only involving the upper layers of the skin. Treatment of bacterial skin infections is accomplished with frequent washings of the skin, warm compresses to enhance healing, topical antibiotic ointments, and oral antibiotics if the infection is spreading, or appears deeper than superficial. Impetigo is usually a direct result of poor hygiene, so attempts to wash the puppy's skin with an antibacterial soap daily will greatly reduce the disease.

Joint Swelling. Commonly afflicted joints are the shoulder, carpus (wrist), stifle (knee), and hock (ankle). Joints swell in response to infection, trauma, dislocation, or immune problems. A bite wound may puncture the joint, introducing bacteria and, along with it, an infection. The joint becomes swollen and painful, and the puppy usually has a fever.

Treatment consists of draining the pus and blood from the joint and prescribing long-term antibiotics. Anti-inflammatory drugs are given to reduce the pain and swelling. Physical therapy may be needed to restore function and flexibility to the joint.

Another cause of joint swelling is dislocation. If a joint dislocates, the bones that make up the joint go out of alignment. This usually occurs after an injury. The joint becomes swollen and painful within an hour or so. The swelling does not subside with time. The dog will not place any weight on the limb, and the pain is severe enough to keep him from letting anyone touch the joint. Depending on the severity of the dislocation and whether there was concurrent ligament or tendon damage, treatment may range from a splint or cast to surgical correction. Anti-inflammatory drugs are given to reduce the pain and swelling.

Lactose Intolerance. This is a problem people and animals share. Lactose is the sugar found in milk and dairy products. Some animals cannot digest it, due to a lack of the enzyme *lactase*, which breaks down the sugar into an absorbable form. The result is stomach distress, abdominal gas, bloating, and diarrhea following consumption of dairy foods. The simplest cure is to stop feeding your puppy dairy foods.

Legg-Calvé-Perthes Disease. This condition is considered the "hip dysplasia" of small breeds, but it's more a deterioration of the hip joint, more specifically the femoral head and neck. The blood supply is shut off to this area, and because the bone cannot live without a proper blood supply, it actually dies. This is called *avascular necrosis*, or death due to reduced blood flow. The first symptoms are the same as for hip dysplasia and start at six months. There is a predilection for males. These dogs have pain on manipulation, especially extension of the hip. They also experience pain when climbing up stairs, jumping, or doing anything that puts additional weight on the hindquarters. Other symptoms include muscle atrophy of the thigh muscles, a bunny-hopping gait, and stiffening of the hind legs. Also the dog sits more than it should. Mild cases can be treated with analgesic and anti-inflammatory medications. More severe cases require surgery.

Lick Granulomas. Other names for this are *lick sore*, and *acral lick granuloma*. These are self-inflicted sores on the extremities of short-coated dogs. I have seen them on the front legs, below the elbow (especially near the wrist joint) and below the knee on the hind legs (especially near the hock joint). What starts these dogs licking their legs is not totally known, but the more the dog licks the spot, the larger, more irritated it gets. This makes him lick more. It's a vicious cycle. The lick sores can be from the size of a dime to a quarter. They are devoid of hair on the top, raised, thickened, round, often ulcerated in the center, and painful to the touch. The skin thickens as a protective response to the constant irritating licking. The licking behavior becomes neurotic or obsessive. The key to treating these cases involves a combination of treatments. Below is a list of treatments I have used to try to cure lick sores. They are listed from the easiest to the most complicated. Not all of them have worked. It's an attempt to find the best technique for the individual patient.

- bandages
- topical anti-inflammatory lotions that may contain cortisone and topical antibiotic ointments
- local injections of cortisone at the base of the sore
- systemic antihistamine and cortisone medications
- antidepressant or psychogenic drugs, such as Prozac
- allergy testing and shots
- Elizabethan collar
- a muzzle
- surgical removal of sore

Megaesophagus. This literally means "large esophagus." The esophagus is the tube that carries the swallowed food into the stomach. If the esophagus is dilated or enlarged, the food collects in it and never reaches the stomach. Factors that can cause a dilated esophagus are: (1) impaired nerve control to the muscles of the esophagus so the normal pushing along of the food (called peristalsis) stops, (2) genetic ballooning of the walls of the esophagus, (3) reduced thyroid function. The main symptom is that the puppy regurgitates within minutes to hours after eating solid foods. Regurgitation means the food he just swallowed comes back up undigested because it never reached the stomach. Also there are no forceful stomach contractions like those in vomiting. There is limited treatment for this, and aspiration pneumonia is a common complication.

Muscle Strains, Pulls, and Cramps. Since each muscle fiber is a finite entity covered with a sheet of fibrous tissue, there are limits to how much it can contract. When these limits are pushed or ignored, damage to the muscle fibers results. If the damage is extensive, there can be bleeding within the muscle, leading to bruising. Inflammation quickly follows; swelling and pain ensues, which can last for days to weeks. Cramping is not as dramatic. Muscle cramps occur when there is oxygen deprivation to the muscle or a buildup of lactic acid, a byproduct of muscle contraction. Cramps are usually temporary, lasting a minute or so. Treatment is not necessary in mild cases. In more severe ones, anti-inflammatory drugs, warm, moist compresses, and rest are needed. If a muscle is actually torn, it can take weeks or months for a complete recovery.

Muscular Dystrophy. This form of canine muscular dystrophy is similar to the *Duchenne* form seen in children. It is a defect in the X chromosome that causes progressive muscle destruction throughout the body. The muscle fibers are destroyed and replaced with fat. Symptoms of muscle weakness, abnormal gait, collapse, overextended joints and a dropped head start at 12 weeks and progress to six months. The dogs can walk and run for only short distances before weakening. The heart and respiratory muscles are affected, which ultimately leads to the demise of the dog. There is no treatment except for a lot of TLC and patience.

Orchitis. *Orchitis* means inflammation of the testicle, the male gonad that manufactures sperm. There are three common causes of a swollen testicle in a puppy: *Trauma*—any kind of blunt trauma to the testicle will result in inflammation, pain, and swelling; *testicular torsions*—when a testicle twists on itself and shuts off the blood supply to the testicle, causing an acute swelling and intense pain of the testicle; and *infectious orchitis*—an infection from either bacterial contamination or venereal diseases. Brucellosis is the most common sexually transmitted venereal disease. This bacteria can cause an infection of the genitals of both males and females. It is passed from dog to bitch or vice versa during breeding, infecting both the male and female genital tracts and causing disease and infertility. Females don't conceive, and males have affected sperm quality. Brucellosis is highly contagious in vaginal secretions, sperm, and urine of infected dogs. People too can become infected with the bacteria, causing a serious illness. The infection is treated with high doses of long-term antibiotics. In some cases, the dog is euthanized because of the possibility of human exposure.

Osteochondritis Dissecans (OCD). This is an inherited defect of cartilage development not bone. We see OCD in large-breed dogs, especially the Labrador Retriever, Golden Retriever and Rottweiler. The defective cartilage actually flakes off the bone, causing pain and inflammation within the joint. Cartilage is the shock-absorbing covering to the ends of bones that is crucial to a properly functioning joint. With OCD, areas of cartilage in certain joints "lift off" the underlying bone; these cartilage flaps cause trauma to the joint, resulting in pain and swelling. The joints most often involved are the shoulder, knee (stifle), hock, and elbow. In most cases, treatment is surgical removal of the cartilage flap.

Otitis Externa (bacterial). The bacterial ear canal infections come in two varieties: *pus producing* and *nonpus producing*. In the pus-producing form there is a yellowish-green discharge from the ear canal and usually a foul odor. The nonpus-producing infections are harder to spot at first. There is no discharge, but there will be an odor, and the ear will be every bit as red and inflamed as the other form. Whether or not an infection is pus producing depends on the type of bacteria growing because some stimulate pus and other don't. Symptoms and treatment are similar to those for a yeast infection. For advice on preventing ear infections, see "Your Puppy's Ears" in Chapter 15.

Otitis Externa (yeast). Yeast is the budding form of fungus. A certain amount normally lives in the ears of dogs. If water gets trapped in the outer ear canal, the yeast will start to flourish. The symptoms of a yeast otitis externa include head shaking; scratching at the ears; a very sour, curdled odor from the ears; red, inflamed and intensely itchy ears; a brown crusty accumulation in the ear canal; self-induced abrasions from the dog's scratching its ear; and a dark brown waxy discharge from the ears. Treatment is usually threefold. First, a thorough cleaning of the ears by the veterinarian to remove all debris and infectious material from the ear canal. Second, topical anti-yeast ointments are squirted into the ear canal once or twice daily for 7 to 10 days. Third, if the infection is severe, the vet may prescribe oral anti-yeast drugs as well.

Overshot and Undershot Jaw. These are the lay terms for bad bites. Overshot jaw (*brachygnathism*) occurs when the upper jaw is longer and extends past the lower jaw. Undershot jaw (*prognathism*) occurs when the lower jaw is longer or extends past the upper jaw. There is no treatment for either condition because it is more of a cosmetic rather than

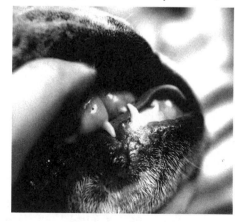

This puppy has an undershot jaw.

functional wrong. Of course, it is a fault in breeding, and these dogs should not be bred.

Panosteitis (growing pains). This is the most common noncongenital bone disorder of young dogs in the six-to-eight-month age group. Breeds at high risk are large, fast-growing breeds. The disorder happens at the age when the long bones are growing the fastest. The puppies come up lame because there is pain associated with panosteitis. There is usually a shifting leg lameness, which means the lameness doesn't stay in the same leg, it goes from leg to leg. Treatment is twofold: anti-inflammatory drugs to reduce the pain, and attempts to slow the puppy's growth rate. This can be accomplished by changing the puppy's diet and by discontinuing the use of any vitamin and mineral supplements.

Patent Ductus Arteriosus (PDA). This condition is the number one congenital heart defect of dogs. During the development of the fetus, a duct develops between the left pulmonary artery and the aorta that causes the blood to bypass the lungs. This development is needed because the lungs are not functional in the fetus. At birth, this channel closes, directing the newborn's blood to the lungs so it can breath air. If the arterial duct remains open (patent), then there is a shunting of blood through the duct from the aorta to the pulmonary artery. This situation overloads the artery and floods the lungs with blood. The consequences are wet lungs, difficulty breathing, rapid respiratory rate, and eventually death. Treatment is always surgical ligation (tying off) of the duct.

Portosystemic Shunts (PSS). This is the most common liver defect seen in young puppies. In the normal puppy, the venous blood circulation from the intestines, which carries most of the nutritional products of digestion, flows through the liver via the *portal* veins. This process is crucial for the liver to metabolize the digestive byproducts. In puppies with portosystemic shunting, much of this intestinal venous blood bypasses the liver by another route, usually a vein other than the portal ones, which means that the blood carrying the digestive materials never gets metabolized through the liver. The consequences are dramatic. These puppies are sickly from birth but by eight weeks show stunted growth; persistent vomiting and diarrhea; weight loss; drug reactions; and neurologic symptoms, including strange behavior and seizures. Blood sugar and protein levels are usually low, and ammonia levels are dangerously high. All these problems are worsened by a large high-protein meal because the venous blood from the intestines that carry the proteins, sugars, ammonia, and waste products never gets processed in the liver. Treatment is surgical ligation (tying off) of the shunting veins to divert the intestinal blood flow back through the liver. These dogs then need to be on a protein-restricted diet for the rest of their lives.

Progressive Retinal Degeneration or Atrophy (PRD or PRA). This is a disorder where the retina of the eye starts to degenerate or atrophy by 6 to 12 months of age. In PDR type 1, degeneration is progressive, starting with poor night vision and progressing to day blindness. It can take years for complete blindness to ensue. The PRD type 2 form is mild compared with type 1 and doesn't generally progress to complete blindness. These dogs retain peripheral vision, while their central vision is lost. This means that objects directly in front of them will be blurred. This form also may take years to progress to a clinical state, but it then stabilizes. The owner first notices a loss of vision and dilated pupils, even in bright daylight. There is no treatment, and the prevention is not to breed dogs that carry this gene. Most breeders of these dogs have the eyes of their breeding stock certified free of this defect by a veterinary ophthalmologist.

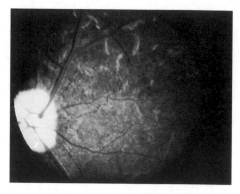

An inside look at an eyeball with progressive retinal atrophy. (Dr. M. Neaderland)

Prostatitis. Prostatitis is the inflammation of the *prostate gland*, a walnut-shaped, spongy gland needed for producing fluid for the semen and for proper breeding. Since this is a puppy book, we will only discuss the infection of the prostate gland in young dogs. The same bacteria that can cause orchitis or cystitis can infect the prostate gland because the urinary bladder, testes and prostate gland are all connected. Symptoms are similar to cystitis. The major difference is that the prostate gland will feel enlarged during a rectal exam. If the dog is a valuable breeding stud, the prostatitis can be treated using long-term antibiotics. Many veterinarians choose sulfur-type antibiotic because they get into the urogenital tract in high concentrations. The dog is not allowed to breed for several months following a prostatitis because of the poor semen quality often seen. If the dog is not a breeding animal, then the best cure of any prostatic disease is neutering. Once the dog is castrated, the prostate gland shrinks to a small nubbin, and the infection clears up, never to return again.

Pulmonic Stenosis. This is the second most common congenital heart defect of puppies. Constriction of the pulmonary artery causes a backup of blood pressure in the right side of the heart, which causes right-sided heart failure. Symptoms include troubled breathing, weakness, and fainting. These signs can be mild at a young age and progress with time. Without treatment, these dogs only live into early adulthood. Surgery is the only corrective option.

Retained deciduous teeth. If a puppy tooth doesn't fall out by six months of age, an extra tooth will be there when the permanent tooth grows in. The retained tooth may inhibit the permanent tooth from growing in (or growing in normally). Treatment involves removing the retained puppy tooth if it hasn't fallen out on its own in six months.

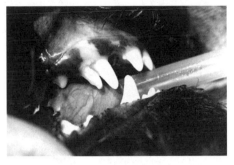

A retained deciduous canine tooth.

Ringworm. The two fungi that can infect skin are *Microsporum* and *Trichophyton*. These fungi grow outside during the late fall and early winter. Animals become infected by touching another animal with the fungus or its contaminated fur. Many wild animals harbor these fungi. The fungus causes a localized skin reaction of redness, itching, hair loss, and crusting, which often occurs in a circular lesion; hence, the name *ringworm*. When this occurs on the eyelids, it is usually very noticeable. The fungus creeps to other areas of the head, muzzle, and ears. There are several ways of treating fungal infections. One is by daily topical application of antifungal creams on the lesions. If the lesions are widespread and severe, oral antifungal medication is used. Ringworm fungus is contagious to people, especially children. Washing hands, vacuuming all dog hair, washing bedding, and generally being conscious of hygiene will keep the fungus from spreading.

Scrotal Dermatitis. As the name implies, this is a dermatitis of the skin of the scrotum. These are very common in young males who are prone to licking themselves. Once the sensitive skin of the scrotum is irritated, it becomes itchy. At this point, the dog licks incessantly at it, causing a worse irritation, or lick sore. Treatment usually includes prescribing antibiotics or topical anti-inflammatory drugs. The essentials in treating a scrotal dermatitis are threefold: 1) antibiotics for the infection, 2) anti-inflammatory and anti-itch drugs (such as cortisone) to calm the itch and reduce the pain and swelling, and 3) an Elizabethan collar to keep to puppy from making it worse.

Sinusitis. Sinusitis is defined as the inflammation of the lining of the sinus cavities. Sinuses are open cavities in the skull where the air breathed in or out must pass. In the sinuses, the air is warmed, cooled and humidified, and fine dirt particles are filtered out before the air passes into the lungs. The sinuses are lined by a moist lining of tissue called a *mucosa*. If this lining becomes irritated, inflamed, infected, or swollen, sinusitis occurs. The symptoms of sinusitis include sneezing, low-grade fever, and a thick yellow nasal discharge, or post-nasal drip into the back of the throat. Treatment is usually long-term antibiotics.

Strangles (puppy). This is another form of *Staphylococcus* infections in young puppies. It is more of a localized, explosive infection that occurs when there is a hypersensitivity (allergy) to the bacteria. The usual areas where it occurs are on the face and neck. The swelling can get so extreme that the eyes swell shut, and the neck lymph nodes get large enough to make breathing difficult. There is often a discharge that breaks from the

Strangles is a condition caused by an allergic reaction to the *Staphylococcus* bacteria.

swelling, draining blood and pus. Since the puppy is allergic to the bacteria, much of the swelling is due to that, as opposed to the infection. Treatment should be instituted at the onset. Warm compresses enhance healing and drainage of the pus, and antibiotics treat the infection. Cortisone drugs are given to counteract the hypersensitivity and reduce swelling. All three must be done for this disease to be cured.

Teething. This stage, when teeth cut through the gum line, is called *teething*. Most puppies start cutting their deciduous (or puppy) teeth at six weeks of age; by four months, the permanent teeth start erupting. The table below summarizes the timing of the permanent teeth:

Permanent Tooth Eruption

Tooth Type	Eruption Time
Incisor	4 months
Canine	5 months
Premolar	6 months
Molars	6–7 months

Tendonitis. *Tendonitis* is defined as inflammation of the tendons. Tendons are the fibrous bands that connect the muscles to bone. If enough stress is placed on the tendon, the filaments of the tendon can tear. These injuries are very common from heavy exercise or work. Any tendon is susceptible to strain. The first symptoms of a strained tendon are acute pain and swelling at the site of injury. Treatment consists of ice packs to reduce acute swelling (within the first 12 hours), then moist warm heat. A soft, padded bandage may be needed to splint and support the damaged muscle and tendon. Prolonged rest is essential for proper healing.

Tonsillitis. This is the most common ailment of the throat of young dogs. The variety of things puppies put in their mouths can infect those who haven't yet developed a resistance to them. The bacteria inhabit the back of the throat where the tonsillar lymph nodes are. Once these become infected, the puppy suffers a sore throat. The tonsils become swollen, red and painful, and the puppy won't eat or tries to eat and can't swallow. Diagnosis is made with a throat culture. *Streptococcus* is a common bacteria. Isolated treatment is to start antibiotics. A minimum 7-to-10-day course is needed to reduce the chances of a relapse.

Trick Knees. The other name for this condition is *medial* or *lateral luxating patella*. Medial means "toward the inside," and lateral means "toward the outside." The medial luxating patella means the patella, or knee cap, luxates (pops out of joint) toward the inside of the leg; lateral luxating patella means it pops out toward the outside. Symptoms include short bouts of lameness on the hind leg when the knee cap pops out and then back into joint. If symptoms are mild and infrequent, no treatment is needed. In more severe cases, surgery is needed to correct the defect.

Umbilical and Inguinal Hernias. Occasionally, puppies are born with a hole in their abdominal wall in the navel area (*umbilicus*) or groin (*inguinal area*). Umbilical hernias are genetic in origin or a result of the bitch chewing the cord too short. Inguinal hernias are usually genetic. Neither is a life-threatening condition unless it is so large that a loop of bowel can strangulate in it.

Undescended Testicles. Breeders call this condition *cryptorchidism*. It's discussed in the "Spaying and Neutering" section of Chapter 15.

Vaginitis (puppy). Young bitches of 6 to 12 months of age often get an inflammation or infection of the vagina. This condition occurs because of the inevitability of contamination from urine and feces. It also occurs more in sexually inactive bitches. The most common symptoms are redness and swelling of the vaginal mucosa (lining); yellow pus discharge; intense vaginal itching; excessive licking at vulva area; and frequent urinations and straining.

Vaginitis is treated with antibiotics for bacterial infections (topical or oral); antifungal medications for yeast infections (topical or oral); douching with antiseptic solutions; and topical cortisone cream to reduce the itching associated with vaginitis.

Vomiting and Inappetence (gastritis). *Gastritis* is defined as an inflammation of the lining of the stomach, which leads to inappetence and vomiting. *Vomiting* is defined as the forceful expelling of stomach contents; it is very different from regurgitation, which is a passive reflux of food out of the esophagus. Inappetence simply means loss of appetite. Inappetence and vomiting go hand in hand. The first thing people notice is that their puppy is quiet and sluggish. This progresses to excess drooling and salivation. Ultimately, the heaving starts. The contractions can seem quite violent at times. Listed below are causes of gastritis. Each is followed by a *V*, meaning it causes primarily vomiting, an *I* for inappetence, or both.

- stuffy nose, I
- any debilitating internal disease, I,V
- certain medications (antibiotics, anti-inflammatory drugs, wormers), I,V
- constipation (severe), I,V
- dietary indiscretion, V
- fever, I
- food poisoning, V
- gastric ulcers, I,V
- heat stroke, V
- infectious bacterial or viral diseases, I,V
- infectious gastroenteritis (usually viral),V
- ingesting a foreign body, I,V
- ingesting poisons or poisonous plants, V
- internal metabolic disorders, I,V
- internal parasites, I,V
- overeating, V
- poor-quality food, I,V
- stress, I
- trauma, I
- vaccinations, I

Many mild, brief cases of vomiting or loss of appetite are treated with symptomatic therapy. *Symptomatic* therapy is when the doctor treats the symptoms, without sometimes knowing what's causing them. It can include restricting food and water for 8 to 12 hours following vomiting, followed by small amounts of water or a bowl of ice cubes, and giving oral antacids or stomach-coating bismuth liquids. Severe cases of gastritis will require aggressive treatment. Because the right treatment depends on the cause, a diagnosis is of utmost importance.

Von Willebrand's Disease (VWD). This is an inherited hemophilia of dogs. *Hemophilia* is defined as a lack of one of eight coagulation factors. The factor missing in this case is Factor VIII. Symptoms include: excessive bleeding, frequent nosebleeds, pale mucous membranes, easy bruising, and bloody urine. The owners notice that small abrasions or minor surgical procedures like tail docking bleed for up to an hour. Treatment is needed when the dog is in danger of hemorrhaging and usually means a whole blood or plasma transfusion. Some veterinarians treat VWD with injections of vitamin K_1, because this vitamin aids in making the coagulation factors. We have also found this to be helpful.

Vulvar Fold Dermatitis. The vulva is the opening to the vagina. Many young bitches have folds of skin on either side of the vulva, due to the fact that they have a small, immature vulva as a puppy. Overweight dogs will have larger creases. The creases formed by these folds of skin become chaffed and irritated. Add to this occasional urine scald from dribbling urine, and the skin can become almost burned. These cases are intensely itchy, so the dogs are constantly licking at themselves. If the skin integrity is broken, infection is a common secondary occurrence. From here, the bacteria can work their way into the vagina and cause a secondary vaginitis. Treatment is similar to that used for any other skin infection.

Wobblers (caudal cervical vertebral malarticulation). This is an inherited defect of the neck vertebrae in the Doberman Pinscher and Great Dane. The sixth and seventh neck vertebrae have an upward displacement, which compresses the spinal cord. Any pressure on the spinal cord leads to weakness (or ataxia) of the hind and sometimes front legs. The dogs appear normal until about six months of age. At that time, symptoms of neck pain on flexing and weakness of the hind legs occur first, which then slowly progress to the front legs. There is also a loss of reflexes and deep pain perception, and an uncoordinated, widely swinging gait and crossed legs occur when the dog walks. As the compression of the spinal cord worsens, so do the symptoms, until the dog is basically paralyzed. The only permanent treatment is to surgically eliminate the cord compression and stabilize the neck.